GEORGE CRABBE'S POETRY

GEORGE CRABBE'S POETRY

PETER NEW
Lecturer in English
University of Exeter

ST. MARTIN'S PRESS NEW YORK

FOR MY PARENTS AND WIFE

Contents

Acknowledgements

I am very grateful to the following individuals and institutions for permission to examine their holdings of Crabbe manuscripts either directly or on microfilm or xerox: Beccles Town Archives, the Bodleian Library, Boston Public Library, the Brotherton Library, University of Leeds, the British Library, Cambridge University Library, the Master and Fellows of Trinity College, Cambridge, Chicago University Library, the Earl of Cranbrook, the Fitzwilliam Museum, the Folger Shakespeare Library, Harvard University Library, the Huntington Library, Ipswich and East Suffolk Record Office, the Earl of Jersey, the John Rylands Library, Mr John Murray, Princeton University Library, the National Library of Scotland, Texas University Library, the Victoria and Albert Museum, Virginia University Library and Yale University Library. To those whose manuscripts were relevant to the present study I am particularly grateful for permission to quote.

I should also like to thank Arthur Pollard, Thomas C. Faulkner, Christopher Hanvey for much useful information, the late John Hutchings for valuable stimulus at an early stage, Myrddin Jones for meticulous reading of two drafts and many very helpful suggestions, John Speirs for advice on the earlier draft, and my father for much typing. But my deepest debt is to my wife for unfailing support and detailed assistance in revision.

Texts and Abbreviations

The text used for poems published during Crabbe's lifetime is the five-volume edition of 1823. The text used for the *Posthumous Tales* is the 1834 edition. Abbreviations used are as follows:

Broadley and Jerrold	A. M. Broadley and W. Jerrold, *The Romance of an Elderly Poet* (1913).
Critical Heritage	Arthur Pollard (ed.), *Crabbe: the Critical Heritage* (1972).
Hastings	J. D. Hastings (ed.), *Posthumous Sermons of George Crabbe* (1850).
Leadbeater Papers	*The Leadbeater Papers* (1862) Vol. II.
Life	*Life of the Rev. George Crabbe* by his son, Vol. I of *The Poetical Works of the Rev. George Crabbe* (1834).
New Poems	*New Poems by George Crabbe*, ed. with an introduction and notes by Arthur Pollard (1960).
Ward	*Poems by George Crabbe*, ed. Adolphus William Ward (1905–7).

1 The Literary and Ethical Context of Crabbe's Poetry

'Crabbe...was hardly at the fine point of consciousness in his time. His sensibility belongs to an order that those who were most alive to the age – who had the most sensitive antennae – had ceased to find sympathetic.' '...he is (or ought to be – for who reads him?) a living classic' (F. R. Leavis, *Revaluation*, 1936). Both these statements are clearly true, but the paradox in their juxtaposition requires examination. One might reasonably expect a 'living classic' to be 'alive' to his own age; a writer dead in the second respect is likely to be presumed dead in the first. By discussing some aspects of the 'order' to which Crabbe's sensibility belonged, so as to make his poetry more accessible to a twentieth-century reader, it will also be possible to indicate the lines of an answer to the question, which haunts Crabbe criticism, of why he ought to be read more than he is.

One way in which he was *alive* to his age can be indicated briefly by juxtaposing a sentence from *The Mill on the Floss* with some lines from *Tales of the Hall*: 'We judge others according to results; how else? – not knowing the process by which results are arrived at' (Book VII, ch. 2);

> How is it, men, when they in judgement sit
> On the same fault, now censure, now acquit?
> Is it not thus, that *here* we view the sin,
> And *there* the powerful cause that drew us in?
>
> (III, ll. 396–9)

The idea that to understand something thoroughly one must know how it has grown, its history, is characteristic of the 'order' which supplanted that of the eighteenth century, and the major interest in most of Crabbe's best work is in the process by which a character becomes what he is. His concern with process is something which links him firmly with the leading minds of the nineteenth century. But before pursuing this point it will be convenient to bring out the aspects of his thought which do not lie 'at the fine point of consciousness in his time'.

RELIGIOUS CONSERVATISM

That his religious beliefs were not disturbed by his interest in fossils is
not surprising: it was not until well after his death that geology gravely
threatened *Genesis*, and not until very near it that Sir Charles Lyell's
Principles of Geology (1830–3) could even have begun to shake the conviction, expressed in Crabbe's 'Opinions in Religion and Morality'
(1779), that 'the wisdom we see in [the World's] Parts calls loudly for a
continually directing Wisdom to keep in Being the Whole.'[1] Nor is it
surprising that this statement and the 'Opinions' as a whole draw, as
early as 1779, on the general teleological argument for the existence of
God, though with Paley behind him he also used it long after the work
of Hume and Kant: in a sermon written in April 1822, he asked his
congregation to envisage a society without religion, and declared that it
'would not last: Some stronger Mind . . . would perceive that Man could
not create . . . the more he saw of Nature the more he would be convinced that all were made and governed by Wisdom' (Chicago Collection, p. 561). But although it was still quite common even after the
middle of the century to use the miracles and prophecies as arguments
for the truth of Christianity, one does not expect an antenna of the race
to contemplate publishing, in 1814, a laborious refutation of Gibbon's
and Hume's attacks on them.[2] However, although he devoted much time
to it, this work was not published, and in the theological discussions
with his son, George, in the last decade of his life, his attitudes on some
points of controversy seem to have become less militant. Fitzgerald
reports that Crabbe's son said his father sometimes 'cut very short' the
arguments about theology in which the son 'delighted'.[3] In a letter to
George of 17 April 1822 Crabbe writes, 'Objections there are of many
kinds and I cannot solve the Difficulties I meet with' (Bodleian Library,
MS. Don. d. 79), and on 4 February 1831,

> Your Method appears to be rational and I trust will be satisfactory
> and yet $^{you}_{we}$ must not expect with all your Care and Pains,
> absolute Conviction . . . conscious that I shall never arrive at the very
> Truth and that there will remain Difficulty in some Questions and
> Uncertainty in some points more or less important I rest quietly in
> those Facts which Reason assents to unforced and as I believe, un-
> biassed and these are sufficient to keep my Mind at Peace.[4]

A similar attitude is expressed in the letters to Miss Waldron of 10 May
1825 and to Mrs Leadbeater of 24 December 1828, which are quoted in
the *Life*, and in another to Miss Waldron of 10 July 1828: 'Books written
on the Evidences of Religion, often take into their Protection too many

Points which they had better have left to themselves ... there is Evidence sufficient I believe for all who will be at the Pains to seek for it, but the Christian certainly sees things in a Light which is not clear to them who say "Prove to us what you assert".' (Harvard Collection)

He continued to attach great importance to the more modest accounts of the 'Evidences' (especially Paley's), but in some of the later sermons there is increased emphasis on some forms of the 'moral proof'. In one first preached on 12 April 1818 he says, selecting and developing one line of thought in the anti-Gibbon writing of 1814, 'If this R[eligion] be not true, some obscure Men who were Imposters and therefore wicked, have given the world the most pure and holy Precepts that Ever were promulgated for the Good of Mankind' (Murray Collection); in the letter to his son of April 1822 quoted above, he says, 'If I could give up the Inspiration of the Writers of the Gospels, I could not the Doctrines they have transmitted to us. The Divine Morality, for I know not what else to call it'; and in another Murray sermon, first used on 22 October 1826, he has moved further: a Christian, he says, 'will be convinced that what was taught him was Truth, because he finds Proof in all his Experience: What he reads in the New Testament agrees with what he finds in himself.' But this shift of emphasis, in which the elderly Crabbe may seem to show some sensitivity to contemporary trends, remains substantially within an eighteenth-century framework. Rational conviction remains at the foundations of his theology. The words 'Reason' and 'rational' are used in the letter of 1831 already quoted; and more emphatically, in a letter to his son of 19 April 1827, he says, 'I have no scruple to say that I believe because my Reason is convinced that I ought to do so.'[5] His reliance on speculative reason was far less than that of the eighteenth-century theologians who had tried to answer the Deists on their own terms – 'Our reason is given us that we may seek the truth and find it; but having found it, reason has done its office, and must submit to that truth which it has found' (Hastings, p. 140) – but he never wavered in 'the confidence that we possess that God is true and that his truth has been made manifest to us' (Hastings, p. 79). To see the consequences for his poetry, we shall have to approach it first from some other directions.

CRABBE AND THE IMAGINATION

When one thinks of Crabbe as not 'at the fine point of consciousness in his time', one is most likely to have in mind a contrast with Wordsworth and Coleridge. This contrast certainly brings out a respect in which Crabbe was intellectually behind his time. But he will also be shown as outflanking the Romantics, both consciously, in his allusion to Johnson's

Shakespeare in the Preface to the 1812 *Tales*, and implicitly, in the resemblance of his imagination to that of the nineteenth-century novelists. Firstly, Crabbe's work is based on the old aesthetic of imitation rather than that of the creative Imagination as conceived by the Romantics. Crabbe believed there to be an independent external reality which it was the function of art to imitate, whereas Wordsworth and Coleridge, who for much of their working lives were contemporary with him, saw the poetic Imagination as essentially creative in its relationship with reality. The shaping spirit of the Imagination transmuted the nature of what was perceived in the process of artistic creation. That the Romantics were aware of this difference is clear from Coleridge's remark that 'in Crabbe there is an absolute defect of the high imagination',[6] and from several of Wordsworth's comments, including one which linked Crabbe with Jane Austen: 'though he [Wordsworth] admitted that her novels were an admirable copy of life, he could not be interested in productions of that kind; unless the truth of nature were presented to him clarified, as it were, by the pervading light of imagination, it had scarce any attraction in his eyes; and for this reason he took little pleasure in the writings of Crabbe.' The writer of the *Quarterly Review* article on *The Borough*, though sufficiently sympathetic to the new ways of thought to regard 'the doctrines of Mr. Crabbe' as 'essentially hostile to the highest exercise of the imagination', also remained sufficiently in touch with the empirical philosophers' views of the imagination to point the contrast more objectively: 'He lives, if we may be allowed the expression, without an atmosphere. Every object is seen in its true situation and dimensions; – there is neither colour nor refraction. No poet was ever less of a visionary.'[8]

Secondly, that Crabbe was not only aware of but consciously rejected the new aesthetic of the Imagination is clearest in the Preface to the *Tales* of 1812, where he borrows the phrase 'without an atmosphere' and relates it, by way of such words as 'naked and unveiled', less to the absence of imagination than to the presence of 'truth and nature'. The boldness of what Crabbe was doing in the Preface is partly concealed by the apparent timidity of his last paragraph, where he claims only a 'negative kind of merit', though even there the Johnsonian resonance of the concluding phrases makes it in fact less diffident than at first it seems. Similarly, although the prevailing impression of the first half of the Preface is of a second-rate poet apologising for 'the only means I possessed' of engaging the reader's attention, he has contrived to suggest that not only Chaucer and Boccaccio but also Johnson's view of Shakespeare provide relevant perspectives on what he has done ('greater variety of incident and more minute display of character ... we pass from gay to grave, from lively to severe, not only without impropriety, but with manifest advantage'). Thus we should already be prepared for the strategy of the central paragraphs, in which, while apparently conceding Shakespeare to his opponents by quoting the famous passage from A *Midsummer Night's Dream*,

> The poet's eye, in a fine frenzy rolling,
> Doth glance from heaven to earth, from earth to heaven;
> And as Imagination bodies forth
> The forms of things unknown, the poet's pen
> Turns them to shapes, and gives to airy nothing
> A local habitation, and a name . . .

which is so apt that to us it also suggests works of Coleridge and Wordsworth written or published after 1812, he is in fact by allusion to Johnson enlisting Shakespeare on his own side. He does this in two ways within a single long sentence. Firstly, he undercuts the transcendent imagination by reference to Chapter IV of *Rasselas*, concerning the 'artist' of whose attempts to fly Rasselas remarks, 'I am afraid that no man will be able to breathe in these regions of speculation and tranquility', and to Chapter X, in which Imlac's description of the task of a poet ironically echoes the 'artist': 'he must . . . rise to general and transcendental truths . . . as a being superiour to time and place.' '. . . Taking captive the imagination of his readers', says Crabbe, 'he elevates them above the grossness of actual being, into the soothing and pleasant atmosphere of supra-mundane existence.' The ironies have accumulated subsequently – for example, Wordsworth complained to Lockhart in 1825 that he found in Crabbe 'a general dryness and knottiness of style and matter which it does not soothe the mind to dwell on'[9] – but Crabbe seems to have had specifically in mind the *Quarterly Review* article on *The Borough*.[10] The second stage of his strategy is to use phrases which purport to praise the visionary poets' work for not possessing qualities fundamental to Johnson's critical thought. One thinks, for example, of the 'Life of Cowley', where Johnson says that the reader's mind is exercised by the Metaphysical poets but that they were not successful in representing or moving the affections, and of the 'Preface to Shakespeare' ('The irregular combinations of fanciful invention may delight a-while, by that novelty of which the common satiety of life sends us all in quest; but the pleasures of sudden wonder are soon exhausted, and the mind can only repose on the stability of truth', Yale ed., Vol. VII, p. 61). Crabbe writes:

> . . . there he obtains for his visionary inhabitants the interest that engages a reader's attention without ruffling his feelings, and excites that moderate kind of sympathy which the realities of nature

often-times fail to produce, either because they are so familiar and insignificant that they excite no determinate emotion, or are so harsh
and powerful that the feelings excited are grating and distasteful.

By this time it will be clear to a reader in sympathy with Johnson's
view of Shakespeare that a definition based on 'the more dignified kind
of composition' is going to exclude 'a vast deal' of 'the greatest of poets,
not divinely inspired', even if he does think that the 'more dignified' is
'the only kind that has pretensions to inspiration', so that when Crabbe
has added Chaucer, Dryden and Pope, he can well afford to concede the
'enchanters, spirits, and monsters of Ariosto and Spenser' – or at least
seem to do so, for we find that what at first seems a timid afterthought,
such as those which appear in the Preface to *The Borough*, has subjected
even these to the criteria of 'truth and nature'. If the manner in which
the poem itself is conducted is 'judiciously managed', '... the imaginary
persons and incidents to which the poet has given "a local habitation
and a name", will make upon the concurring feelings of the reader the
same impressions with those taken from truth and nature, because they
will appear to be derived from that source ...' Here again Crabbe has
Johnson's Shakespeare behind him: 'Even where the agency is supernatural the dialogue is level with life' ('Preface'); and referring to
Caliban in particular, 'let any other being entertain the same thoughts
and he will find them easily issue in the same expressions' (note to
The Tempest, I, ii, l. 321). All he has conceded in fact is that he has no
answer to someone who begs the question: 'it must be granted that the
pretensions of any composition to be regarded as poetry will depend
upon that definition of the poetic character which he who undertakes
to determine the question has considered as decisive.'[11]

    That Crabbe rejected certain theories of poetic Imagination developed
by Coleridge and Wordsworth and deliberately stood by the older
aesthetic conception of imitation, does not of course make his poetry
colourless or unoriginal. Without any irony P. E. More wrote that
Crabbe 'has succeeded in giving his work a tone or atmosphere
peculiarly and consistently his own',[12] and E. M. Forster was attracted
by what he called 'a curious flavour', 'an unusual atmosphere'.[13]
Crabbe would, however, undoubtedly have preferred Johnson's way of
expressing a similar observation: 'The reader of *The Seasons* wonders
that he never saw before what Thomson shews him, and that he never
yet has felt what Thomson impresses.' Some forms of imagination are
possessed by Crabbe and others are relevant only to metaphysical
systems peculiar to the Romantics. It will, for example, be shown later
how deeply Crabbe could enter into the spirit of a man he disapproved
of, and how ironic it was in view of Crabbe's debt to Hogarth that

Wordsworth should have used in his description of the Imagination in the 1815 Preface a quotation from Lamb on the genius of Hogarth ('which makes things animate or inanimate, beings with their attributes, subjects with their accessories, take one colour and serve to one effect'). Where, on the other hand, Wordsworth's and Coleridge's views of the imagination become entangled with the conception of intellectual intuition derived from the Cambridge Platonists, and where Coleridge is drawn more deeply into Schelling's transcendental idealism, it is not only Crabbe who is left behind, but everyone who cannot share the remote and eclectic metaphysics, without which their terminology has no authority.

It is here, however, that it becomes necessary to distinguish between specific theories of the Imagination which are embedded in a metaphysical system that can no longer be believed in, and the general, and indeed commonplace, view that the act of perception is necessarily partly or largely creative. We know from the *Life* that his father used to read out passages of Young to the family, so it is unlikely that Crabbe did not know the famous lines of *Night Thoughts* (VI, ll. 420–40) which Wordsworth acknowledged in a note to 'Tintern Abbey': 'Our senses, as our reason, are divine', 'And half create the wondrous world they see', even though he made no reference to them in the paragraph on Young in 'Midnight' (ll. 79–85). But he evidently did not find them very interesting. The comedy of 'The Lover's Journey' depends as much on the premise that an objectively accurate description of the scenery is possible as on the perception of how subjective the mind can be in certain moods. As John Speirs has noted in *Poetry towards Novel* (1971) the comic effect is 'chastening to our human pride', and this is very remote from the spirit of Young's passage. It is a commonplace in criticism of Crabbe that he uses external description to convey a state of mind, but on the comparatively few occasions where the mind of the beholder is in active relationship with the scenery, the purpose is usually ironic. In Book VI of *Tales of the Hall*, for example, Richard's enjoyment of the 'spacious bay' and the view of the 'large fleet' in 'full sail' is coloured by his confidence in the love of Matilda whom he is going to visit:

> For where does man evince his full control
> ... with more effect ...
> Than when man guides the ship man's art has made,
> And makes the winds and waters yield him aid?
>
> (ll. 184, 186, 188–9)

Unlike the Murray draft of this passage, the final version emphasises the irony here by preceding Richard's musings with the image of a storm –

> As in the storm that pours destruction round,
> Is here and there a ship in safety found;
> So in the storms of life some days appear ...
> Like spots in deserts   (ll. 156–8, 161)

and by following it with the image of the 'rude icy wind' (l. 204). We should be more prepared than Richard is for the 'lightning' shock of seeing Matilda with the 'rival soldier'. But the passage was conceived in ironic terms even before these revisions, for in the Murray draft also Richard chooses the upper of the two routes to Brandon, keeping away from the small pebbles which give their 'reflected lustre' to the new day when 'wetted by the wave'. They might have reminded him that the lustre he was conferring on the scene was by temporary courtesy of the elements.

In the much-quoted passage from 'Delay has Danger' describing Henry's state of mind on the evening of his engagement to Fanny, Crabbe is simply uninterested in the theory of perception:

> All these were sad in nature, or they took
> Sadness from him, the likeness of his look,
> And of his mind – he ponder'd for a while,
> Then met his Fanny with a borrow'd smile.   (ll. 721–4)

It is left uncertain whether the scene was 'sad in nature' or the sadness was imposed in the act of perception, for the important facts are, firstly that the scene gives the likeness of his mind, and secondly that it is quite certain that the smile was 'borrow'd'. This paragraph was not in the early Murray draft of the poem. In the Huntington draft there is considerable verbal difference in the description, though the feeling rendered is the same; but in the four lines which were replaced by lines 721–4, Crabbe gives a third possible version of the relation between the landscape and Henry's mind:

> And all these objects had their full Effect
> On Henry's Mind now sad and incorrect
> But still he met his Fanny as a Man
> Who proves his Duty and does all he can.

The main reason for rejecting this attempt was probably dissatisfaction with the second couplet, on which Crabbe's marginal self-criticism, 'not very good lines', understates the case; but if his first thoughts were of the objects having a dejecting 'Effect' on Henry's mind, the idea of the mind half-creating what it sees was clearly not central to his conception of the passage.

Obviously, the conception of the half-creating mind made possible most of the greatest parts of *The Prelude* and many shorter poems of

major stature. Making a rough distinction between writers who have
changed the consciousness of their age and those who have only
enriched what was already charted for them, it is clear that Crabbe is,
in one respect at least, not of Wordsworth's significance. On the other
hand, it may be questioned, setting the tale of Margaret in 'The Ruined
Cottage' against, for example, 'Resolution and Independence', whether
Wordsworth's originality was wholly a gain. One important sense of
the word imagination is the capacity to treat other minds *as* other,
which Wordsworth's kind of imaginative response to the Leech-gatherer
precludes. Crabbe's view of the relation between the objective nature
of a scene and the subjective distortion of it may be compared with,
say, George Eliot's use of the narrative voice, and it is not fortuitous that
George Eliot was also the creator of Casaubon. In comparison with the
Wordsworth of *The Prelude*, a limitation in Crabbe is apparent when
one contrasts the plan for the 'Farewell and Return' series of the
Posthumous Tales,

1. The Place itself and its Improvements
2. The Change in a Man's self –
3. That in others,[14]

with the failure in the tales as we have them to treat the second subject
and the explicit evasion of it at the end of the last, 'Preaching and
Practice'. That Crabbe used a great deal of his own experience in his
writing is known from the letter to Mrs Leadbeater quoted in the *Life*
(p. 232) and from the comments in Fitzgerald's copy of the *Works*, some
of which are printed by Huchon; but when he wrote *about* himself, in
'Infancy', his manner (as noted by Mrs Haddakin) resembles that of the
tales, and the result is uninteresting. His imagination is of the kind of
the novelists, of Jane Austen and George Eliot, rather than that of
Wordsworth or Coleridge. Although he was not responsive to the
newest conceptions of the Imagination in his time, he has roots in a
tradition which survived them.

CRABBE AND MORAL LAW

The effect of Crabbe's religious conservatism on his poetry is greatest
where it is combined with the assumption that the truth about the
external world is knowable in the objective manner discussed in the
previous section. To him it was clear that the world was governed by
moral laws which were both absolute and, as far as was relevant, known
to man. In a sermon on *St Luke* 13. 23 ('Then said one unto him, Lord,
are there few that be saved? And he said unto them, Strive to enter in
at the strait gate'), he suggests that Christ deliberately did not answer
the question and put the emphasis instead on the relevant imperative:

As we must be completely ignorant of the divine dispensation, we may rest assured that the Judge of all the earth will do that which is righteous and just, and may cease from all further inquiry. . . . Many things we may be anxious to know, but they are hidden from us; there is sufficient, there is all that is requisite for our conduct in this life, and our happiness in a life to come' (Hastings, p. 83–4).

In a number of extant sermons Crabbe admits that obedience to these laws is clearly not rewarded in this life. For example, in one now in the Chicago Collection (p. 643) he interprets the story of Job as a means of showing the Jews that they were mistaken in believing 'that Prosperity was the Reward of Virtue'. In one of the published sermons he develops the point: 'Let no man be deceived by his religion . . . [St Paul] did not hold out prospects of what we call pleasure in this life, but . . . indescribable blessings in the life that is to come' (Hastings, p. 13). But he does not regard the reward as coming wholly in the 'life that is to come'; the quality of this life is also directly affected. In the sentence last quoted, the first phrase following 'but' is 'present inward satisfaction and content'; conversely, in another Chicago sermon (p. 401), he says of the envious, for example, 'they bear a Hell within who feel the constant Spur of ungratified Desire'. In the poetry he sometimes feels it necessary to anticipate the judgement to come by external manipulation of the events, but there are also extreme cases of poetic injustice. Although there are instances of it, which will be noted later, he would generally speaking have found the cruder forms of poetic justice objectionable not only on aesthetic but also on moral and religious grounds. He would have agreed strongly with Sydney Smith's remarks in an article on R. A. Ingram's book on Methodism in the *Edinburgh Review* of January 1808: 'If two men travel the same road, the one to rob, the other to relieve a fellow creature who is starving; will any but the most fanatic contend, that they do not both run the same chance of falling over a stone, and breaking their legs? . . . The honest and the orthodox method, is to prepare young people for the world, as it actually exists.' The usual form in which Crabbe shows the temporal working of the moral laws is by tracing through time the consequences of moral choices on the quality of life.

Before examining this more fully, three pitfalls in the view of moral law held by Crabbe must be noted, and some contemporary opinions of the status of moral law must be discussed. Firstly there is the danger that the basis of moral behaviour will be reduced to enlightened self-interest. In many sermons Crabbe speaks of the 'heavenly treasure' and balances it against the pleasures of the world in such a way that choice of the former seems a matter of *prudence*, in a debased sense of the word. The poetry is frequently criticised along the lines of Varley Lang's comment 'Prudential morality is often in evidence – be sincere and honest because you'll get along better.'[15] This is more true of the sermons than of the poetry, which will be considered in detail later. But even in the sermons Crabbe shows by some more careful discussions that, like Butler, he sometimes placed his emphasis less to suit his own more acute perceptions than to meet the attitudes of his listeners, who were most likely to be moved by self-interest. In the Huntington sermon first preached on 12 September 1784, he shows an understanding of Prudence far beyond the prissy form which is commonplace in the minor novel of the eighteenth century and beyond the kind of commonsensical appendage to good-nature in Fielding – though the latter is included within it. Prudence, he says,

> ... is the mean between trust and distrust, Credulity and incredulity. For some rush upon the nets and traps of designing and wicked Men, incautious and full of Confidence in themselves and others; and become an easy prey to the treachery, which prudence would teach them to avoid; and others are ever too wary and mistrustful, doubting everybody and looking upon all Mankind as Creatures prone to prey upon them, as Enemies rather than as fellow Creatures, so they contract a hard and callous heart and become miserable to themselves by their Caution as they are disgusting to others in their Suspicion.

The description of the 'others' who are 'ever too wary' shows more understanding than Fielding's treatment of Blifil and Bridget Allworthy; but 'callous' is a strong word. Later in the same sermon Crabbe stresses the limited value of the prudence which coincides with self-interest: 'Prudence is a Virtue that brings its own reward with it, and consequently being rewarded in this world, the prudent Man has little pretence to value himself upon that account or to deem himself worthy of a future and spiritual Blessing, for his good Quality which is so amply recompensed in this world.'

Crabbe was in fact less successful in overcoming a second limitation in the view of moral law he held, which is not so often noted. In his world it is excessively easy to distinguish good from evil. He knew the attractions of evil sufficiently well to be able in some of his better work to make it really appear attractive, but there are very few occasions where it is not clear that a mistake has been made. This is not to say that his poetry would have been more interesting if it left the reader morally confused or gave him the cheap satisfaction of seeing a clergyman attracted by the values it is his vocation to warn men against. The important thing is that it deprives him of the possibility of writing some of the higher forms of tragedy, those in which there is an insoluble conflict between different goods or obligations, such as there is in Sophocles' *Antigone*. He stresses, as we have seen, that we must remain 'completely ignorant of the divine dispensation', but he does not seem to have entertained the possibility that in some situations a man, striving to do what is best according to Crabbe's own understanding of what is 'requisite for our conduct', may not know what to do. Similarly, although he does represent characters who suffer undeservedly, he never explores the implications on a larger scale. He does not envisage metaphysically meaningless suffering, or to put it in Christian terms, suffering which must appear meaningless for self-sacrifice to be most demanding: he assumes too readily that 'the afflictions and troubles of the religious and devout person are really trials, and will conduce to his present or his eternal welfare' (Hastings, p. 182). A minor exception is in *The Parish Register* (ii, ll. 581–634). The characteristic forms of his more tragic tales are pathos in the more sinned against than sinning, as illustrated by the aspect of *King Lear* he selects in the epigraph to 'Resentment', and realisation of a mistake when it is too late to go back, which is probably why he seems to have been moved most by *Macbeth*.

The third limitation, to some extent related to the second, is a tendency to find human behaviour too readily explicable in causal terms. John Wilson had this in mind when he contrasted Crabbe with the Greek tragedians:

> These dark dim visions of the world of man, which show him living in part in intelligible sufferings, and in part under unintelligible agencies, if they exaggerate his condition, show it at least in the colours in which it appears to the troubled and awful imagination. . . . The stories of Crabbe are on the other extreme point of the line. His causes of events are sedulously chosen out of the most intelligible, and incontestable realities; and he makes the current of human life run yet shallower than it appears even to the undiscerning eyes of ordinary experience.'[16]

Clearly one must beware of making false inferences from the form of fiction: there may be a reason for every event in a narrative not because the writer is in any sense a determinist, but because it gives his work shape. This is particularly the case in the line of aesthetic thought Crabbe was working within. John Dennis in 1712 – 'The second Reason why the Fiction of a Fable pleases us more, than an Historical Relation can do, is, because in an Historical Relation we seldom are acquainted with the true Causes of Events, whereas in a feign'd Action which is duly constituted . . . those Causes always appear'[17] – is echoed a century later by Mrs Barbauld: 'Every incident in a well written composition is introduced for a certain purpose, and made to forward a certain plan. . . .

The great author of the drama of life has not finished his piece; but the author must finish his'.[18] But we do know that Crabbe was influenced in his early moral thought by the well-known deterministic work, Joseph Priestley's *Doctrine of Philosophical Necessity* (1777). In both drafts of the 1779 'Opinions' in the Murray notebooks, Crabbe uses Priestley's arguments, and in the first he refers to him by name. With some timidity, Crabbe accepts Priestley's views against his numerous opponents who thought the possibility of Free Will was in jeopardy: 'How far each may be right, tho' I do not pretend to determine I have certainly a Freedom of Judging, and will confess I lean to the Doctors Argument.'[19] Priestley's exposition of the doctrine of necessity was not original and not very sophisticated (he does not, for example, distinguish between a cause and a reason), but he makes it quite clear that it does not entail the exclusion of Free Will – 'The choice is, indeed, [a man's] own making, and voluntary; but in voluntarily making it, he follows the laws of his nature, and invariably makes it in a certain definite manner' (pp. 16–17) – and he regards the indeterminist as introducing an element of randomness which throws moral philosophy into considerable difficulty: 'If nothing in the preceding state of his mind ... contributed to [an action], how did *he* contribute to it? and therefore in what sense can he call it *his*?' (p. 71). As well as reserving his 'Freedom of Judging', Crabbe devotes most of his comments on Priestley to the question of Free Will, and his main purpose in adducing him is to argue that if nothing happens by chance, the universe must have been created by a Designer. The word 'necessity' is often used in the eighteenth century to refer to fatalism, the view that what we do is wholly controlled by something which is independent of our own will; Crabbe strongly opposed this, representing it as one means by which men try to justify evil behaviour to themselves.[20] But in Priestley's system not only does human behaviour become as wholly intelligible as Newtonian physics, but human responsibility is maintained: 'In fact, the system of necessity makes every man the *maker of his own fortune*, in a stricter sense than any other system whatever' (p. 99, Priestley's italics). Yet in the sense that a man *has* to follow 'the laws of his nature' he must, when punishment has been administered with the intention of changing that nature, be regarded with more compassion than blame: 'as a necessarian, I cease to *blame* men for their vices in the ultimate sense of the word ... I, on my system, cannot help viewing them with *tenderness* and compassion' (p. 112, Priestley's italics). Crabbe must clearly have found this work attractive for several reasons, though it is unlikely that he retained conscious sympathy with the doctrine of necessity for long: Priestley was a Unitarian, one of his sources was Hume, and on the publication of Godwin's *Enquiry*

Concerning Political Justice in 1793, the doctrine was adopted into
another uncongenial context of thought. But the tendency in Crabbe
for human action to be a little too easily explicable in terms of previous
experiences or events was probably increased (if not caused) by this
early influence. It is, however, *only* a tendency, and only impresses one
as a limitation when one thinks by contrast, as Wilson did, of writers
of the highest order; for not only does Crabbe often exploit it to good
effect in the way suggested by Dennis and Mrs Barbauld, but in ways
which will be examined in detail in subsequent chapters he qualifies the
doctrine considerably.

Crabbe shows little interest in abstract thought about the authority
of law, but in order to appreciate the moral attitudes which recur
explicitly and implicitly in his tales, it is necessary to understand the
contemporary ways of thought they embody and oppose. In the
Huntington sermon quoted earlier (p. 11) he makes a conventional
distinction between the 'Laws which Men receive from the Light of
Nature', the Mosaic Law, and the laws revealed by Christ, and in a
Murray sermon (first preached 30 August 1801) he says that the third
of these did not set aside the first two. It is clear that he regarded the
moral laws as absolute. In one of the published sermons he will not allow
the fact that a lie injured no one to be morally relevant: 'suppose it be not
injurious, yet truth is violated, and that is sinful' (Hastings, p. 50); and
in another he says that good men would not 'on any consideration' have
'done anything wrong that good might come of it' (Hastings, p. 189).
Beyond this most of his thinking was based either on Butler's view of
the Conscience or on the theory of habit, which will be discussed later.
    The question of whether moral law was absolute or was subject to
question appears very frequently in eighteenth-century fiction. In
Joseph Andrews Mr Wilson relates how he became involved with a
London set, one of whom professed that 'there was nothing absolutely
good or evil in itself'. Ellis Cornelia Knight showed in her 'Continuation
of *Rasselas*', *Dinarbus* (1790), that she understood at least something of
Johnson's moral thought: 'to open a letter addressed to another, is a
breach of confidence, which political reasons may authorize, but which
honour and delicacy must ever reject' (4th ed., p. 119). In her *Tales
of the Castle*, of which Crabbe possessed a copy,[21] Mme la Comtesse de
Genlis tells a story, embodying the moral that 'nothing can sanctify a
lie', about an Arab who frees a prisoner for telling the truth when to
have lied seemed an obvious and simple way of escaping death. Unfortunately the pat reward undermines the moral point, not only
throughout the *Tales of the Castle*, but very frequently in the work of
other novelists of the period.

This question became a major preoccupation in the novel in response to Godwin's *Enquiry Concerning Political Justice* of 1793, that is, during the years of which we know from the *Life* that Crabbe 'seldom passed a day without reading part of some such work' (p. 158). It is worth dwelling at some length on Godwin and the novelists he influenced in order to see the ways of thought Crabbe was reacting against. Although there are so many important differences between Godwin and Bentham that F. E. L. Priestley has argued in his edition of the *Enquiry* that Godwin 'overturns the whole utilitarian scheme', it was Godwin who had by far the greater effect on contemporary fiction as a representative of moral thinking based not on the conception of absolute law, but on the calculation of consequences. According to Godwin, one should decide what is morally right to do in a given situation not according to any law, natural or revealed, but according to one's assessment of which action will bring about the greatest good to society. 'Morality itself is nothing but a calculation of consequences'; 'He that is not governed by the moral arithmetic of the case, or who acts from a disposition directly at war with that arithmetic, is unjust' (*Enquiry*, ed. K. Codell Carter (1971) pp. 38, 92 . This went straight into the novel, both in the form of dogma, as in Mary Hays's *Memoirs of Emma Courtney* (1796) – 'What is virtue, but a calculation of *the consequences of our actions* (Vol. II, p. 91, her italics) – and providing a new form of dramatic interest, as in the *Anna St. Ives* (1792) of Thomas Holcroft, who knew Godwin and was influenced by him before Godwin's important publications. Anna writes to her friend Louisa on the question of whether she should marry her social inferior Frank Henley: 'He thinks that the marriage of two such people can benefit society at large. I am persuaded that the little influence which it would have in the world would be injurious' (Oxford English Novels ed. (1970) p. 261). On this, Mrs Barbauld's comment 'What can be more absurd than to represent a young lady gravely considering, in the disposal of her hand, how she shall promote the greatest possible good of the system?'[22] is not altogether too cutting. But in Godwin's own far more gripping novels, especially *Caleb Williams*, one can see how far the interest in representing inner conflict in the novel was stimulated by the belief that 'Every case is a rule to itself' (*Enquiry*, p. 273). In these early years, however, the commoner reaction was horror at some of the implications of the new philosophy. Elizabeth Hamilton's *Memoirs of Modern Philosophers* (1800), a general satirical attack, parodies the ethical calculus in the remarks of the philosopher Myope: 'The most atrocious *crime* (as it is vulgarly termed) that ever was perpetrated, amounts to no more than a mere mistake; and whose conscience ever smote him for a mistake?' (Vol. 1, p. 84).

The commonest argument against utilitarianism brought to bear by writers of fiction was that, given the indefinite range of possible consequences which might be envisaged, there was permanent danger of emphasising only those which supported a decision already made on non-rational grounds. Elizabeth Hamilton exploits the ironies of rationalisation in *Memoirs of Modern Philosophers*. Vallaton persuades himself he is justified in sending to the guillotine an old man whose large sum of money he is commissioned to deliver: 'Of what utility is his life to society? ... Does not the philosophy, I now profess, teach that there is no such thing as right? From thence the inference is plain, that the gold ought in justice to be disposed of in the way that will be most conducive to the general interests of society' (Vol. 1, p. 73). Similarly, in Jane West's *Tale of the Times*, the villain asks, 'Is it not a general advantage, that property should be transferred from an indolent sensualist to an active enterprizing citizen, who would turn it to beneficial purposes?' (Vol. 11, p. 294) And similarly Crabbe's Jachin in *The Borough*, Letter XIX:

> 'these have cash and give it to the poor.'
> A second thought from this to work began –
> 'And can they give it to a poorer man?'   (ll. 157–9)

One protection against this danger in utilitarian thought was the insistence on the absolute nature of law which we saw in Crabbe on p. 14: under *no* circumstances should a moral law be broken 'that good might come of it'. Following Butler, Crabbe also put considerable emphasis on the role of Conscience. In Butler, Conscience is the 'superior principle of reflection' in man

> which distinguishes between the internal principles of his heart, as well as his external actions: which passes judgement upon himself and them; pronounces determinately some actions to be in themselves just, right, good; others to be in themselves evil, wrong, unjust: which, without being consulted, without being advised with, magisterially exerts itself, and approves or condemns him the doer of them accordingly. (*Fifteen Sermons* (1726) Sermon 2, §8)

Butler sees that 'a great part, perhaps the greatest part, of the intercourse amongst mankind, cannot be reduced to fixed determinate rules. Yet in these cases there is a right and a wrong: a merciful, a liberal, a kind and compassionate behaviour, which surely is our duty; and an unmerciful contracted spirit, an hard and oppressive course of behaviour, which is most certainly immoral and vicious' (10. 10). In this area conscience can guide where rules cannot; and on major issues it 'magisterially exerts itself'. Although he regards conscience as our chief defence against self-deceit, Butler does not think it is infallible: in sermons on Balaam and on David's murder of Uriah, he dwells at length on the *prima facie* incredible fact that men who are on the whole good can show 'total insensibility of mind' (10. 10) towards major crimes, and on the habitual self-deceit which eventually 'corrupts conscience' (10. 16). But he does believe that if strenuous efforts at self-honesty are made, conscience will give true guidance. To most modern commentators this seems a serious error, since in the course of history many atrocities seem to have been committed for conscientious motives. In this respect, Crabbe is substantially with Butler, even though he sometimes expresses himself differently. We noted earlier (p. 12) that Crabbe does not probe issues of insoluble perplexity. In a Murray sermon first preached on 22 August 1790, he says, 'Let the voice of Conscience, in its stillest whispers be always attended to. If so, it will answer rightly, but if you seldom ask it, the answer of Conscience is vague and deceitful, and if you neglect it, will be callous to Sin.' There is a slight modification of Butler here, in that Butler almost always reserved the word 'Conscience' for what answers rightly; but the more important point is that Crabbe follows him in thinking that a conscience well 'attended to ... will answer rightly'. 'A conscience, when pure and just ... cannot err' (Hastings, p. 46). Sometimes Crabbe follows Butler in thinking of conscience as a 'divine Preceptor'[23] which magisterially exerts itself, but at others his looser use of language allows him to represent the relationship between a man and his conscience more as one between equals, in a way which resembles 'The Struggles of Conscience' (*Tales* (1812) XIV). In one sermon he speaks of 'the thoughtless and wicked, who make a kind of compromise with conscience by resolutions to become faithful and obedient at a later period' (Hastings, p. 43). But despite the slight modification, he is here drawing both on Butler's imagery ('they are for making a composition with the Almighty' (7. 13)) and on one detail of his profound analysis of the many forms of self-deceit.

Small as it is in its effect on the theory of conscience as the light of God within, this change of emphasis shows that Crabbe did not accept Butler's distinctive basis for an ethic fundamentally opposed to any kind of utilitarianism. Butler vigorously rejected the calculation of consequences as an ethical principle not only because he saw that it could 'in supposable cases' lead to 'the most shocking instances of injustice, adultery, murder, perjury, and even of persecution',[24] but because he regarded it as a fact of human nature that

there are certain dispositions of mind, and certain actions, which are in themselves approved or disapproved by mankind, abstracted from

the consideration of their tendency to the happiness or misery of the
world . . . There are pieces of treachery, which in themselves appear
base and detestable to every one . . . Fidelity, honour, strict justice,
are in themselves approved in the highest degree, abstracted from the
consideration of their tendency. (footnote to 12. 31)

To argue that these responses are natural, Butler of course had to make
a distinction (2. 5–8) between two senses of 'following nature'; that of
obeying every impulse and that of acting in the way most suited to the
distinctively human form of life. In Butler's account of this form of life,
conscience has the highest authority, so that to act according to it is to
obey the law of our being, to behave in the distinctively human way.
He distinguishes authority from strength, since men obviously do not
always obey; but to disobey is a 'violation of the constitution of man'
(2. 13). In slightly shifting the usage of the word 'Conscience', Crabbe
loses this particular conception of human nature.

But although he does not follow Butler in detail here, Crabbe does
draw on a tradition of thought which law behind Butler. We may now
begin to see more adequately Crabbe's conception of the temporal
working of the moral laws, tracing through time the consequences of
moral choices on the quality of life. To Crabbe moral action was, as we
have seen, partly a matter of divine command, revealed through the
Old and New Testaments; but it was also a matter of fulfilling human
nature, of becoming more fully human or becoming inhuman. In so far
as consequences entered into it, the focus was less on the consequences
of actions, than on the consequences on the nature of the agent. Actions
could not be weighed in isolation, as if by a creature of angelic stature,
but were the expression of a character which had been formed largely
by what it had done. Moral action or inaction was momentous not
because one had to calculate the effect on the good of the human race,
but because in the course of time, what one did had a direct effect on
what one became: by one's choices one largely created one's own moral
nature, sometimes on single occasions of abnormal significance, more
often by the repetition of similar choices which became habits.

Crabbe shares the basic distinction between the two senses of
'following nature', though he is not concerned to make it with Butler's
precision. He affirms in one sermon, for example, that in following
Christ there is necessarily 'much opposition to the nature of man'
(Hastings, p. 18). In many sermons he develops or refers to the parable
of the talents as a way of expressing the fulfilment of human nature in
terms of obligation; in one he says characteristically, 'in the early
repentant and religious mind, improvement of the talents becomes its
natural and pleasant occupation' (Hastings, p. 41). His conception of

how to achieve the more fully human nature is thus nearer to William Law than to Butler. To Law, 'The measure of our love to God, seems in justice to be the measure of our love of every virtue. We are to love and practise it with all our heart, with all our soul, with all our mind, and with all our strength. And when we cease to live with this regard to virtue, we live below our nature'.[25] The practice of the virtues has a divine sanction, but it is the only way to develop *human* nature. A classic exposition of this way of thought is John Scott's *Christian Life* (1681), of which Crabbe possessed a copy. The distinction between the two senses of nature is fundamental in Scott's thought: 'to be a perfect Man, is to live up to the highest Principle of Human Nature, which is *Reason*; and till we are once released from the Slavery of *Sense* and Passion . . . we are in a *maimed* and *imperfect* Condition . . . And till we are in some measure arrived to this, our Nature is so far from being *perfect*, that it is the most *wretched* and *confused* Thing in the whole World'. (9th ed. (1729) p. 14) This gives the individual two basic processes to choose between: 'in the Practice of Virtue [men] are more and more *inclined* and *disposed* to it, and so by degrees it becomes *easy* and *natural* to them' (p. 12); 'when we have *carelessly* permitted *one* Sin to break thro' our Fence, that will open a Gap for *another* to follow; and if this be not presently *stopt* by Repentance, 'twill make the Breach yet *wider* for *others*, and those again for *others*, till at last they have made a *Thorow-fare* in our Wills for a Custom of sinning'. (p. 104)

Although man is quite free to choose between these alternatives, habitual choice in either direction steadily decreases the freedom as character is formed. The virtuous man is unlikely to be dismayed at being less disposed to act badly; but the vicious man can be held responsible for actions which, given his character, might seem inevitable, because earlier actions have to a crucial extent created that character. Although this idea that a man, within limits, creates himself is associated most readily now with existentialism, it can be seen that the emphasis is quite different. The freedom is not valued as an end in itself: the authentically human is not the most free action, but the most virtuous. This way of thought in fact goes back to Aristotle, who in a discussion of free will argues that one cannot excuse law-breaking, for example, by saying that the agent is 'just that sort of man'. 'Such people have only themselves to blame for having acquired a character like that by their loose living, just as they have only themselves to blame for being unjust, if they make a practice of unjust behaviour, or intemperate, if they spend their time in drinking or other forms of dissipation. It is their persistent activities in certain directions that make them what they are' (*Nicomachean Ethics*, Penguin transl., pp. 90–91). The tradition is kept alive in our time not by the existentialists but by those who draw on Aristotle.[26] But in the eighteenth century it was common currency. In Lillo's immensely popular *London Merchant* (1731), for example, the ruined hero, Barnwell, says towards the end: 'What avails it to think on what I might have been? I now am – what I have made myself'. Thinking similarly, but of the cultivation of virtue rather than vice, Young writes in the sixth Night of his *Night Thoughts* (1744):

> Each man makes his own stature, builds himself:
> Virtue alone outbuilds the pyramids.   (ll. 311–12)

It was given currency in the later seventeenth and the eighteenth centuries both through Christian apologetics and sermons, and through the theories of education which derived largely from them. Although Aristotle had, through Aquinas, passed into the central line of Roman Catholic thought, Jeremy Taylor felt able to use arguments drawn from the theory of habit to attack Roman Catholic doctrines in *Unum Necessarium*: 'We can efform our nature over anew, and create ourselves again, and make ourselves bad when God hath made us good ... or on the contrary, what was crooked in nature, we can make straight by ... customs' (*The Whole Works*, ed. R. Heber (1839) Vol. VIII, p. 419). The Latitudinarian divines who had so much influence on eighteenth-century Anglicanism generally laid more emphasis on the natural goodness of man than Crabbe found justified. To Tillotson, to act virtuously 'is the most pleasant enjoyment in the world. It is natural, and whatever is so, is delightful. We do like ourselves, whenever we relieve the wants and distresses of others' (*Works* (1820) Vol. I, p. 205). When Crabbe says anything approaching this in his sermons, it is almost always in the form of a qualification to a more sombre argument. The quotations on p. 10 from Hastings, p. 13 and on p. 18 from Hastings, p. 41 (concerning the pleasures of acting well) do not by any means indicate the major emphasis of the arguments in the sermons they are taken from. But both directly and through the innumerable imitations, he must have been influenced by Tillotson's accounts of vice as habit.[27] Tillotson's sermon, 'Of the deceitfulness and danger of sin', in particular, although not by any means original, brings together three key images for the growth of vice, the progress, the seed, and hardening, in a way which makes it a classic statement:

> he that once engages in a vicious course is in danger to proceed in it, being insensibly trained on from one degree of wickedness to another; so that the farther he advanceth, his retreat grows more difficult, because he is still pushed on with a greater violence. All error, as well of practice as of judgement, is endless; and when a man is once out of the way, the farther he shall go on the harder he will find it to return

into the right way ... by frequency of acts, a thing grows into a habit; and a confirmed habit is a second kind of nature.... But vicious habits have a greater advantage, and are of a quicker growth. For the corrupt nature of man is a rank soil, to which vice takes easily, and wherein it thrives apace. The mind of man hath need to be prepared for piety and virtue; it must be cultivated to that end, and ordered with great care and pains; but vices are weeds that grow wild, and spring up of themselves. They are, in some sort, natural to the soil, and, therefore, they need not to be planted and watered, it is sufficient if they be neglected and let alone ... by passing from one degree of sin to another, the sinner becomes hardened in his wickedness, and does insensibly slide into that, in which, without a miraculous grace of God, he is like for ever to continue. (Vol. II, pp. 19–25)

In many of his sermons Crabbe traces the 'progress' of vice. In a Murray sermon first preached on 19 March 1797, he says, 'there is commonly a visible Progress both in Godliness and in Guilt ... Our life is progressive. We do not stand still', and he invites his listeners to consider in detail 'by what ways, some who are called Christians fall from Good to Evil, from one Sin to an Excess of Sinning, from little Omissions to enormous Crimes, and from forgetfulness of God to their Soul's Perdition'. Towards the end, Conscience is asleep, but 'it is not dead, and sometimes before it is hardened it rises unexpectedly and frights the Soul by telling its Sins, and representing its Fall, so that the Sinner hurries to his Favourite Companions, his favourite Pleasures, to drown its voice and lay it asleep again. And now when this be completely done, the last Step of this sad Progress is taken.' The parables he dwells on most frequently are those of the prodigal son, the talents, and the sower. In a Murray sermon on the sower first preached on 30 May 1813, he links the seed image with that of the talents: 'if we do not cultivate good thoughts, Evil will come of themselves.... There are those who disliking the Labour of Improvement, will deny the Ability to improve, that is, they will bury the Talent in the Napkin.' Elsewhere the image of the progress is exploited to bring out the irony of a creature whose 'life is progressive' trying to find satisfaction in finite pleasures:

His Desires and Appetites his Eagerness and Longings for the Pleasures will increase and the Pleasures themselves will diminish and become Pleasures no more: then he will seek for an Increase of them and that also if he finds it, will become of no Value and he will soon long for more variety and for more sinful Gratifications, till at last there will be no bounds to his Wishes and no End to his Disappointments. (Murray Collection, 26 August 1827)

Death in remorse is the natural end to the progress. One thinks most immediately here of 'Peter Grimes'.

This degeration of conscience into intolerable remorse was not, however, the invariable end of these representations of the progress of vice: often the breaker of moral law was left in ironic enslavement. Here one thinks of, for example, 'Procrastination' or 'The Mother'. Butler coolly remarks that 'the tyranny of our own lawless passions is the nearest and most dangerous of all tyrannies', and Blair, in a sermon 'On the slavery of vice', losing the edge of the irony, explains at length that 'The sinner yields to the impulse, merely because he cannot resist it. . . . He does not go, but is driven. . . . Vice confirms its dominion, and extends it still farther over the soul, by compelling the sinner to support one crime by means of another.' In a Murray sermon first used on 3 July 1796, Crabbe asks, with an ironic glance at Paine, 'what were indeed the Rights of Man in his State of Freedom and Innocence?' and continues, 'the World is not our only Tyrant. We are ourselves the Enemies of ourselves, and miserable is the Yoke our own Passions and Evil Habits, our Humours and Sins make for us . . . The Yoke of Christ, truly taken upon us, will entirely release us from this Bondage.' It is characteristic that Crabbe leaves open here the possibility of release; but his usual emphasis is on the increasing difficulty of it as the progress continues.

To summarise the conclusions so far reached: in holding to a conception of absolute moral law, as against the expedences of contemporary utilitarianism, Crabbe drew to some extent on Butler's view of the role of Conscience, but placed more emphasis on the conception of a self created through time, which either became more fully human through virtuous choices or followed a degenerative 'progress' towards inhumanity through evil choices.

HABIT AND THE 'PROGRESS' FORM

In order to understand Crabbe's views on habit more fully, it is necessary to look at Locke, who although he probably did not have much direct influence on Crabbe (an exceptional instance is the portrait of Richard Monday: see p. 56), greatly influenced the literary expressions of 'progress' which Crabbe certainly was acquainted with. The influence of the tradition of Christian thought about habit on the fiction of the eighteenth century was greatly strengthened by Locke's *Thoughts concerning Education* (1692). To Locke, 'the great thing to be minded in education is, what *habits* you settle' (§18). The pupil must have desirable 'habits woven into the very principles of his nature' (§42), and the seeds of vicious habits must be vigilantly extracted. 'Those seeds of vice are not to be suffered to take root, but must be carefully weeded out as soon as ever they begin to show themselves' (§100), otherwise, 'all the force, skill, and diligence we can use is scarce enough to cleanse the vitiated seed-plot' (§84). The image of the hardening effect of habit is also taken over: the fundamental aim must always be to make the pupil's mind 'supple and pliant to what their parents' reason advises them now, and so prepare them to obey what their own reason shall advise hereafter' (§112). The extent of Locke's influence, as in so any areas of his thought, was increased by a fundamental uncertainty about the nature of the mind before the educative process started. At the end, for example, he describes the child's mind in his famous image as 'white paper, or wax, to be molded and fashioned as one pleases' (§217). But elsewhere he insisted that 'God has stamped certain characters upon men's minds', so that the educator should 'observe what their native stock is, how it may be improved, and what it is fit for. . . . For in many cases, all that we can do, or should aim at, is to make the best of what nature has given. . . . Everyone's natural genius should be carried as far as it could; but to attempt the putting another upon him will be but labour in vain' (§66).

Thus on one hand he was enlisted by such a pillar of orthodoxy as *The Lady's Magazine*. In a story called 'The Assignation' (Vol. III (1772) p. 545 ff.), the parents of Flirtilla treat her 'with too much fondness in her tender years'. 'The twig may be bent when young, but will preserve all its growing deformity when it has shot into a tree; and parents frequently find it is too late to begin, what once to have begun it was not too early.' Consequently she makes a 'precipitative choice' and is eventually found 'hanging in her own garters . . . a warning of the dangerous effects of indiscreet fondness'. The orthodox influence continued after the turn of the century. In *The Disgraceful Effects of Falsehood and the Fruits of Early Indulgence; Exemplified in the Histories of Percival Pembroke and Augustus Fitzhue* (1807), Mrs Pilkington shows herself better able to paraphrase Locke than to write cautionary tales: 'Though Education may have the power of improving the disposition, it can never entirely change the natural propensities of the mind' (p. 64).

The other possibility, that the educator was confronted by a sheet of 'white paper', was developed by Hartley, whose fundamental doctrine in psychology was described by Mill as 'the formation of all human character by circumstances, through the universal Principle of Association, and the consequent unlimited possibility of improving the moral and intellectual condition of mankind by education' (*Autobiography*, World's Classics ed., p. 91). From Hartley it passed to Godwin ('it is impression that makes the man. . . . Children are a sort of raw material put into our hands', *Enquiry*, pp. 34–7) and thence to, for example, Mary Hays, who writes in *Memoirs of Emma Courtney* (1796) of 'those associations and habits which make us what we are; for without outward impressions we should be nothing' (Vol. I, p. 7). Godwin himself writes very vividly of the powers of habit and early impression in his novels, but representing it as an evil, for 'the perfection of the human character consists in approaching as nearly as possible to the perfectly voluntary state' (*Enquiry*, p. 46).

The paradox here is one that runs throughout Godwin's thought, but in relation to education it draws on Rousseau, to whom Godwin acknowledges much indebtedness. Rousseau's most important contribution was the idea that the child's mind should be encouraged to develop at its own ('natural') pace, but his confessedly unsystematic way of expressing himself left him highly vulnerable to ironic attack. His way of teaching pliancy and self-control is precisely opposite to Locke's: 'The only habit the child should be allowed to contract is that of having no habits. . . . Prepare the way for his control of his liberty and the use of his strength by leaving his body its natural habit, by making him capable of lasting self-control, of doing all that he wills when his will is formed' (*Emile*, Everyman transl., p. 30). Yet later he wants to re-introduce teaching by habituation: 'you must make children copy the deeds you wish to grow into habits, until they can do them with understanding and for the love of what is good' (p. 68). Similarly, although the child should do 'nothing because of other people, but only what nature asks of him' and the mind 'should be left undisturbed till its faculties have developed' (p. 57), this is in fact an illusion: 'There is no subjection so complete as that which preserves the forms of freedom. . . . Is not this poor child, without knowledge, strength, or wisdom, entirely at your mercy? . . . He should never take a step you have not foreseen, nor utter a word you could not foretell' (pp. 84–5). As will be shown later, Crabbe's exploitation of similar ironies was possibly based on first-hand knowledge of *Emile*; but we know from the *Life* that he was certainly acquainted with the sensible application of Rousseau's ideas by Mrs Inchbald in *Nature and Art* (1796), and he is unlikely not to have read Bage's *Hermsprong* (1796). In another work published the same year, the anonymous *Berkeley Hall, or the Pupil of Experience*, he may have encountered some typical satire against Rousseau from Locke's point of view: 'I was not restrained in any whim . . . for fear of breaking my spirit. . . . I naturally grew up unaccustomed to discipline or subordination, proud, obstinate, self-opinionated, and incorrigible' (Vol. III, pp. 13–14). When the father of this man attempted 'to *sow the ground* which he had so long suffered to remain *fallow*, he found it was already covered with tares and noxious weeds, which all his labour could not eradicate' (Vol. III, p. 14, original italics).

Thus the idea of 'creating' one's self, through habitual choice (free, guided, or determined) gradually settling into confirmed character, was common to writers who on most issues were radically opposed to each other. One of the commonest ways of exploiting it in fiction was the representation of extremes of remorse. In Sophia King's highly orthodox *Waldorf, or the Dangers of Philosophy* (1798) the eponymous hero, who 'entered into a sort of compromise with his conscience, *never* to suggest his sorrows' (Vol. II, p. 152), is nonetheless so tormented by his crimes that he kills himself through remorse, and in case the point is missed Lok, the philosopher who corrupted him, asks his father at the end, 'what is conscience? It is the creature of instruction' (Vol. II, p. 211), and is then struck by remorse himself and dies weeping over the tombs of Waldorf and his chief victim. In *Nature and Art*, Mrs Inchbald, herself influenced by one of the dreaded philosophers, describes the feelings of William, who becomes a judge, when he discovers that the prostitute he has condemned to death is the girl he first seduced: 'wonder, astonishment, horror, and every other sensation was absorbed by – Remorse: – it wounded, it stabbed, it rent his hard heart, as it would do a tender one. It havocked on his firm inflexible mind, as it would on a weak and pliant brain! Spirit of Agnes! Look down, and behold all your wrongs revenged! William feels – Remorse!' (1820 ed., p. 354)

An even more frequent motif was the 'progress' (which often, but not always, culminated in remorse). It is found not only in writers of the most diverse beliefs, but in diverse genres: novel, drama, verse, periodical essay, biography, and, of course, painting and engraving. G. A. Starr has shown in *Defoe and Spiritual Autobiography* (1965) that an early version of the 'progress' form developed out of the popular spiritual autobiographies of dissenters: '[Crusoe's] running off to sea is not ... the direct cause of all later vicissitudes, but it does initiate a pattern of wrong-doing which has far-reaching consequences.'[28] It seems probable from the passage in the Preface to *The Borough* which refers to Letter IV that Crabbe was acquainted with this sort of autobiography and the patterns it often adopted, even though *The Memoirs ... of James Lackington ... Written by Himself*, on which the well-selected quotations given as footnotes in the 1834 edition suggest 'The Convert' may have been based, does not show any sense of the sort of structure the tale assumed. The crude 'progress' pattern was already current in Grub Street: Ned Ward's *Rise and Fall of Madam Coming-Sir* (?1720) is a hack prose narration of a country-girl's history as, in turn, barmaid, mistress, prostitute and brothel-servant, ending with premature death from venereal disease. But in the early 1730s it acquired much greater sophistication in the work of Lillo and Hogarth. In *The London Merchant* (1731), Barnwell, the once virtuous apprentice, is seduced by a prostitute, Millwood, and from then on 'one vice as naturally begets another as a father a son' (II, xiii, l. 9). But within the basic 'progress' structure, the moral issues are seen in some complexity.

Crabbe was certainly acquainted with the tradition of popular prints which lay behind Hogarth's work,[29] and although contemporary comparisons are limited to remarks about the detailed depiction of low life, Crabbe probably owed more directly to Hogarth's own handling of the 'progress' form than to the literary work which came between them, so it is worth examining the resemblances. Although the division of Hogarth's progresses into separate pictures seems to suggest only the earlier work of Crabbe, organised around quasi-pictorial contrasts, the best plates in fact, like episodes in Crabbe's maturer works, imply a narrative continuity. As Ronald Paulson has pointed out,[30] the first plate of *The Harlot's Progress* (1732) suggests the past, through the York wagon on the left, and the future, through Chartres standing in the doorway on the right, as well as the present in the central group formed by the girl and the procuress. In a famous remark in the Preface to *Joseph Andrews*, Fielding said of Hogarth's figures that 'they appear to think'; one has to add, however ungraciously, that they appear to feel much more than Fielding's own characters, who outwardly owe so much to them. Crabbe was able to move beyond Hogarth in this respect, as will be shown later, but there is little in the fine last three paragraphs of 'Procrastination', for example, which Hogarth could not have achieved in a painting or engraving. The major central figures in Hogarth are not merely *exempla* though they do exemplify: the harlot's face is recognisably that of a particular individual in all five plates on which it appears. Crabbe maintains a similar poise between individuality and generality, even though his means of registering the continuity of personal identity are more various. In his mature work Crabbe is usually concerned with the feelings of at least one other character than the main one. Similarly, the harlot's child, bewildered and peripheral in the fifth plate, becomes central in the last; and more obviously the girl rejected by her seducer in the first plate of *The Rake's Progress* is the only person who pities him in the last. It is equally characteristic of Crabbe and Hogarth that this remarkable purity and durability of feeling should be emphasised by the specific contrast with the trivial prurience of the other two visitors to Bedlam. Finally, Crabbe's famous ability to describe characters and feelings through description of possessions or surroundings was noted in Hogarth by Walpole in his *Anecdotes of Painting* (1762), of which Crabbe possessed a copy: 'The very furniture of his rooms describes the characters of the persons to whom they belong; a lesson that might be of use to comic authors' (*Works* (1798) Vol. III, p. 457).

After Hogarth's major Progresses, criminals seem, to judge from the Ordinary of Newgate's accounts, to have become more regular in their development. On Wednesday 4 February 1736, for example, Burton Brace, in a letter to his former fellow drawers in the taverns of London, warned them how to avoid his fate: 'if you once come to think Cheating a small Fault, or Fraud in any Degree excusable, you will quickly advance farther in the same unhappy Path, and come at last to Practices as bad as mine.' The Grub Street tradition was directly stimulated, though in Eliza Haywood's *Life's Progress through the Passions, or the Adventures of Natura* (1748), for example, the respectable morals to be drawn from the progress are chiefly confined to the chapter-headings, leaving Natura to pursue his more or less salacious adventures, seldom hampered by comment, in the chapters themselves. But the influence on serious fiction was slow in developing. Although Lovelace, for example, degenerates, Richardson's concern with the development of character through time is on a minute-by-minute scale which makes the deliberately erratic pace of the 'progress' uninteresting to him. Fielding's conception of character is too static for time to be of major moral significance in his novels. He introduces progresses in the form of digressions which critics either regard as irrelevant or have to see in some special relationship to the main plot. For example, Mr Wilson's Progress in *Joseph Andrews* has been interpreted as a forceful qualification to any inference which might be made from the main plot that Joseph's sexual continence is absurd because it is comic.[31] Whether such views are accepted or not, the histories of Mr Wilson, of the Man of the Hill in *Tom Jones*, and of Miss Matthews in *Amelia* are fully coherent and could be detached from the novels. This practice was commonly imitated by Fielding's contemporaries and in the following decades: Miss Williams in *Roderick Random* (1748), George Primrose in *The Vicar of Wakefield* (1766), and Miss Atkins in *The Man of Feeling* (1771) are all relatively short and self-sufficient histories, and they were in fact commonly reprinted separately in miscellanies, as they formed a useful supply of free copy.[32] The basic form is of some kind of initial moral error leading to a series of worsening incidents, and culminating in either disaster or providential rescue. The initial error was often due to bad education and the stages of the progress frequently followed each other causally as well as temporally; but the emphasis varied very widely. There was a natural tendency for the form to lose itself in the ancient romance tradition of narrative digression. The moral interest was usually focused either on specific issues (in Mr Wilson's case, the inadequacy of the view that the intrinsic beauty of virtue is sufficient motive to good action, and the mistake of trusting to Fortune rather than Providence) or on the pathos of the protagonist (in Miss Atkins' case the misery of women who, more sinned against than sinning, are trapped into prostitution).

Of the literary versions of the 'progress' form, however, it is the periodical essays, particularly of Johnson, which most directly influenced Crabbe. It is clear that a direct influence on MacKenzie's Miss Atkins was Johnson's more restrained and deeply moving papers on Misella, in *The Rambler* (nos. 170–1), in which the prostitute herself, with quiet dignity and acceptance of limited guilt, tells how she was abused by her first seducer, on whom she was dependent, and how her subsequent progress was caused by social prejudice and financial necessity. These particular papers are in a 'progress' form, but although Johnson admired Hogarth, they seem less to be indebted to him than to stand in the line of Johnson's general development of the preceptive tales which were used in the *Tatler* and the *Spectator* and their imitators. Before Johnson, the interest was usually in illustrating a precept, and often Johnson's is also. But in many of the narrative papers, which are usually in the form of a supposed autobiographical letter, although there is seldom a formal progress, the emphasis is very largely on what it felt like to live the kind of life or the moral attitude described; and often this involves, as in Crabbe, seeing the effect of the passage of time. Captator, for example, a legacy-hunter, not only portrays the difficulties and humiliations of spending his youth in flattering his relatives, but describes the long-term consequences: 'I am arrived at manhood without any useful art or generous sentiment' (*Rambler* 198, Yale ed., Vol. v, p. 270). Pertinax, in *Rambler* 95, describes his childhood in a 'house of discord', which causes him to be 'trained up in all the arts of domestic sophistry', and the habit of sophistical argument, which eventually contaminates him intellectually and morally: 'I had perplexed truth with falsehood till my ideas were confused. ... It was at last the sport of my vanity to weaken the obligations of moral duty, and efface the distinctions of good and evil' (Yale ed., Vol. iv, pp. 146–7). But instead of the outward form of a progress, we are taken deeper into the development of his inner life: 'I soon had the mortification of seeing my conversation courted only by the ignorant or wicked, by either boys who were enchanted by novelty, or wretches who having long disobeyed virtue and reason, were now desirous of my assistance to dethrone them.' Mortification develops into shame and together with sheer weariness finally leads to a reorientation of his way of life.

John Hawkesworth clearly owed a great deal to Johnson, but by placing more emphasis on the use of incidents to dramatise the states and changes of mind which interested his master, he prepared the way for a different aspect of Crabbe's art. In *Adventurer* 4 (1752: almost exactly a year after the Misella papers) he argued that the events in a narrative should follow 'in a regular and connected series'. For this reason, among others, he particularly admired drama, but, admitting some boldness, linked it with the kind of narrative suitable to a periodical such as the *Adventurer*: 'such pieces, although formed upon a single incident, if that incident be sufficiently uncommon to gratify curiosity, and sufficiently interesting to engage the passions, may afford an entertainment, which, if it is not lasting, is yet of the highest kind.' In *Adventurer* 18, he went a little further (adducing the commonplace distinction between tales based on a precept and those based on passions):

> Fables of the preceptive kind should always include the precept in the event, and the event should be related with such circumstances as render the precept sufficiently evident. As the incident should be simple, the inference should be in the highest degree natural and obvious. Those that produce their effect upon the passions, should excite them strongly, and always connect them with their proper objects.

Of Hawkesworth's own tales the one which comes nearest to Crabbe (to 'Edward Shore' in particular) is that of Opsinous, in papers 12–14, though the comparison brings out the delicacy of Crabbe's handling. Hawkesworth's tale keeps closely to the 'progress' form: Opsinous wants 'to communicate the series of events, by which I have been led on in an insensible deviation from felicity, and at last plunged in irremediable calamity.' The first step is to engage in a sophistical dispute with a lawyer who offers to maintain that there is no divine Revelation. Opsinous is defeated and is pushed further into scepticism, at a club for free-thinkers, until he resembles Pertinax. Johnson's paper is clearly in mind: 'I sometimes, indeed, reflected, that I was propagating opinions by which I had myself become vicious and wretched.' But the emphasis is on incident. Ospinous's crowning achievement is to seduce the lawyer's daughter. The ending is rapid and absurdly melodramatic: the girl conceives, Opsinous insists on an abortion, she dies, Opsinous is accused and convicted of murder, is reprieved, swallows an overdose of poison, vomits most of it, but retains enough to die slowly in desperate remorse. But although this loss of control violates Hawkesworth's own principle that the incident should be 'simple', he is still attempting, however unsuccessfully, to 'include the precept in the event'. Such tales as this were, like the extracted progresses from the novels, frequently reprinted and imitated in popular magazines of the kind which Crabbe not only read widely, during his early years, but occasionally contributed to. His own tales owe much more to them than to eighteenth-century narrative verse.³³ The deep human sympathy which Johnson brought to bear on the brief histories in his papers is evident throughout Crabbe's work, and the close relationship which Hawkesworth wanted to see between incident and moral inference is particularly clear in, for example, 'Resentment'.

This influence was reinforced by a development in the novel during the years when his son tells us that Crabbe read from novels almost daily. John Moore's *Zeluco* (1789) is the first powerful attempt to base a full-length novel on the sustained close analysis of the progress of a mind, in a manner drawing on the Hogarth tradition. Zeluco moves through the stages of cruelty from killing a sparrow to the murder of his own child, but although the plot is often excessively lurid, Moore's chief interest is in the process of mental change. Godwin's *Caleb Williams* (1794), a far more gripping and accomplished development of this sort of fiction, is listed in the Cambridge notebook as contained in Crabbe's library. His disciple, Mary Hays, indicates a major source of Godwin's interest: 'the most useful fictions are, perhaps, such, as delineating the progress, and tracing the consequences, of one strong, indulged passion, or prejudice, afford materials, by which the philosopher may calculate the powers of the human mind, and learn the springs which set it in motion.' (*Memoirs of Emma Courtney* (1799) Vol. I, p. 5) But the novel has an imaginative power which goes far beyond such a mechanistic philosophical intention. Apart from its insight into the workings of the mind, two major contributions made by it to the development of the novel are particularly relevant to Crabbe. Firstly, against the general trend of eighteenth-century fiction, it demonstrates repeatedly that virtuous and vicious characters are not conveniently distinguishable in their every action. When Laura naïvely says, even faced with Caleb, 'The good man and the bad, are characters precisely opposite, not characters disinguished from each other by imperceptible shades' (Oxford English Novels ed. (1970) p. 299), the whole book weighs against her with crushing irony. Secondly, one of the novel's chief structural principles is the series of parallels and contrasts between different characters and their situations, which usually carry an ironic force. Not only does Falkland come to resemble Tyrrel, whose values he wholly despises, but Caleb in turn comes to resemble Falkland. Falkland's resemblance to Tyrrel is shown, for example, in the parallel between Tyrrel's despotic treatment of his cousin Emily and Falkland's treatment of Caleb. Both try to force repentance from a weaker person while desiring 'the respect and applause of every one' (p. 57). Falkland, defending his reputation in an informal trial, ironically realises that it is a false god: 'Reputation has been the idol, the jewel of my life' (p. 102). Caleb later thinks he is free of the irony when he uses the same reference to *Othello*: 'Of what value is a fair fame? It is the jewel of men formed to be amused with baubles'. (p. 182) But by the end he has realised that his writing of the book itself shows the same irony: 'I began these memoirs with the idea of vindicating my character' (p. 326).

Caleb Williams is an exception: Godwin's other novels show the fascination with the forms of 'progress', but lack the complex ironic structure, which, as subsequent discussion of major tales will show, equally stimulated Crabbe's imagination, despite the radical intellectual differences between the two men. Far more characteristic of the decade is *Nature and Art*, which does not develop the line Moore and Godwin had taken, though it has moved beyond the earlier habit of isolating the 'progress' in a digression. Several of the characters' actions become hardened into the habit which is a 'second kind of nature', and the main progress, that of Agnes, is integrated with the main plot.

In the 'progress' as it had developed up to the turn of the century, Crabbe clearly found a congenial form. Hawkesworth's limitation to either a single central incident or a 'regular and connected series' accorded with Crabbe's conception of his own abilities. In a letter of 1816, printed by Broadley and Jerrold, he says he has received material for a new story from a lady at Bath, but fears that 'it is too complicated and loaded with incident' to suit him (p. 140). Rejecting the advice to attempt a longer work, he says in the 1812 Preface that he is unfitted to write a poem 'where no one pursues his peculiar objects and adventures', and goes on in an apt image to compare his tales to a group of pilgrims as opposed to a disciplined army. Of 'Peter Grimes', the *Critical Review* (1810) said, 'The greater part of this hideous story is told in the Ordinary of Newgate style' (p. 302), and indeed Crabbe wrote to Scott, 'I have often thought that I should love to read *Reports*, that is, brief Histories of extraordinary Cases with the Judgements.'[34] Critics have frequently shown his use of aspects of the 'progress' form. In the best chapter of her book on Crabbe, Mrs Haddakin analyses his increasing 'concern with process' (p. 102). T. N. Talfourd's emphasis reminds one of Butler: 'he sets forth the humbler charities, and traces out the miserable and often fatal consequences, which flow from habits and affectations which we are disposed to consider as venial.' T. Bareham notes at the other end of the scale that Crabbe's representations of ghosts and of insanity usually convey extreme states of remorse or other moral derangement.[35] Vague awareness of the 'progress' pattern has, however, often led to an exaggeration of a bias towards degeneration which is certainly present but not exclusive. Leslie Stephen put it drily: 'No-one describes better the process of going to the dogs',[36] and the point is repeatedly made by Crabbe's critics, more heavy-handedly.

Only detailed examination of a wide range of his work can provide a sufficiently qualified answer, but it will be convenient to indicate here a recurring form. At the centre of Crabbe's understanding of man lies the perception of the moral significance of time. An attitude towards life, or a particular conception of the priorities of value, or a predisposition, is projected through time in order to expose its degree of viability: whether it is a possible basis for a way of life, and, if so, what happens to a person who lives it. It is true that the curve of the projection is often downward; but it will be shown later that it is sometimes upward, that some of the most disturbing histories are those which do not curve at all, and that many are deflected in quite unexpected ways by a sudden event or the influence of another person. The major Augustan tradition lying behind Crabbe centres on seeing things clearly through seeing them in perspective: Sir Balaam's acquisitive pertness against the dignity of Job, for example, or Timon in his Brobdingnagian house. Crabbe's main contribution to that tradition is to develop more fully perspective through time. Johnson frequently urges us to acquire more sense of perspective by emphasising the fact of death:

> Let us therefore make haste to do what we shall certainly at last wish to have done; let us return the caresses of our friends, and endeavour by mutual endearments to heighten that tenderness which is the balm of life. Let us be quick to repent of injuries while repentance may not be a barren anguish, and let us open our eyes to every rival excellence, and pay early and willingly those honours which justice will compel us to pay at last. (*Rambler* 54, Yale ed., Vol. III, p. 294)

Crabbe sometimes follows him; for example, in a Murray sermon for 27 June 1784, on the text which meant so much to Johnson (*St John* 9. 4: 'The night cometh when no man can work'), he says: 'At the hour of Death, I suppose every one will wish their life had been a good one, but is it not equally reasonable to wish it a little before, and before that and so backward till the present Day.' But even in the sermons, his attention is more characteristically on the intervening process or stages of it, most often in negative terms – 'for who is there in youth so daring and impious as to think without terror of becoming an old and confirmed sinner' (Hastings, p. 39) – but also in positive terms, referring to the parable of the 'talents distributed for increase and improvement', or the parable of the leaven: 'in time, but not without, the whole is leavened' (Hastings, p. 41).

It is possible to see a biographical influence here. Crabbe's engagement to Sarah Elmy was protracted through ten years, and his son brings out the kind of impact his return to Aldeburgh must have had: 'He left his home a deserter from his profession. . . . He returned . . . a successful author, patronised and befriended by some of the leading characters in the kingdom.' (*Life*, p. 103) But despite facile generalisations from the form of Augustan satire, a sense of the importance of time runs back through the century, not only in the profounder minds of Butler ('rational agents . . . are naturally directed to form each his own manners and character, by the gradual gaining of knowledge and experience, and by a long course of action', *Analogy*, Part II, ch. IV) and Johnson ('Our minds, like our bodies, are in a continual flux; something is hourly lost, and something acquired', *Rasselas*, ch. XXXV), but also in men such as Lillo ('Will yesterday return? . . . never yet did time, once past, return', *The London Merchant*, II, ii) and Young (*Night Thoughts*, *passim*, especially Night II). Crabbe's understanding of character not as static but as evolving and sometimes changing largely and unexpectedly was certainly in accord with the new historical consciousness we associate with the nineteenth century, and it may have owed something to the accidents of his own experience, but it had deep eighteenth-century roots.

AIMS AND INTENTIONS IN CRABBE'S POETRY

It was shown earlier that Crabbe consciously stood by the traditional aesthetic of imitation; we can now begin to see how the aspects of the tradition he emphasised were those which passed on into the most vital form in the nineteenth century, the novel. Not only did his sophistications of the 'progress' form foreshadow the tracing of individual lives through time which became a major strength of the novel, but the lives he chose to trace covered a very wide range of social status as well as moral character. The most original part of this, as remarked by the more perceptive of the contemporary reviews, was the capacity not merely to represent characters from the lowest social levels, which had been done before, but to explore what it felt like to live their lives. But this important extension should not be allowed to obscure the fact that he more frequently wrote about the various levels of the middle classes than the extremely poor, partly, as he says in the note appended to the Preface to *The Borough* in the 1834 edition, because it affords 'more originality of character, more variety of fortune', and partly perhaps because he wanted to deal directly with the areas of life his readers were best acquainted with. This too both reaches forward to the nineteenth-century novel and has strong roots in the eighteenth century. In language anticipating his description of Shakespeare, Johnson said in

the fourth *Rambler* essay (1750) that unlike the old romances, contemporary novels 'exhibit life in its true state, diversified only by
accidents that daily happen in the world, and influenced by passions
and qualities which are really to be found in conversing with mankind'.
(Yale ed., Vol. III, p. 19) When he said in Rambler 60 that 'Histories of
the downfall of kingdoms, and revolutions of empires are read with
great tranquillity' (Vol III, p. 319), he might have been thinking of
Tatler 172 (1710), in which Steele suggested that 'such adventures as
befal persons not exalted above the common level' might have more
effect than 'the history of princes', or of the Preface to Rowe's *Fair
Penitent* (1703):

> Long has the fate of kings and empires been
> The common business of the tragic scene . . .
> But far remote, and in a higher sphere,
> We ne'er can pity what we ne'er can share.

Although the romance tradition remained strong enough for Crabbe to
feel it necessary to complain at length in 'Ellen Orford'

> That books, which promise much of life to give,
> Should show so little how we truly live,   (ll. 15–16)

he was repeating what it had been thought important to repeat before,
and would need repeating later.

His purposes in showing 'how we truly live' were various, and can
again mostly be related both backwards and forwards. At the end of
The Borough one line of thought is that it is in itself pleasing to
perceive truth:

> 'Tis good to know, 'tis pleasant to impart,
> These turns and movements of the human heart.   (ll. 436–7)

As to its moral efficacy, he shows a healthy ironic self-detachment:

> I search (a Quixote!) all the land about,
> To find its giants and enchanters out, –
> (The giant-folly, the enchanter-vice,
> Whom doubtless I shall vanquish in a trice);   (ll. 452–5)

but goes on to write of aiding 'the cause of virtue'. When he wrote to
Hatchard on 11 November 1819, 'Little I am afraid can be effected by
the Muse of most moral and even seraphic endowments. . . . Creating in
the Reader a general sobriety and some Elevation of Mind is all I think
that can be expected' (Broadley and Jerrold, p. 242), his emphasis was
in response to the review from the *Christian Observer* which Hatchard
had sent him: 'we should have the effusions of a vigorous and masculine

understanding, leading us to all that is great and noble and generous in our common nature, and bearing us on lofty measures and daring thoughts, as on eagle-wings, towards heaven.' (repr. in *Critical Heritage*, p. 269) He had already dissociated himself from Imlac's 'enthusiastic fit' in describing the poet at the end of *The Borough*: 'Silent he walks the road of life along' (l. 430). Similarly, in the Preface to *Tales of the Hall*, the declaration, 'I will not assume the tone of a moralist', needs to be seen in relation to contemporary criticism such as the *Eclectic Review*'s objection to 'The Parish Clerk', that it was improper to represent a man who believed in the 'agency of evil spirits on the mind and the sinfulness of mental adultery' as 'a hypocrite and a thief' – especially if it were done 'in terms of indecent and prophane jocularity' (repr. in *Critical Heritage*, p. 103). Following Johnson, Crabbe clearly realised that the aim of the poet must be to give pleasure, 'to engage the mind of his readers, as, failing in that point, he will scarcely succeed in any other',[37] but that to do so in a way which was in any important sense untrue was not just trivial but immoral. As Johnson puts it in the 'Life of Waller', referring to his representations of romantic love, 'Such books ... may be considered as showing the world under a false appearance, and, so far as they obtain credit from the young and inexperienced, as misleading expectation, and misguiding practice.' Crabbe's poetry is profoundly moral in intention, and much of its characteristic strength arises from this.

Apart from having this value of representing truth – 'Man as he is' – for its own sake, Crabbe's poetry works morally in two ways, which can be related, one to eighteenth-century, the other to nineteenth-century conceptions, yet which are in fact both reflected in eighteenth-century thinking about fiction. The first derives from the very ancient idea, running back to Polybius and frequently repeated, which is expressed in Crabbe's published sermon, *The Variation of Public Opinion* (1817): 'History, we are informed, is philosophy teaching by example.' He develops it in a way more relevant to his own work in the Chicago sermon of 29 April 1821, referring to Isaac and Rebecca at the end of *Genesis*, Chapter 24:

> We may dress our Stories in the Habits of Pomp and Circumstance. We may add Adventures and descriptions, but these simple Relations of natural Manners and common Events are not only more true but they are more affecting; they do not bring to our View extraordinary Situations and Trials that no one undergoes, but they teach us by Example what is our Duty. (p. 443)

It was a commonplace of this line of thought that to learn from historical examples was less painful than learning by experience, but

Crabbe would also have seen it as less arrogant than learning through judgement of other men. In a published sermon he says, 'We are not the judges of our fellow-sinners, neither, generally speaking, do we approach near enough to discern the secrets of the heart' (Hastings, p. 98), and in an unpublished one (Murray Collection, 30 August 1801) he adds that those who do judge 'are not accustomed to look at their own Hearts, nor to study their own Defects and Follies'. The short poem entitled 'Satire' is not, as one might think from its relative glibness, merely a reflection of the general contemporary reaction against satire. The end of *The Borough* carries a very bold double allusion to the biblical woman taken in adultery and the lines in the second dialogue of the 'Epilogue to the Satires' in which Pope, admitting to a pride he thinks justified, writes of his satire as a 'sacred weapon' in 'Heav'n-directed hands':[38]

> No! let the guiltless, if there such be found,
> Launch forth the spear, and deal the deadly wound.
> How can I so the cause of Virtue aid,
> Who am myself attainted and afraid?   (ll. 460–3)

Like Johnson,[39] he knew he was too 'attainted' to aid the 'cause of Virtue' thus, and it is very unlikely that he would have approved his son's notes referring his characters back to the originals from which, as he explains in the first letter to Mrs Leadbeater quoted in the *Life*, he had been careful to distinguish them. In a literature which portrays 'Man as he is' one can make the sort of judgements which if made of living men are arrogant and cruel.

The other way in which Crabbe saw his work as having moral effect is best expressed in the Preface to *The Borough*: 'it ties and binds us to all mankind by sensations common to us all, and in some degree connects us, without degradation, even to the most miserable and guilty of our fellow-men.' The rather escapist conception expressed in *The Library*, that books

> By mix'd sensations ease th'afflicted mind,
> And steal our grief away, and leave their own behind;
> A lighter grief! which feeling hearts endure
> Without regret, nor e'en demand a cure,   (ll. 33–6)

gives way to the idea that the literary 'grief' is of positive value in educating the sensibility. As Crabbe puts it in the fragment 'Tragic Tales, Why?' (Ward, Vol. III, p. 474):

> The Mind enlarges as its Grief extends;
> And Grief that's painted true improves the Heart it rends.

According to this view, we grow morally not through judgement but through feeling:

> In judging others we can see too well
> Their grievous fall, but not how grieved they fell.
>
> (*Tales of the Hall*, III, ll. 402–3)

It is clear from a Murray sermon of 30 August 1801 that Crabbe saw the two ways of achieving moral effect as complementary, not contradictory: 'Many Things which we condemn in other people, may not be worthy of Condemnation. We see not their Causes, the Reasons which led them, nay perhaps the Necessity. The same Action is not the same Fault in one as in another – only he who can behold the Heart can properly judge it.' Since by the convention of Crabbe's poetry, we can behold his characters' hearts, we can both sympathise fully with the 'Reasons' and make judgement without arrogance.

So it is possible to see Crabbe as poised between characteristically eighteenth- and nineteenth-century views of the moral effect of literature. The first is easily associated with the eighteenth century by thinking of the first chapter of *Amelia*, in which Fielding writes of 'histories of this kind' as 'models of HUMAN LIFE' which can instruct his readers in 'the ART of LIFE,' or of the Preface to the anonymous *Constantia, or a True Picture of Human Life* (1751): 'We may consider works of this kind, also, as a sort of artificial experience, by which the nature of mankind and an acquaintance with the world may be infused imperceptibly without fatigue and without danger.'[40] The second view, on the other hand, suggests Wordsworth's shift of emphasis towards the education of the feelings: 'a great Poet ought ... to a certain degree, to rectify men's feelings, to render their feelings more sane, pure and permanent, in short, more consonant to nature' ('Letter to John Wilson'), thus counteracting the 'craving for extraordinary incident, which the rapid communication of intelligence hourly gratifies', and which blunts 'the discriminating powers of the mind' (Preface to *Lyrical Ballads*). Snipped out of context, these quotations, suggest vividly a major value of Crabbe's work: it is, to borrow an even finer phrase from Wordsworth's Preface, 'a rock of defence for human nature'.

The view that literature works morally through educating the feelings was, however, current in the eighteenth century, chiefly in critical thought about the novel. At first the emphasis was more frequently on the dangers: the fear is expressed, curiously often in novels, that reading novels corrupted young ladies. Miss Williams in *Roderick Random* is typical in blaming her fall partly on her reading of romances: 'cursed be my education, that, by refining my sentiments, made my heart the more susceptible!' (ch. XXII) But Richard Graves was also expressing a commonplace when in *Eugenius* (1785), he put more weight on the positive effect: 'For who can read the affecting narratives of Richardson, or Miss B-rney, and not be excited to acts of benevolence and generosity; or, on the other hand, not be deterred from the mean pursuits of selfishness, avarice, and fraud?' (2nd ed., p. 10) MacKenzie's *Man of Feeling* (1771) clearly encouraged this view of the novel, but it was current previously. Charles Jenner in his *Placid Man* (1770) writes similarly: 'The account of a generous action may raise a warmth in the heart very likely to incite to the doing one; the sympathetic tenderness which may arise in the breast from the history of a feigned distress may open the heart to an attention to real misery.'[41] This argument also was stood on its head as the cult of sensibility increased in popularity. Dugald Stewart thought that too much feeling good in response to the printed page might prevent doing good in response to actual people (*Collected Works*, ed. W. Hamilton (1854) Vol. II, pp. 464–6). Crabbe is more likely to have read Secker's similar argument that people can 'weep over even a feigned distress, when well described, or barely represented to them by fancy; and perhaps weep a second time at reflecting on their own meritorious tenderness; yet, in real cases that come before them, can see the heaviest afflictions without being moved. . . . And thus they cultivate, in idea, the most refined and exalted sentiments of humanity, which no one living is ever the better for.'[42] Crabbe of course, like Jane Austen, satirises this sort of fiction. He reached the kind of balance described by Fanny Burney in the Dedication to *The Wanderer* (1814), where she says that the novel holds 'in its hands our best affections, it exercises our imaginations; it points out the paths of honour; and gives . . . the lessons of experience without its tears.'

It is in such old-fashioned terms as these that Crabbe's claim to be a 'living classic' is best stated. In a famous remark in *Lady Chatterly's Lover* Lawrence wrote of the power of the novel to 'lead into new places the flow of our sympathetic consciousness'; but with an eye on what happens to our feelings for Clifford, one feels the need to insist that the new is not necessarily the good. Sometimes defence is more necessary than exploration. Crabbe did, in fact, lead his readers' sympathies into places not previously explored well in English. Johnson praised *The Village* as 'original', and Henry Giles summed up many earlier reactions when he wrote in 1850: 'among our moral poets, Crabbe, as the critics admit, is the most original, the most original in topics, thought and style.'[43] His strongest advocate, Jeffrey, even thought that Crabbe had gone too far in exploring depraved minds in *The Borough*, exceeding the 'unalterable laws by which nature has regulated our sympathies' (repr. in *Critical Heritage*, p. 93). But more important, especially in our time, than this breaking of new ground, is his representation in his characters and his provocation in his readers of human feelings and experiences of permanent value. His poems depict, in many different ways, what happens to the quality of life when a particular attitude is adopted, asking the implicit question, is this an attitude worth taking? The attitudes are shown with such imagination and yet criticised so firmly that the reader is developed in his capacities both to sympathise and to discriminate. If a man becomes what he is as a result of his actions and of his interactions with other people, so also, to some extent, does he as a result of what he reads. As Johnson puts it in *Adventurer* 137: 'That a writer, however zealous or eloquent, seldom works a visible effect upon cities or nations, will readily be granted ... [But] books have always a secret influence on the understanding; we cannot at pleasure obliterate ideas.' (Yale ed., Vol. II, pp. 490–1) Both kinds of moral effect have been crudely stated, and in Crabbe's time they were stated with the crudity which led to the cautionary tales of Mrs Pilkington. It is not a question of learning *a* good example or acquiring *an* emotion which is of value, but of gradually becoming habituated to a humane understanding of characteristic patterns of human behaviour. Such understanding is pursued not because it leads to greater happiness or to a better specific action, but firstly because it is a good in itself ('' 'tis good to know') and secondly because it is one means of sensing the frontiers of what one would care to describe as human when using 'human' as a value-term. Naturally the effect this influence has on an individual, if it has any at all, will depend on what other influences are operative, and on his choice. For those who wish to look, Crabbe stands as a 'rock of defence for human nature' not so much in the way Wordsworth had in mind as in the way Johnson read Shakespeare: 'he who has mazed his imagination, in following the phantoms which other writers raise up before him, may here be cured of his delirious extasies, by reading human sentiments in human language'. (Yale ed., Vol. VII, p. 65)

This way of reading literature must be firmly distinguished from the Existentialist use of the novel. Crabbe says in the sermon quoted on p. 37, 'The same Action is not the same Fault in one as in another', but the intention of his art is to provide us with the particulars which will enable us to 'properly judge it'. Particular situations are explored in detail not in order to illustrate that every moral situation must be faced on its own unique terms, but to develop the capacity to behave or judge well in other particular situations. What is seen as a moral development according to this way of thinking would to an Existentialist be an impingement on his freedom. But although Crabbe's poetry is naturally most fully appreciated by someone who shares his sort of views of moral law, its more general accessibility is conveniently indicated by the similarities to that of Godwin, who, though far from existentialism, held as a fundamental maxim that 'every case is a rule to itself'. It has direct relevance for anyone who thinks that, whether desirably or not, 'Man is the creature of habit' (*Enquiry*, p. 175).

There is not much on the surface of Crabbe's work which reflects the *Zeitgeist* of the early nineteenth century, but (with the qualifications already touched on and later to be developed) the core of it belongs substantially between Johnson's Shakespeare and the major English novels of the following five decades.

2 Poems up to 1807

The best poems Crabbe wrote in the period up to 1807 were *The Village* (1783) and *The Parish Register*, which was the main new work published in the 1807 collection. But in order to see these achievements in perspective it is necessary to look also at the minor verse he wrote during the period, some of which was quite different in kind. Although almost all Crabbe's mature poetry is in decasyllabic couplets, he did not settle on this form before considerable experimentation with others: it was not laziness or lack of initiative which made him choose the metre of Pope. The poetry sections of the *Lady's Magazines* he contributed to did not provide much scope, but even the poems of 1772, written when he was eighteen, include octosyllabic quatrains, blank verse and Spenserian stanzas. One of the most interesting contributions was in fact a short prose piece, using a variation of the 'progress' form, and written with a terseness rare in his later prose.

Inebriety (1775) is by far the liveliest of the very early works. There is little sign of the original imagination which makes the club of smokers in *The Borough* X so vivid, but the imitation and parody of Pope encourage both economy and verbal energy, especially in Part II. The cleverness, into which the parody often degenerates, at times gives way to a more genial and evocative humour:

> Old Torpio nods, and, as the laugh goes round,
> Grunts through the nasal Duct, and joins the sound;
> Then sleeps again, and, as the liquors pass,
> Wakes at the friendly Jog, and takes his Glass.   (II, ll. 31–4)

In contrast, 'Midnight', in which Crabbe was imitating Young's blank verse, is as turgid as the original and duller. It is interesting only in that it emphasises Crabbe's awareness of the minor line of eighteenth-century verse, which is usually obscured by his obviously much greater debt to Dryden, Pope and Johnson: after Homer, Virgil and Milton, the poets he refers to here are Young, Thomson and Akenside. In addition to these experiments, we know from the *Life* that early during his stay in London he had 'composed two dramas and a variety of prose essays, in imitation, some of Swift, others of Addison' (p. 51).

Most of the poems of 1780 show a self-conscious poeticism. Young's reflections on Time in *Night Thoughts* must have sunk deep into his mind during his father's readings, but in the little poem 'Time' he invokes Young only to elevate the poet, 'all big with vision', above concern with 'those vile mechanic things', clocks; and when he thinks a little further, it is only to wish against the known reality that 'Time would hold his tongue':

> It calls the duns to crowd my hapless gate;
> It tells my heart the paralysing tale
> Of hours to come, when Misery must prevail.   (ll. 16–18)

The two 'Poetical Epistles' (Ward, Vol. III, p. 376 ff.) show further experiment, imitations of Goldsmith's 'Retaliation' so jerky and clogged that they are difficult to read. In the second, 'To Mira', there is an almost Keatsian rejection of the systems of scientific thought which

> Have robb'd my poor Muse of her Plume and her Wings;
> Consum'd the Phlogiston you us'd to admire.   (ll. 56–7)

In *The Candidate*, he says that he does not want to write of Wolfe or Rodney, but

> Of laughing girls in smiling couplets tell,
> And paint the dark-brow'd grove, where wood-nymphs dwell.
>   (ll. 236–7)

As in the poem 'Time', he is aware that this entails self-deception, but is willing to indulge nonetheless:

> Ah! tell me not these empty joys to fly;
> If they deceive, I would deluded die.   (ll. 298–9)

The Library (1781) is the earliest of Crabbe's poems which he cared to reprint in later editions of his Works, though in a revised form. In the interests of propriety, Divinity was moved from the shelves following the books of Law to the place of honour, in front of Philosophy. Unfortunately Crabbe also made the tone more solemn, omitting among other couplets on the theologians:

> There the devout an awful station keep,
> Vigils advise and yet dispose to sleep.

Similarly, he cut out the witty exploitation of Linnaeus' use of sexual terms in the description of flower reproduction in the passage on Philosophy.[1] The most important difference between the printed text and the Murray manuscript, from which extracts are printed as footnotes in the 1834 edition, is that Crabbe originally gave much more space to romances and novels and was less dismissive. The introductory tone was not given by

> Now in disgrace. What, though by time is spread
> Polluting dust o'er every reverend head,   (ll. 537–8)

but by

> Huge, pond'rous, vast and mighty volumes lie
> In dusty State and proud Obscurity.

In the printed version, 'too dearly bought' emphasises the time wasted in reading romances:

> But lost, for ever lost, to me these joys,
> Which Reason scatters, and which Time destroys;
> Too dearly bought: maturer judgement calls
> My busied mind from tales and madrigals.   (ll. 571–4)

The punctuation of the 1834 quotation obscures the fact that originally the phrase qualified 'maturer judgement'; the manuscript reads:

> Ah! lost, for ever lost to me these Charms,
> These lofty Notions and divine Alarms,
> To[o] dearly brought, maturer Judgement calls
> My pensive soul, from Tales and Madrigals
> For who so blest . . .

The original attitude was much closer to that of the earlier poems, stressing the loss of 'th'imagined paradise' more than its falsity. What was lost was both integrated ('The tear and smile that once together rose') and pure (in the draft, the 'infant mind' was 'to Guilt unknown' rather than 'to care unknown'); so the concluding line held far more tension between 'make' and 'mar': 'And Pain and Prudence make and mar the man' (l. 594). The passage on novels quoted in the 1834 edition, however, contrasts them with the innocent imagination of the romances: their writers mix fantasy and realism in ways which may, in Johnson's terms, mislead expectation ('rakes repenting, clogg'd in Hymen's chains') and misguide practice ('nymph reclined by unpresuming swain'). The fantasy is not the 'delightful Dream' of children's romances, but the dangerous wish-fulfilment which 'wake[s] the soul to life': 'humbler nymphs' are encouraged to imagine 'captains, colonels, lords' whose immoral habits are charmed away by beauty:

> A virtue, just before the rover's jest,
> Grows like a mushroom in his melting breast.

The looser structure of the draft allows Crabbe to parody at some length the style of sentimental epistolary novels. It shows an early stirring of his interest in narrative, but is fully controlled by its context. The waking from the dream within the narrative also represents the fantasy of the reader outside it, so that the summarising lines can refer both to the writer of the letter and to the reader of the novel:

> Thus, gentle passions warm the generous maid,
> No more reluctant, and no more afraid.

At the three known stages of its development, the poem was progressively tidier and less interesting.

Although the degree of Burke's share in revising *The Library* is unknown, we can see that the changed attitude towards romance was Crabbe's own from the difference between the lines in *The Village* which Johnson rewrote and Crabbe's draft. Whereas Crabbe opposed both Virgil and Fancy to 'Truth and Nature', in lines 19–20, Johnson aligned 'Fancy' with 'Truth and Nature', reserving his criticism only for 'Mechanic echoes' of Virgil. Much of the distinctive strength and weakness of the poem derive fom the over-simple opposition of Truth and Fancy. It has long been recognised that Crabbe was by no means the first poet to reject the pastoral version of village life. Goldsmith's is a *deserted* village, and there was a substantial tradition of anti-pastoral poetry, of which Langhorne's *Country Justice* (1774–5) bears the closest resemblance to Crabbe.[2] But although it is unfair to Goldsmith to take the allusion to his vicar, 'passing rich with forty pounds a year', as a specific satire, most of the verbal and emotional energy of *The Village* derives from a self-conscious anti-pastoralism. The tone of the first paragraph is muted: 'care' may carry its conventional pastoral sense and 'declining' and 'Age' do not seem at first to have the force they gain later, so that in 'the real Picture of the Poor' we do not expect to meet militancy. The second paragraph begins with an elegiac note – 'Fled are those times' – which dominates the tone until the sudden release of cutting irony, the more effective because delayed:

> And shepherds' boys their amorous pains reveal,
> The only pains, alas! they never feel.   (ll. 13–14)

The use of a word in an unexpectedly literal sense is thoroughly Augustan – Pope's ironic use of 'frightful' in the Narcissa passage of the first *Moral Essay* is comparable: 'One would not, sure, be frightful when one's dead' – and one need not labour the later resemblance to Johnson's 'Review of Soame Jenyns' *Free Enquiry*' ('This author and Pope perhaps never saw the miseries which they imagine thus easy to be borne') when a ponderous first line with uncompleted syntax, deflated by the swiftly moving completion of both couplet and syntax, registers the point that those who praise the labourer's 'homely, healthy fare' should taste it:

> Homely, not wholesome, plain, not plenteous, such
> As you who praise would never deign to touch.   (ll. 170–1)

To achieve such force, Crabbe needed to have more behind him than the poeticism of the earlier pieces, and the emotional drive is clear in the young man's manifesto: 'I paint the Cot,/As Truth will paint it, and as Bards will not' (ll. 53–4). But that it is the work of a *young* man is equally clear from the insistence, which, by the time we have reached the old shepherd's white hair made whiter by the snow, has shown an absence of poetic tact. The excessive emotionalism drifts with ironic ease into a mannerism as sentimental as that it is repudiating:

> A lonely, wretched man, in pain I go,
> None need my help, and none relieve my wo.   (ll. 222–3)

The indignation engendered also becomes greater than the ostensible structure of the poem can accommodate. In Book II Crabbe attempts to pull the poem together by arguing in lines 87–100 that the 'great' should lose their pride when shown that the poor are their equals in vice, and in lines 107–14 that the poor should accept their 'lot in peace' when they learn that the well-born Manners gave his life for their country. It seems unlikely that the rich will be made humbler by the discovery that their vices are shared by the poor, but it is even more unlikely when the vices of the poor have been seen to depend partly on appalling conditions under the threat of destruction by the sea and partly on a system mal-administered by their social superiors. The ending in general is very badly managed: the image of Manners as the 'tall Oak' in line 119 uncomfortably recalls the 'withering tree' which was the old shepherd's 'sad emblem'; it is rather tasteless to refer to Manners' 'gen'rous spirit, mounting high' in the same poem as the descriptions of the villagers' inescapable poverty of spirit; and the thesis about pride is gravely endangered by the line, 'If Passion rule us, be that passion pride' (II, l. 184).

The strength of the poem is clearly in the first part, in the passages where the anti-pastoralism conveys the real plight of the 'poor, blind, bewilder'd erring race' and does not become an end in itself. Despite the sentimentality of much of the passage on the old shepherd, the paragraph from lines 188 to 199 takes us successfully into the feelings of a redundant man, through his response to the memory of the straight furrows he once ploughed – 'He hears and smiles, then thinks again and sighs' (l. 193) – and through the practical detail of the 'alternate

masters', which registers very precisely the nature of the indignity he is
subjected to. The phrase near the beginning, 'smooth alternate verse',
may well, as Arthur Sale suggests, allude to Gay's *Shepherd's Week*
('Monday', l. 32), but in a way later exploited more fully by Crabbe, it
also both pulls the poem together and adds another ironic resonance to
the re-use of the word here and in line 148: 'See them alternate suns
and showers engage'. The description of the labourers leaning on their
scythes recalls Langhorne:

> When the poor hind, with length of years decay'd,
> Leans feebly on his once subduing spade.
>
> (The Country Justice, II, ll. 43–4)

But Langhorne has little of Crabbe's power to represent what it felt like
to stand 'beneath the dog-star's raging heat,/When the knees tremble
and the temples beat' (ll. 144–5). If we put the retrospectively applied
thesis out of our minds, the transition from the sufferings of the
villagers to their vices is well managed in the phrase 'sullen wo' (I, l. 86),
and although the reference to pastoral games is a little laboured, Crabbe,
while firmly insisting on the criminality of the smugglers, retains a
balancing sense of their wretchedness and the evil which surrounds
them. The introduction of the poet in the 'poetic' image of a swallow
with 'ready wing' spread is inept (as well as ornithologically inaccurate), but man and nature are elsewhere seen as united in a way which
is shockingly apt: wrecked vessels are 'Theirs, or the ocean's, miserable
prey' (l. 118). The Augustan irony which Crabbe has re-learned through
anti-pastoral use of pastoral words is deployed more delicately in the
description of the poor-house. Vapours 'play' rather than children and
even they are 'flagging'; only the dull wheel 'hums'. The suffering is
emphasised by the way so many people with broken relationships are
thrown together yet dwell essentially alone with their 'unheeded tears';
and the sheer irrationality of the system is rendered in the jarring
repetition of the words: the sick are brought 'amid the scenes of grief,
to grieve'. The already 'sorrowing' are forced to 'each kindred sorrow
scan', while those who would benefit from scanning the scene remain
coldly aloof, bartering charity for pride.

The rest of the book (line 262 onwards) is done chiefly in a series of
Hogarthian pictures. The room in which the man is dying is clearly
written with Pope's treatment of Villiers (*Moral Essay* III) in mind, but
Crabbe's attention is primarily on the visible squalour and neglect. The
picture is framed by the beam and rafters, and the 'drooping wretch'
evokes a Hogarthian curve in the foreground. In the second picture, the
quack, 'quaintly neat' and 'all bustle and conceit', provides a visual
contrast with the 'languid' dying man. There is no attempt to catch the

'habitual queries' in the texture of the verse as in Crabbe's later work: his attitude is represented chiefly by the impatience in his 'averted eyes' and the contempt in his 'sapient sneer'. The parish priest is rendered in more literary terms, with the allusion to Goldsmith and the verbal irony that he is 'better skill'd the noisy pack to guide' than his 'little flock'; and we are given a glimpse into his rationalising mind as he excuses himself for not trying 'To combat fears that e'en the pious feel' (l. 317). But the last 'gloomy scene' is depicted not only through the literary allusion to *Isaiah* 53. 3 ('man of sorrows'), which points the outrage to Christian values, and the not too obtrusive irony of 'the happy dead', but largely through the mourners' expressions, which are a comic-pathetic mixture of dignity, piety and dullness – 'Sedately torpid and devoutly dumb' (l. 330) – and through the children whose inquisitive inspection of the unearthed bones, more typical of Hogarth than of Crabbe, holds in check the potential sentimentality of 'gazing, hand in hand' and of the reference to the cricket games of the past. The bell and the owl seem at first to be standard graveyard machinery, but after 'Fear marks the flight and magnifies the sound' (l. 342), the nature of the fear is immediately defined in a way which is effectively unexpected.

The famous paragraph beginning 'Lo! where the heath' (l. 63 ff.) epitomises the curious degree of unevenness which *The Village* contains and which in fact continued to run through most of Crabbe's work. The first sixteen lines of it are extraordinarily packed with relevant irony. One expects 'light turf' to mean springy to the tread, until it is clear that its low calorific value is the main point: it is the sand which is most powerfully 'burning'. After the repetition, 'withering' and 'wither'd', and mention of the 'thin harvest', '*rank* weeds' comes as a sudden shock, which is reinforced by the imagery of hostility ('rob', 'threaten war'). But the mockery – 'There poppies, nodding, mock the hope of toil' (l. 71) – is driven home by the contrast between the images of hostility and a chain of words which suggest apparent benignity: 'nodding', 'paints', 'waves', 'throws a shade', 'clasping'. The sterility and sickliness are mocked by the 'splendour' and vigour of the weeds, and, more particularly, the 'silky leaf' of the mallow, given associations of insidiousness by 'slimy', mocks the 'ragged infant'. Not only does the verbal energy hold the reader's fullest attention, but the lines work successfully on the three levels of describing the landscape, representing the harsh relationship between the villagers and nature, and evoking the general feel of life to them. Yet having done this, Crabbe exasperatingly ends the paragraph with a pseudo-witty comparison to the cliché of the painted prostitute. The last line is conceivably relevant, though redundant, but her 'sad eyes' and 'troubled breast' belong in

Goldsmith and are nothing to the purpose here, while 'betray'd by man'
is as precisely irrelevant as possible. It is an extreme case, but the poem
as a whole shows an analogous mixture of great power to represent
feelings vividly through the close interaction of words, and a curious
degree of incompetence. When incompetence shows in the later work,
critics usually ascribe it to carelessness, but the badness in this poem,
for example, occurs in some of the places where he is obviously strug-
gling hardest. A label is not an explanation, but perhaps we can call it an
inability to intelligently criticise his own work.

Despite its blemishes however, *The Village* is by far the best of
Crabbe's earliest works. The verbal energy is far greater than in
anything he wrote before the best parts of *The Parish Register* and it
succeeds vividly in its primary intention of confronting the reader with
the reality of late eighteenth-century village life in a poor part of the
country.

After *The Newspaper* (1785), a very dull poem put together hastily
to earn a little money,[3] there followed the twenty-two years before his
next publication, during which, his son tells us, he wrote a great deal of
verse and of prose fiction, destroying almost all of it, partly on the
advice of others, but partly on his own judgement. He clearly had *some*
powers of self-criticism, but often of this all-or-nothing kind. A few
scraps of verse preserved in botanical notebooks are interesting only in
so far as they are all that has survived from these years. The three
fragments printed by Ward (Vol. III, p. 497) belong to this period and
are parts of a single poem. They are written on some spare pages in a
botanical notebook given to Trinity College Library, Cambridge, by
Fitzgerald. Neither they nor the botanical notes are dated, but at the
end of the book there are more verses, written with the book upside
down, which are dated 23 September 1793. This book contains a few
more lines clearly belonging to 'The Curate's Progress' (to adopt Ward's
title) which show even more autobiographical content, particularly the
following:

> Oh! give me then induring much I cry'd
> A little Portion! be it thine reply'd –
> I say not who! but dear I hold the Debt
> 'And God forget me when I him forget.'
> As Thurlow said! when Heavn affecting Lot
> Possessed his Soveraign Mind and some forgot.

Of the verses following the date 23 September 1793, some are couplets,
which may also belong to the same work, drawing on the experience of
Crabbe's visits to Belvoir:

The loving Mistress of the [?Mansion] sends
And quits him kindly by her kindly friends ...
The Sum on Dress by this fair Creature spent
Would more than equal Colin's yearly rent.

But there are also eight lines of a blank-verse poem which are headed

Plan of a Poem, the Seasons –
Spring. the Visitation. Etc.

and which begin with an invocation of the 'Genius of Milton'. It is clear from the *Life* that wide experimentation continued at least until 1799, when Crabbe had thoughts of publishing, among other things, a versification of the story of Naaman. The Fitzgerald copy of the 1834 *Works* attributes the novel 'The Widow Grey' to 1801. In another botanical notebook (belonging to the Murray Collection), under the date 12 June 1800, there survives a fragment of a narrative poem. It is written in alternately rhyming octosyllabic lines arranged in stanzas of varying length, and represents a dialogue between a sailor who wishes to marry and his girl who thinks it is wiser to wait till they are less poor. It shows some movement towards what later became his characteristic material, but the form of the dialogue is nearer 'smooth alternate verse' than Crabbe's maturer achievements.

The same measure is used for most of the poems first published in 1807 with *The Parish Register* and an eight-six measure for 'Hester', which is the only other extant work of this period. Although the copy, dated 1804, from which 'Hester' was printed in *New Poems*, seems to be a fair one, Crabbe's judgement in rejecting it was sound: its only merit lies in the description of the misery of prostitution to the prostitute (ll. 449–68). Less judgement was shown in admitting the turgid 'Birth of Flattery' and the vapid 'Woman!' 'Reflections' is of chiefly biographical interest in showing Crabbe's reliance on an eighteenth-century version of the 'moral proof' of personal immortality, but the paradoxes are expressed with some wit. Victory over the passions comes only when it is too late; when we gain enough sense of perspective to be able to reprove our warmest friend or praise our fiercest foe, both are dead. Perhaps remembering Young, Crabbe argues from this irony to immorality:

Since virtue's recompence is doubtful here,
If man dies wholly, well may he demand,
Why is man suffer'd to be good in vain?

(Night, VII, ll. 177–9)[4]

'Sir Eustace Grey', much admired by his contemporaries and subsequently by those with a preference for the eccentric, is only superficially

like Romantic poems about abnormal states of mind: it is offered as an
attempt to take us deeper not into the nature of reality but into what it
may feel like to be mad. It is headed, pointedly, 'Scene – a Madhouse',
and Sir Eustace's speeches are those of a 'Patient'. The madness has a
specific moral cause, pride –

> 'With men I would be great and high,
> But with my God so lost, that He,
> In his large view, should pass me by' –   (ll. 105–7)

and is triggered by particular events narrated with contrived inco-
herence. The sensation of being whirled through a succession of nightmare experiences is expressed very vividly with usually just enough
detail to make each specific before passing to the next. But the most
powerful lines are 196–211, in which everything seems capable of sleep
except Sir Eustace, and the horror lies chiefly in the magnitude of the
beauty at which he is 'condemn'd' to gaze.

The best of the minor poems of this period is 'The Hall of Justice',
written, according to the 1807 Preface, in 1798. Unlike 'Hester' it is
not cluttered with extensive descriptions, but clipped to a degree of
understatement which conveys both an urgency and an integrity in the
speaker. The role of the Magistrate, although implausible in terms of
realism, is a skilful rhetorical manoeuvre. His attitude seems clear –
'Thy crime is proved, thou know'st thy fate' – so we expect that pity
for the Vagrant will be qualified by a judgement made through him.
But his frown at the end of Part I is only at her language, not at her
story, and when *he* expresses sympathy the attitude of judgement is
denied to us. The manoeuvre is needed to counterbalance the progressive
unfolding of her vicious life. At first our sympathy is easily held by a
woman whose only guilt seems to be stealing to feed a starving child;
though on reflecting with the perspective of the whole poem in mind,
we can see that it was least deserved at that point: from a specious
self-justification by appeal to 'a stronger law' she moves to contrition
and submission – 'punish whom 'twere sin to save!' The shift is not too
contrived, for at the end of Part I she curses Aaron's father, and in Part
II (ll. 61–2) there is some self-pity; but in general it is from

> 'Could I a better life embrace,
> Or live as virtue dictates?   No!   (I, ll. 51–2)

to

> 'True I was not to virtue train'd;
> Yet well I knew my deeds were ill.'   (II, ll. 69–70)

But while *she* comes to accept responsibility, *our* focus is on her as victim: when Aaron's father raped her, for example, 'The clan were all at his command', and Aaron's frown, unlike the Magistrate's, includes no pity. The irony of 'He bade me lay down and sleep' is built up steadily as the restlessness of her life comes across, and Aaron, despite his crime, 'yet took his rest'. The major emotional moments of losing and finding her daughter are handled with an extreme understatement which makes them very moving:

> ' "Where is my child?" – "Thy child is dead."
> 'Twas false . . .'   (II, ll. 52–3)

> She knew my name – we met in pain.'   (II, l. 97)

At the end there is no self-pity or self-justification, but a genuine reaching out towards the goodness she thinks is beyond herself, so that the Magistrate is right to emphasise that the pardon extends to her, though he is careful to put it finally in terms which will discourage her from feeling elect.

But the pace of the octosyllabic lines, the measure most frequently used for narrative verse in the eighteenth century, does not admit much variety of mood: suited as it was to the frenzy of Sir Eustace and the Vagrant, it would clearly not do for the wide range of responses needed in *The Parish Register*. According to the *Life*, *The Parish Register* was begun about 1800. In conception it is very simple: a record of the differing ways in which groups of ordinary people have responded to three major events in life, birth, marriage and death, represented in such a way as to make the reader react as if to actual individuals. (Crabbe's theory of literary characters was as unashamedly unsophisticated as the maiden's in the little poem called by Ward '[Horatio]', Vol. III, p. 513).[5] One is reminded clearly of Johnson's remarks on biography in *Rambler* 60: 'I have often thought that there has rarely passed a life of which a judicious and faithful narrative would not be useful' (Yale ed., Vol. III, p. 320). The clergyman browsing over his register, an obvious persona for Crabbe to assume, is ideally placed to make such observations, having all kinds of people pass before him, but committed by his role in society to viewing them both critically and sympathetically. The simplicity is part of the strength: we are invited to make a human response to the behaviour of real people at crucial events. As Jeffrey put it: 'Mr. Crabbe, in short, shows us something which we have all seen, or may see, in real life; and draws from it such feelings and such reflections as every human being must acknowledge that it is calculated to excite.'[6]

These immensely important steps beyond painting the 'real Picture

of the Poor' are obscured both by the 1807 Preface and by the first 276
lines of the poem. The main intention in these seems to be to correct
inferences which might be made from *The Village*: the new villagers
are 'contented or miserable' wholly in accordance with their own
behaviour, rather than the inescapable conditions they have to contend
with. But this is pressed much further than an insistence that his
interest is moral rather than sociological: through a very loaded description of first industrious and then idle families, Crabbe seems to present
the untenable and un-Christian thesis, that though good and evil are
mixed in this life, man has 'power to part them, when he feels the will',
in a way which will be evident in material well-being. In the cottage of
the industrious peasant, all is in its proper order: the books are 'each
within its place' (ironically unlike Crabbe's own – see *Life*, pp. 262–3);
and as well as playing with his children, the peasant has enough spare
time and energy not only to maintain his cottage in good repair but to
cultivate a remarkable variety of flowers, fruit and vegetables.[7] By a
strange irony, Crabbe not only adopts a very Goldsmithian tone – 'the
same stories are for ever told' comes straight from 'news much older
than their ale went round' – but applies it, as Goldsmith did not, to a
present situation. Whereas the abstemious happy peasants gather so
idyllically on Sunday evenings, the 'disputatious crew/Each evening
meet' to curse, cry, beat, shriek, and swear. Smuggling is not, as in
The Village, the village sport, but confined to this 'infected row'. The
emphasis is on confusion – 'mingled masses' of rubbish on the floor,
pigs mixed with chickens, parents and children in the same bedroom,
garments 'worn by each sex', pistols 'unpair'd', and the palings which
once separated the gardens broken down. The only things which 'yet
remain in rows' are the 'chalky tallies' of drinks or card games. To
complete our self-righteous (and very unCrabbe-like) withdrawal of
sympathy from these people we are offered the callousness of 'th'inhuman cocker' who has no sense of his bird's suffering.

> Whence all these woes? – From want of virtuous will . . .
> And want of ev'ry kind but want of power.   (ll. 226, 229)

But having got his thesis out of the way, Crabbe can respond more
sensitively to the following 'Portraits'.

The first four births are patterned in a clear alternation of children of
sin and children of virtue, but the most interesting is the first, which
has already developed into a form of narrative containing its own
internal pattern of relationships. Lucy herself is not handled very well.
We discover little of what she feels when she learns she is pregnant:
after the suggestive line, 'The forced sad smiles that follow'd sudden
sighs' (l. 350), Crabbe falls back on the personification of Scandal,

Folly and Malice, which derives from *The Vanity of Human Wishes* (ll. 333–42), but does not fit the present idiom. In the dialogue with her father she only gives a flat statement of information; the baptism is uncertainly rendered – the 'noisy sparrows' are aptly discordant and mundane, but the 'bats on their webby wings' are much too Gothic – and the ending is in sentimental cliché. The greater interest lies in her father, the Miller, and the way the relationships form round him. His boasting at the market about his daughter and the money which will go with her directly provokes the sailor, William, to set his sights on her. Lucy's accurate perception of her father's values – 'I'm like his steed, prized highly as his own' (l. 318) – makes her too react against him. So when William's premature suggestions of equality with the Miller ('Both live by Heaven's free gale') are bluntly rejected ('Where thy notes and cash?'), William's revenge seems to her a rescue and seduction is simple. When he discovers he has been thwarted, the Miller's feelings of revenge extend as far as wishing William will never gain enough money to marry the otherwise ruined Lucy. The seraglio he later keeps not only shows his hypocrisy in speaking of Lucy's 'shame', but helps him maintain the new expression of his pride: Lucy has to walk to the mill for her weekly pittance and is compelled to stay long enough to see the plenty she has been cut off from. His half-rescued pride totally outweighs any sense of pity for the degradation of the woman who was once 'my Lucy'. The sentimental final paragraph is unfortunately irrelevant to the main interest of the tale, which lies in the interaction of the three characters, of whom the most guilty remains in material terms the most successful.

The 'decent couple', Robert and Susan, are placed for local contrast between the imprudent Lucy and the harlot, but, as Fitzgerald noted in his copy, they belong more to 'Marriages' than to 'Baptisms', with their mature relationship explicitly set against the romantic fantasies of 'Love all made up of torture and delight' (l. 409). In fact, they act as a standard against which other kinds of failure are seen, in 'Burials' also, with their right ordering of priorities, the

> wise frugality, that does not give
> A life to saving, but that saves to live. (ll. 445–6)

The contrast with their stability gives added irony to the phrase used of the child produced by the harlot, 'babe of love'. In the 1807 version the harlot tried to justify herself, using similarly debased language:

> ''Twas pure good nature, not a wanton will;
> ... all my failing is a tender heart.'

This is consistent with her superstitious observation of the 'rite of churching', which is not only mocked by the satirical reference to the prayer-book phrase 'great pain and peril of childbirth' – she is 'still in peril of that pain to be' – but is also seen as a need in her: 'she humbly knelt' and 'their comforts felt'. In the revised version, sympathy is greater when, instead of trying to justify her past behaviour, the harlot emphasises her present plight. She rejects the clergyman's too easy admonition by admitting it was once relevant but insisting through the pun that it no longer remains so:

> 'Alas! your reverence, wanton thoughts, I grant,
> Were once my motive, now the thoughts of want.'
>
> (ll. 453–4)

The 1834 edition aptly quotes Johnson on Misella, for Crabbe also emphasises that once fallen she is trapped:

> 'Your sex pursue us, and our own disdain;
> Return is dreadful, and escape is vain.'   (ll. 457–8)

But the revision spoils the paragraph of the 'rite of churching'. The knowledge of herself and of the social code which she shows in the revised version makes it improbable that she would naïvely go to the church 'In dread of scandal'.

The first 276 lines are uncharacteristic of the poem as a whole in their humourlessness as well as in ways already indicated. The comic touches in the story of Lucy are clearer if one does not concentrate too heavily on the pathos of the heroine. In Gerard Ablett the humour is more direct. The reference to his 'overflowing cup' of joy, which we expect to be cliché, is seen to be comically exact as the image of the fruitful vine is developed:

> Those playful branches now disturb his peace:
> Them he beholds around his tables spread,
> But finds, the more the branch, the less the bread.
>
> (ll. 478–80)

'Playful' keeps the image focused on the children and also qualifies 'disturb his peace', showing that at least something of what he anticipated in his look of 'joyful love' at the wedding has been fulfilled, even though the look now seems rather naïve. The following paragraphs on why Gerard should cease to grieve are a very flat-footed recurrence of the thesis that the rich have as many cares as the poor.

Although the illegitimate son of Ditchem's wife maintains the basic alternation of children born in and out of wedlock, the main principle of organisation in the next section is clearly the much tighter and more

significant mesh of comparisons and contrasts between Ditchem and
Dawkins. They each form distinctive views about marriage and we are
asked explicitly to see what happens to them as time passes: 'Observe
them as they go,/Comparing fear with fear and wo with wo' (ll. 538–9).
Both form their ideas of marriage around calculations based on money,
and both think they are sufficiently in control of their fate and of time
to delay until they can achieve what they envisage. These similarities
both emphasise the basic mistakes and focus more clearly the details
over which the two men differ. In this way the moral and psychological
observations gain greater clarity, and the passage is given aesthetic
unity. Dawkins has a confidence based on his success as a dealer: he
assumes that it will be as easy to gain a fruitful bed as to fleece his
neighbours. Time shows his confidence to be misplaced, and he and his
wife spend their lives envying Ditchem and blaming each other. That
they do blame each other shows that their experience has still not fully
taught them the point of the reference to Jacob and Rachel ('Am I in
God's stead, who hath withheld from thee the fruit of the womb?'
Genesis 30. 2). Ditchem, on the other hand, is afraid of 'fierce intruding
heirs', so he pauses and then chooses a 'staid' widow whose fair looks
he sees chiefly as providing a self-deceiving justification for spending on
himself the money he would resent spending on children:

> 'Fair as she is, I would my widow take,
> And live more largely for my partner's sake.'   (ll. 534–5)

Time's irony is to grant him no children, and his wife five, so that his
jealousy is equal to Dawkins' envy. There are intruders, though not
of the kind he feared: 'A gay pert guest – Heav'n knows his business
– came' (l. 570). But although the ending is thus partly comic, the
emphasis lies on the effect on the quality of their lives: Dawkins
spending his time in despondency and recrimination, and Ditchem's
emotional as well as physical impotence rendered in his house filled with
his wife's gay friends, 'While I in silence sate, revolving all' (l. 568), his
inarticulate growls being met in turn with silent contempt:

> 'My tender partner not a word or sigh
> Gives to my wrath, nor to my speech reply.'   (ll. 576–7)

The surface tone of the description of Richard Monday's naming is
comic. The Latin sense of 'frequent' gives a mock-heroic flavour to a
phrase in which 'full' refers as much to the rural sages' stomachs as to
their meeting: 'Frequent and full, the rural sages sate' (l. 690). The
quasi-judicial solemnity of their procedure is undermined by the nature
of the evidence (''Twas pinch'd, it roar'd') and the long search for a
name which will not incriminate any of them becomes particularly

comic when we realise that 'they gravely spoke to all' means no more
than making sure that no one among them is called Richard. But
'frequent and full' has more than a general mock-heroic flavour: it is
used of the conclave of devils at the end of Book I of *Paradise Lost*, so
that the sages are not well placed to dismiss the apparent culprits as
'harden'd knaves'. Their scale of values is indicated by the use of the
word 'unlucky' to describe the peasant who found the baby, rather
than the baby itself: the unfortunate thing is not that a baby has been
abandoned, but that it has been found in a healthy enough state to
require money for maintenance from the ratepayers. The phrase which
seems to continue the deflating mockery, 'with all their words and work
content', is made more bitter by the reference to the impending reality
of the 'workhouse'; and while the vestry return 'content,/Back to their
homes', the object of their discussion, hitherto referred to chiefly as 'it',
is seen more clearly as a particular person with a particular future by
the first use of his full name: 'Richard Monday to the workhouse sent'.

In the description of his treatment there, we are made to sympathise
with the child's bewilderment at the meaningless whirl of punishment
and reward – 'There was he pinch'd and pitied, thump'd and fed' (l.
711) – which it seems very sensible to resign himself to accepting
patiently. But the consequence is a grotesque perversion of the Lockean
ideal: he becomes 'supple' and 'pliant', and 'his passions he suppress'd',
yet he develops no moral sense at all. 'Contempt and kicking have their
use' in giving him the self-control to do anything which will gain
favour, and thus making himself indispensable. The amorality gradually
shifts towards immorality as his perverted will is formed – 'he stole/As
others order'd' – then acts on his own – 'In all disputes, on either part
he lied' (l. 727) – and then initiates acts of betrayal – 'In all detections
Richard first confess'd (l. 730). But his will remains sufficiently 'pliant'
for him to maintain self-control even though it is for no moral end: 'he
watch'd his time so well,/He rose in favour, when in fame he fell'
(ll. 731–2). In case the vestry are inclined to think they have no
responsibility for the voluntary self-abasement of a pauper who obeys
the orders of criminals, Crabbe adds,

> Base was his usage, vile his whole employ,
> And all despised and fed the pliant boy.   (ll. 733–4)

The unexpected word 'fed' reminds them that it is their ministration
which has fostered this boy and sustained the conditions under which
his moral nature has formed. It is not only the criminals whose usage of
him has been 'base' and 'vile'; this is the vestry's 'work'.

> 'One morn they call'd him, Richard answer'd not'   (l. 737)

recalls the meeting to decide on his name, when he was so clearly not wanted, so the 'clan' who find they 'had better spared a better man' are evidently not restricted to the inmates of the workhouse. At an early stage, 'his very soul was not his own', so it is not surprising that his 'talents for the world were fit'. The description of his success is spoilt by the ponderously handled image of the magnet and there are only the barest hints of his methods in his calm look and 'complacent speech that nothing meant'; but his loneliness emerges across the mixture of distress and success in his 'fortune': 'This fortune's child had neither friend nor foe' (l. 752). At the end there remains a degree of ambivalence about him: 'He gave reforming charities a sum', yet he 'bought the blessings of the blind and dumb'. It remains obscure what the bequest of two pounds to his native parish meant to him – whether it shows a revengeful venom accumulated through the years, or a vestigial sense of justice which the parish itself warped (a 'rigid trust' to repay the education of a 'pliant soul'). But as judgement on the vestry it is an apt parody of pseudo-religious ('at church produced') cold charity.

The subject of 'Baptisms' is not a very successful one. The most striking passages are those on Lucy, on Dawkins and Ditchem, and on Richard Monday, but of these only the last is really concerned with childhood. The chief interest of all three is in the foreshadowing of Crabbe's later work – the structure of relationships in the first, the irony of time in the second, and the tracing of a complete life-history in the third – but only the third shows evidence of the verbal energy he had already achieved with the easier subject of *The Village* and was later to bring to bear on more complex material.

Like *The Library*, the second part of *The Parish Register* ('Marriages') suffered in revision as a result of the increasing prudishness of the early nineteenth century. In the revised version of old Nathan Kirk's marriage, the sufferings his young wife will inflict have to be invented for the purpose: 'Clamorous her tongue will be … thy money she will waste/In the vain ramblings of a vulgar taste' (ll. 42, 44–5). In the 1807 version, they arise naturally and comically from the basic fact of the marriage: poor Nathan's 'slumbering Fire' is stirred but can only remain an 'idle Wish'.

The pathos of Phoebe Dawson is set against this comedy in very sharp contrast, and her history is itself conceived in the three contrasted pictures of the wedding, the courtship and the degenerated marriage. The first is done powerfully: we see vividly the 'long rent cloak, hung loosely' to disguise the pregnancy, the boy-bridegroom shuffling and stammering, 'confused with muddy ale', and Phoebe's futile attempts to evoke some more timely response by lisping and mincing at him as he strides on ahead to spend their last shilling on more ale. There is a black comedy (its tone defined by contrast with the lighter comedy of Nathan) in the attempts to conceal the reality, which makes the finger-wagging refrain quite superflous. The warrant vulgarises 'strong passions': 'Brought by strong passions and a warrant there' (l. 105). With her torn cloak Phoebe tries 'From ev'ry eye, what all perceived to hide' (l. 107); and the bridegroom 'Now hid awhile and then exposed his face' (l. 110), the anger breaking through the veneer of shame. This pattern of concealment running through the section prevents a merely sentimental response to Phoebe's final attempts to disguise her submission to a 'tyrant' with the 'soften'd speech' of 'departed love'.

Varying the normal 'progress' form, Crabbe then moves backwards in time in the second section to trace what culminated in such a wedding. From being 'In haste to see and happy to be seen' (l. 134), Phoebe becomes involved in a situation where she is 'Seen by but few, and blushing to be seen' (l. 166). But although this early incidence of what becomes in the wedding scene the dominant pattern is aesthetically satisfying, and we glimpse the future of a lover who is 'Fierce in his air, and voluble of tongue' (l. 158), this section as a whole, though twice the length of the first, tells us little about Phoebe. We know she 'felt, and felt she gave, delight', but the 'secret joy' she feels in her 'beauty's power' does not seem strong enough to blind her to the quality of a man who, having shown a 'scorn of trade' could speak of how 'With her should years of growing love be spent,/And growing wealth' (ll. 163–4). It is not that she is simply infatuated by 'manners most unlike her own', for she is 'Dejected, thoughtful, anxious, and afraid' (l. 167). This pile of emotional adjectives tells us very little of her actual feelings, for the nature of the relationship is so vague that we have nothing specific to attach them to. The seduction itself is through appeal to her pity, but that is equally unconvincing as she has shown no previous tendency to indulge in pity: what initially pleased her was his 'bolder spirit'. In fact Crabbe was clearly not very interested in Phoebe as a particular individual, for in the final paragraph of her history he asserts quite falsely that 'Compassion first assail'd her gentle heart' (l. 232). His interest lies chiefly in the major contrast of the first and last pictures.

The last section shows some strength of detail: her gown is 'torn', not deliberately 'rent' like the cloak she wore at the wedding and has been unable to afford to replace; and there is a powerful representation of what grief physically feels like in the word 'inflation: 'she feels th'inflating grief,/That shuts the swelling bosom from relief' (ll. 217–218). Tennyson achieves the same effect less economically in one of the best lyrics of *In Memoriam* ('The Danube to the Severn gave', XIX). But there is also some of the mannered self-conscious pathos of the Old Man in *The Village*, which is comic in an altogether undesirable way:

> Her home she reaches, open leaves the door,
> And placing first her infant on the floor,
> She bares her bosom to the wind, and sits ...   (ll. 213–15)

The 'neighbour-matron's' homely assistance might have helped to control the sentimentality, but the final couplet sentimentalises her as well. The interest of the paragraph lies in its central intention: to render a single significant episode in such a way as to form the dramatic definition of a character's whole tenor of life. She is seen going to fill her pitcher from the village pool, a physically laborious task, for she is carrying her infant as well as being pregnant again, so she has particular reasons for anxiety, in addition to the general ones which contrast with the Lammas Fair when she 'gaily cross'd the Green'. On the way back she puts a foot wrong; it sticks deep in the mud and this makes her break down. It is psychologically accurate that such a trivial incident should trigger off her hysteria; and the incident itself stands as a kind of symbol of her anxious, clogged life. It is a delicate kind of symbol, for it is the sort of thing which might happen to a village woman quite naturally any winter day: it is a selection of the significant from observed life, not merely something set up to make an abstract point.

The portrait of Phoebe Dawson is more interesting in conception than in execution. The tripartite structure of the whole might have offered an interesting variation on the 'before-and-after' pattern, and the significant episode in the last section foreshadows an important technique in the later Crabbe. But although the first section is done well, the second is diffusely and lazily written and the third is spoilt by sentimentality.

Like that of Nathan Kirk's, the description of old Lodge's marriage is spoilt in the bowdlerised revision. The image of him and his wife as owls is feeble in itself and makes the following image of the withered trees seem mannered; whereas the 1807 lines it replaced were both funny in themselves and by using a related image brought out the comic effect of the deliberately pseudo-poetic trees:

> So two dried Sticks, all fled the vital juice,
> When rubb'd and chaf'd, their latent Heat produce ...
> So two sear trees, dry, stunted, and unsound,
> Each other catch, when dropping to the ground ...

The more broadly comic tone also blended more successfully with the indignation in the preceding paragraph at the more serious aspects of the couple's failure to come to terms with their age:

Relating idly, at the closing eve,
The youthful follies he disdains to leave.   (ll. 368–9)

Although three of them are treated humorously, the first six marriages
are all more or less seriously flawed. To some extent this was a
deliberate reflection of Crabbe's view of life, which he consciously
shared with Johnson: 'they who most enjoy shall much endure' is
clearly intended to recall *Rasselas* (ch. XI) 'Human life is every where
a state in which much is to be endured, and little to be enjoyed.' But
although he recognised the need to give content to the last phrase, to
assert, against the impression the six flawed marriages might give, that
happy ones may not be 'frequent, but they may be found', he is unable
to produce much to substantiate the assertion. At this stage of his work
the nature of his talents (in treating comic as well as more directly
serious material) gives the impression of a greater pessimism than he
actually felt. In the paragraphs purporting to show the sober happiness
of some of the farmers and their wives, his attention is quickly deflected
into indirect criticism of girls' schools, a puzzling contrast between the
'noisy drudge' who 'gave/Her soul to gain' and her daughter whose
only stated superiority lies in her ability to boast 'a decent room', and
a description of the art, attributed to 'English wives alone', of gossiping.
The marriage of Reuben and Rachel is important to the structure of
'Marriages' in referring back to the opening paragraph on the wisdom
of delay, in adding to the qualification of the pessimism with a relationship 'By time confirmed', and, by representing a class lower than the
farmers, in inferring a social range such as is indicated by the juxtaposition of Phoebe and her upper-class counterpart. But the details of
their savings and their purchases of furniture remain merely factual,
failing to carry any suggestion of their feelings; and the image of the
'tall elms', although perhaps deliberately set against old Lodge's trees,
has not been given enough emotional content for the contrast to work
poetically.

The last marriage, Fanny Price's, is very much better handled, but
here too there is very little about the marriage itself: the energy derives
from the satire of Sir Edward Archer's debased romantic clichés and
from the unexpected departure from a commonplace literary pattern.
Sir Edward's clichés would have emerged even more clearly as puerile if
the preceding passages had been better written. 'Hope of my life' is
vapid in itself but gains additional effect from the contrast with the
long hope of Reuben and Rachel; and his breast which 'knows not joy
nor rest' seems particularly trivial beside the couple who 'feel their
lingering woes/Receding slowly, till they find repose' (ll. 473–4). But
although these contrasts are less effective than they might have been,

the effeteness of Sir Edward's 'taste' is conveyed well in his little
parentheses, '(what on earth so fair!)' and '(oh! the torment!)', and his
disdainful reference to 'some coarse peasant's sprawling heir'. He
attempts to enlist Time on his side:

> 'want and deep regret those charms destroy,
> That time would spare, if time were pass'd in joy';   (ll. 520–1)

but undermines his own case by going on to offer Fanny 'all the young
desire'. His vision of the possibilities of a love relationship is restricted
to providing her with wine, 'fruit so tempting' (with its obvious
allusion), carpets, pictures and mirrors, and to provoking other women
to envy. The mirrors are linked ironically with the pictures:

> 'Pictures of happiest loves shall meet your eye,
> And tallest mirrors, reaching to the floor,
> Shall show you all the object I adore.'   (ll. 543–5)

Fanny is an object to him, and one which, although he does not admit
it, will change in time to a degree the pictures will not. The pictures
and mirrors probably only fortuitously recall Sir Epicure Mammon
(*The Alchemist*, II, ii, ll. 41–8), but there is that sort of poverty of
imagination. Fanny's reply is an effectively terse dismissal of his puerile
fantasies: 'My mother loved, was married, toil'd, and died' (l. 559). She
knows her social position and she knows that sexual relations include
matters more substantial than 'taste':

> 'With joys, she'd griefs, had troubles in her course,
> But not one grief was pointed by remorse.'   (ll. 560–1)

The relationship between Sir Edward and Fanny is of a kind commonplace in contemporary fiction. The usual conclusion is either for each
to pursue his own path, like the more famous Fanny Price and Henry
Crawford, or for the seduction to succeed to the disaster of the girl, or
for a fantastic reformation to take place in the seducer, of the kind
satirised in the manuscript draft of *The Library*. Here we are led in the
opening lines to expect the third form, with what may be a note of
foreboding in the last phrase:

> Last on my list appears a match of love,
> And one of virtue; – happy may it prove!   (ll. 500–1)

It is not until the end that we find the marriage is a more realistic one,
requiring a more credible degree of virtue in Sir Edward: he feels 'the
transient power of virtue' rather than undergoing a total moral revolution. But although the impulse is transient, it gives him something more
living than his pictures and more lasting than the images in his mirrors:

> A living joy, that shall its spirit keep,
> When every beauty fades, and all the passions sleep.
>
> (ll. 572–3)

Fanny Price's marriage is handled in a more accomplished way than any other in this part of the *Register*, though the passage on Phoebe is probably more interesting. Besides these two, the remaining passages are very slight and in most cases not worth discussion.

In 'Burials' there is more attempt than in the other two parts to give a sense of unity to the whole by relating the beginning and the end. One means of doing this is by making the narrator enter the poem more himself at both points. At the beginning a brooding melancholic presence is felt, without the humour that emerges later:

> When these my records I reflecting read . . .
> Mine I conceive a melancholy book.   (ll. 17, 22)

The other chief means of relating beginning to end is the contrast between the dying man at the beginning, self-justifying and lacking any real sense of sin – 'His merits thus and not his sins confess'd' (l. 57) – and the 'Youth from Cambridge' at the end, who thinks that all human action is so necessarily contaminated by evil that 'The good I've wrought still rankles in my mind' (l. 994). The first man also serves to introduce a reflection which runs through most of the following portraits: the strange blindness people show to the fact and implications of death. On the very point of dying, he tries to procrastinate:

> 'But now, if spared, it is my full intent
> On all the past to ponder and repent.'   (ll. 53–4)

In Andrew Collett, the blindness is literal as well as metaphorical. He is an early example of Crabbe's ability to dramatise the zest of a character whose moral attitudes he totally rejects. The Falstaff parts of *Henry IV* are explicitly evoked in the quotation used in the portrait of Richard Monday and at the end of 'Burials', where 'and is old *Dibble* dead?' recalls 'And is old Double dead' (*Henry IV* Part 2, III, ii, l. 52) There is less imaginative sympathy with Collett than with Benbow, but both were clearly inspired by Falstaff. The condemnation is at times very direct – 'Cheats were his boast and drunkards had his praise' (l. 84) – and Crabbe feels it necessary to add the final reflective paragraph invoking Young. The point is expressed more effectively when Collett's zest is made through the surface tone to appear attractive –

> He praised a poacher, precious child of fun!
> Who shot the keeper with his own spring-gun –   (ll. 93–4)

leaving the word 'child' to draw quiet ironic attention to the fact that
the speaker is now old and near his death. His own boasts show,
beneath the gay tone, both the misapplication of his talent in youth
and his present failure to make any inference from the fact that he has
now lost it. His 'dexterous hand' was applied to a tap, and when
'bless'd with sight alert and gay' he was creating the conditions of his
present blindness.

The Widow Goe, on the other hand, is blinded by the sustained
application of her 'matchless skill' for thirty years. She has no need to
boast, for she is 'Famed ten miles round, and worthy all her fame'
(l. 126). Unlike Collett, she remains 'alert', but her field of vision
is limited:

> Her maidens told she was all eye and ear . . .
> She look'd on want with judgement clear and cool;
>
> (ll. 137, 145)

and with an irony pointed neatly by the parenthetic 'she heard', she
thinks herself qualified to see other people's business more clearly
than they can: she 'lent them eyes, for Love, she heard, was blind'.
Throughout, there is emphasis on the success she achieves within her
limited range of values: she gives appropriately 'brief concern' to her
toilet, and spends her evenings in conversation with her friends, even
though there is a hint that this is more to sustain good opinion of
herself than for direct pleasure. But the cost is indicated both by the
sadder glances of the impoverishment of her life ('No time for love')
and the silent passage of time:

> Not unemploy'd her evenings pass'd away,
> Amusement closed, as business walked the day.   (ll. 155–6)

She balances her 'business' with 'amusement', but the very neatness of
the arrangement (and the negativity of 'Not unemploy'd') shows where
the priority lies, and shows that it excludes anything further. Thus her
life 'pass'd away'.

The syntax of the description of spring registers the surprise with
which she finds herself facing death: the reader too is caught up in the
'lively hope' which in its busy-ness takes for granted that September
will pay what April promises, and death is not mentioned until the last
line of a twelve-line sentence. The sudden realisation can only channel
the busy-ness into panic: no 'reparation' can take place for her soul's
affairs when there has been no preparation, and her attention, deflected
towards repairs to the barn, dithers between 'accounts perplex'd' and
'mind unsettled'; but the general tenor of her thinking becomes clear
in: 'A lawyer haste, and in your way, a priest' (l. 181). Even now, when

she cannot avoid seeing clearly, what she holds on to, and more tightly as the end approaches, are the useless symbols of a lost power and security:

> Heaven in her eye, and in her hand her keys;
> And still the more she found her life decay,
> With greater force she grasp'd those signs of sway.
>
> (ll. 184–6)

A final indication of one price she has paid is the quality of the 'haste' with which her sons return and, having 'dropp'd, in haste, the tributary tear', turn their attention, like their mother, to the keys. 'No time for love . . .'

In the Widow Goe Crabbe has succeeded in portraying a sharply delineated individual, giving vivid insights into the quality of her life but bringing them particularly into focus in the manner in which she faces death. He is almost ready for the final step of rendering a character's response to the passage of time in the form of fully developed narrative.

The Lady, a 'daughter of Indulgence', has this much in common with Collett, the Widow Goe standing between them as an exemplar of futile industry; but beyond this we learn nothing about her except her neglect of the estate. She remains anonymous and as shadowy to us as to the villagers. The description of the hall clearly draws on Old Cotta's house in Pope's third *Moral Essay*, but the indignation is qualified by a whimsically grotesque irony. The only eating is done by worms; the only wooing on 'the bed of state' is done by the bats. The funeral procession consists of actors who cannot even create the illusion of 'mimic miseries': the whole 'farce' is simply 'unmeaning'.

> Slow to the vault they come, with heavy tread,
> Bending beneath the Lady and her lead:　　　　　(ll. 284–5)

the funereal words 'slow' and 'heavy' are made comic by the explanatory 'lead'; and the grotesque whimsy is brought to a climax in the description of the strong coffin which deprives the worms of their due as futilely as the tenants were deprived of theirs. As their brother worms have already eaten the floors of the hall, the 'niggard-caution' is doubly foolish. The whimsy is justified by the Lady's own irresponsibility: her epitaph will be as vacuous as her social conscience. The appropriate response to a hypocrisy which will perpetuate itself by cluttering the church with weeping stone cherubs is simple 'disdain'.

The response to Catherine Lloyd is more complex, despite the sharp satire of the central paragraphs. By setting the neatness of her garden in the past, Crabbe communicates an initial sense of loss:

> those dark shrubs, that now grow wild at will,
> Were clipp'd in form and tantalized with skill.   (ll. 316–17)

There is only a hint, to which we do not yet know how much weight to give, of repression in the opposition of 'tantalized' to 'now grow wild at will'. The 'cockles blanch'd and pebbles neatly spread' evoke only a 'nice' petite bourgeoisie; the content of 'wise, austere, and nice' is on present evidence only partly emptied by 'Who show'd her virtue by her scorn of vice' (l. 321); and the failure to take account of the passage of time seems to have taken a harmless form: 'In the dear fashions of her youth she dress'd' (l. 322). It is only when she assumes the unmistakable traits of the archetypal prude, with tight stays in the present related to a dubious relationship in the past, that this failure is seen to be of profound seriousness: she is 'in maiden-state immured' not only from any repetition of her indiscretion but from all 'looks of love'. Whereas the Lady of the Hall neglected her possessions, Catherine Lloyd's have, in John Speirs' neat phrase, taken possession of her (*Poetry towards Novel* (1971) p. 160). The things, which she gains her only pleasure from displaying, have by their very nature to be 'shut with secret springs' and (a word added in revision) 'conceal'd'; but the sharper irony lies in the assimilation of the woman to the things – the 'pictured wealth', 'Like its cold mistress, shunn'd the eye of man' (l. 351) – and in the reduction of love letters to documents preserved for their prim prettiness and gratifying factual proof of emotions now shut out of her life:

> Letters, long proofs of love, and verses fine
> Round the pink'd rims of crisped Valentine.   (ll. 346–7)

The sole embodiment of active independent life in her 'neat small room', the unfortunate parrot who can only express his 'gratitude and and love' in 'frightful words' which provoke a dangerously spontaneous spinsterly blush, has to be killed and 'stuff'd with art'. Catherine can only tolerate the self-absorption of the cat, the silent encapsulated beauty of the fish, and the fawning of the dog and of the aunt who has learnt to hide her real feelings beneath a mimicking of the animals she obsequiously feeds.

As time passes, Catherine becomes steadily more attached to her possessions, and her wisdom now becomes totally debased: her things

> are wisely hoarded to bestow
> The kind of pleasure that with years will grow.   (ll. 380–1)

She has come to see them, absurdly, as a kind of insurance against time. When the self-delusion is punctured by the approach of death, she begins, like the Widow Goe, to dither between, in this case, her 'stores' and her Book of Prayer, itself contaminated by the false values: it is 'rich-bound', a present from the Captain whose wealth has damaged her more than his illicit love, and valued more for its previous owner ('Some Princess') than its contents. But the tone now ceases to be dominated by the irony of judgement, not because there is any doubt about her, as there was at the beginning, but because the judgement having been already made with such clarity, our attitude can now centre on pity. It is 'an anxious look' she turns on the prayer-book, and the 'stores ... draw a sigh so piteous and profound'. Our response is as to Johnson's miser in *The Vanity of Human Wishes* (ll. 287–8):

> He turns, with anxious heart and cripled hands,
> His bonds of debt, and mortgages of lands.

Her own words, 'Alas! how hard from these to part', are sympathetically confirmed by the narrator: 'Alas! 'twas hard.' Obvious as the answer is, there is an unsentimentalised pathos in her repeated cry, 'What shall I do?' which draws a human response to a woman who has almost stifled her own humanity. Room for doubt is left, though the probability is against any death-bed transformation:

> Nor change appear'd: for when her race was run,
> Doubtful we all exclaim'd, 'What has been done?'
>
> (ll. 407–8)

The certainty and the pity of it is that she lived and died alone: 'Apart she lived, and still she lies alone' (l. 409).

The depiction of Catherine Lloyd is one of the earliest accomplished examples of Crabbe's use of what has become generally known as 'psychological landscape', that is, the rendering of character or feeling through description, often of a natural landsape, but equally often of possessions or furniture, as here or in Walpole's remark about Hogarth quoted above (p. 26). He does not use it as an alternative to statement but as a means of fulfilling or qualifying statement. The description of Catherine Lloyd's house only begins to accumulate significance as we absorb the factual details of the history it reflects, and to achieve the shift of focus when her death approaches, Crabbe moves away from description, using the pointer-words 'anxious' and 'piteous' to give the tone to the repetitions of 'Alas! how hard' and 'What shall I do?' which would otherwise have appeared to be further ironic emphasis on her emotional atrophy. In this Crabbe differs from the characteristic procedure of Tennyson, who is commonly regarded as the classic poet of 'psychological landscape' in English. By omitting or reducing the statement or narrative necessary to give referential content to emotionally charged descriptions, Tennyson constantly runs the risks of repetition (as in 'Mariana') or obscurity (as in the fifteenth lyric of *In Memoriam*, 'Tonight the winds begin to rise', where all we know of the emotion, despite the brilliance of the descriptive phrases, is that it is violent). The dangers Crabbe most often runs are either relying too much on statement, as in the description of Phoebe Dawson quoted above – 'Dejected, thoughtful, anxious, and afraid'[8] – or failing to give significance to factual description: some details even of Catherine Lloyd's possessions could be omitted without loss.

But in spite of some redundancy, a major quality of the passage on Catherine is clearly this rendering of her character though description of her possessions and surroundings. The other major strength lies in the skilful modulation of the reader's attitude from doubt to clear judgement and from judgement to pity.

Despite occasional lapses, the description of Mrs Frankford's death is moving, and of major importance in the structure of 'Burials'. Death does not only take by surprise those who should reasonably be expecting it. She is 'fast-bound' not to her possessions or her 'business' or an inglorious past, but in the relationships which rightly preoccupy her, with her children and her husband. Time has not been able to perform its beneficent function of loosening the ties which give such pain when broken, but without which life would be crucially impoverished. The description of her funeral contrasts with that of the Lady of the Hall: all feel emotionally implicated, not only for the self-centred reasons which help to prevent a sentimentality – 'fear with pity mingled in each mind' – but also for disinterested reasons which emphasise the pathos: 'For good-man Frankford was to all a friend' (l. 604). Unfortunately the husband's grief is rendered in the dreadful line, 'Swell'd the full cadence of the grief by groans' (l. 610), and the village lads are idle machinery, not contributing anything significant, as those at the funeral in *The Village* do. Perhaps for the autobiographical reason suggested by Crabbe's son in the 1834 edition, the feeling becomes more vivid again in the restrained description of the places associated with Mrs Frankford's presence, where the oppressive emptiness and the sense that they retain some sort of sacredness, make the explicit mention of welling tears quite unneccessary. The lines on 'sacred sorrow' are moving in their context, which throws the emphasis on the beseeching of the last couplet, rather than on the easy explanation of the first, which sets the tone when the lines are reprinted by mistake out of context in Ward's edition (Vol. III, p. 496).

The story of Roger Cuff is, as Fitzgerald noted on his copy, very like 'The Deserted Family' of the *Posthumous Tales*. In neither version is it particularly moving, and here it gains nothing from and gives nothing to its context. Its interest lies in the introduction of more characters than the framework of the *Register* generally encouraged and the attempt to represent character through speech, which Crabbe later developed much further. George is blunt and hard. James is piously hypocritical:

'But plead I will thy cause and I will pray:
And so farewell! Heaven help thee on thy way!'   (ll. 765–6)

Peter hides from self-knowledge by prevarication:

'The rates are high; we have a-many poor;
But I will think,' – he said, and shut the door.   (ll. 769–70)

Nancy has the cruel affectation of a prude: 'I hate thee, beast; thy look my spirit shocks.' (l. 777)

The experimenting with direct speech is carried further in old Dibble's loquacious description of the five rectors he has buried. The Author-Rector and the Youth from Cambridge emerge as distinct characters but the first three are mere sketches: the interest is in Dibble more than the men he is describing. His sense of humour dominates the tone, whether the joke is shared with the rector, as in Doctor Grand-spear's punning generosity –

'Thy coat is thin; why, man, thou'rt *barely* dress'd;
It's worn to th'thread: but I have nappy beer;
Clap that within, and see how they will wear!'   (ll. 858–60)

or shared with Crabbe, as in the ironic response to the Youth's excessive anxiety about his 'moral rags' –

'If I of pardon for my sins were sure,
About my goodness I would rest secure' –   (ll. 951–2)

or confined to his own relish of having survived five younger men, as in the comic anticlimax with which he exorcises his fear of Addle's 'stride majestic, and his frown severe' –

'For while the anthem swell'd, and when it ceased,
'Th'expecting people view'd their slumbering priest:
Who, dozing, died.'   (ll. 829–31)

There is nothing in this approaching the degree of Collett's blindness: the atmosphere of the *Hamlet* gravediggers and the Gloucestershire scenes of *Henry IV* is fully present. Yet part of the point of adducing *Henry IV* is to underline the insentience of Dibble's passing within a single line from one rector to the next: 'Who, dozing, died. – Our Parson Peele was next' (l. 831). Shallow's question 'And is old Double dead?' is sandwiched between remarks on the price of ewes and Silence's announcement that Falstaff's men are coming. More importantly, it emphasises the failure to connect the frequency of death with his own old age: a little earlier Shallow says, 'Death, as the Psalmist saith, is certain to all, all shall die. How a good yoke of bullocks at Stamford fair?' (*Henry IV Part 2*, III, ii, ll. 36–8) In Dibble this takes the comic form of the 'variance' between his words 'Heaven grant, I lose no more!' and the look which expresses 'I yet may bear thee forth.' The tone has to be, and is, very delicately poised: the comedy has to be sufficient to distance Dibble from Crabbe, yet not see him with the detachment Dibble himself shows. The function of Dibble in the structure of the work as a whole is to act as a kind of parody of the rector, who hitherto has been objectively surveying the lives of his parishioners as if he were a kind of Gulliver watching 'the annual succession of pinks and tulips in his garden', from another order of existence. Such detachment has to be disowned both explicitly – 'and WE are going all;/Like flowers we wither, and like leaves we fall' (ll. 957–8) – and by contrasting Dibble's dismissal of the rector he liked best – 'but what's the gain of grief?' – with the saddened repetition of 'And is old Dibble dead?' We share the sadness through having come, despite reservations, to like his sense of humour. In these ways, Crabbe has made the points clearly enough to be able to end not on the dramatic, potentially stereotyped note of 'But hark! e'en now I hear/The bell of death, and know not whose to fear' (ll. 801–2), but with the quiet, self-effacing phrase 'one like me' in

> Ere I again, or one like me, explore
> These simple annals of the VILLAGE POOR.   (ll. 969–70)

'Burials' is by far the best of the three parts of *The Parish Register*. The portraits of the Widow Goe and of Catherine Lloyd are the best achieved art in Crabbe before *The Borough*, and there is more attempt to give unity to the whole than in 'Baptisms' or 'Marriages', though some of the minor figures who have not been discussed above could still have been omitted without serious loss.

3 *The Borough*, 1810

According to a note in Fitzgerald's copy of the 1834 edition, *The Borough* was begun in 1804, three years before *The Parish Register* was published. For this reason and also because the order in which the letters of *The Borough* were written is largely unknown, discussions of this crucial phase of Crabbe's development as a narrative poet can only be in terms of probabilities: the development may well have been less steady than critical argument may suggest. The basic form, from which there is considerable variation, is the presentation of a theme or opinion regarding or connected with the ostensible subject, culminating in an illustrative narrative. The framing situation of a man writing a series of letters to a friend living in a very different environment is only used to describe by contrast the scenery of the Borough in the first letter: neither the relationship nor the character of either correspondent is explored at all. The Preface accurately describes the writer of the letters as 'a man of straw'. The most obviously tendentious of the letters is the fourth, on Sects, but almost all of them present a case or attitude, which, although limiting their scope as social history, goes some way towards imposing a form on rather intractable material and more importantly, providing a focus for the narrative passages. In the Almshouse series, the major biographies are given in separate letters, but are clearly linked together through their relationship to the character of Sir Denys Brand. In the series on the Poor, which includes the two best letters, on Jachin and on Peter Grimes, the narratives are even more self-sufficient, more like the *Tales* of 1812. Only two of the letters are organised, in the manner of *The Parish Register*, around the contrasts of a group of fairly rapidly sketched characters. Referring in the Preface to one of them, 'The Alms-house and Trustees', which will be discussed later, Crabbe says of Sir Denys that he has been 'many years prepared for the public', and of the other, 'The Hospital and Governors', he says that the characters 'were written many years since'. The more characteristic letters, although containing some less interesting discursive material, thus seem to have cleared the way for an eventually more developed narrative form, in which Crabbe certainly continued to use internal contrasts of various kinds, but did not have to rely on them as his chief structural technique.[1]

At the beginning of the poem Crabbe says, perhaps to the surprise of a reader who notes that he has over eight and a half thousand lines before him, that he will not be able to describe 'all that gives distinction' to the Borough: 'A part I paint – let fancy form the rest' (l. 6). What he does in the opening letter of 'General Description' is to concentrate on brief suggestive sketches and on the pervading influence of the river and the sea. We are given a quick picture of a very characteristic part of Borough life: the nets hanging at open doors, women mending them, the weariness of the men as they throw aside the 'living mass' of fish for the women to deal with. Then, with the friend's inland stream set up for contrast, so shallow that a small boat has to be 'urged on by pains' and with its fish so distinct as to be 'scaly people' rather than a 'living mass', we turn to the river itself, sweeping inland with the tide and then back to the sea with a 'ceaseless motion', which is in a way 'majestic', yet 'terrible' and associated with the 'sea-weeds withering' and 'a ridge of all things base'. When it seems that the inhabitants escape from it to their food and drink, the word 'painful', referring to the preceding detailed description of the oyster-dredger's pains (very different from those required by the inland steam), brings a reminder of the river into their 'favourite rooms'; 'They hear the painful dredger's welcome sound' (l. 66). The sensuous impression is not merely visual: there is a vivid sense of noise and effort ('laden', 'clamour', 'lumbering', 'loud', 'bellow', 'bolts yielding slowly') and of smell (the 'warm pungence' of the tar and the 'stifling smoke' of the lime-kilns). The activity of the men follows the ebb and flow of the river: the hoys bring down goods from the town, the wagons carry back country-produce in return; sailor and peasant are swept together, 'the loud seamen and the angry hind,/Mingling in business'; and the busy-ness is mimicked by the boys who crowd over shore, sea and ships.

Against the 'wealth that lies in public view' as heaps of coal and coke, is set the countryside of the friend, 'rich in beauty'. Instead of the ceaseless motion of river and men, there is a pleasant variety of the 'lively' and the 'serene': the liveliness of hammer and saw, but the serenity of the soothing smell of jasmine. The scenery varies picturesquely from wood to lake to ruins, and the smoke which one can only just perceive conveniently hides the town. Instead of the crowding and mingling, the 'cattle slowly cross' and the peasants 'part upon the way'. In the Borough, man's mechanical order is imposed on the hedges and trees, so that nothing looks at ease. The smell of the sea similarly invades, spreading inland over heath and vale. Although man seems to defile nature with his 'broad-beaten paths' and the 'sewers' by the roadside banks, his monotony ('from stile to stile') in fact echoes that of river and sea. The 'fences form'd of wreck', representing the victory of

sea over man, seem at first to be used defiantly as defences against the
flooding of crops by the sea, but '(with tenters tipp'd)' makes it clear
that they show the aggressiveness between man and man which mirrors
that between sea and man. One cottage with 'undefended blooms' and
a still spinning-wheel gives brief hope that the pervading aggression and
ceaseless activity has not penetrated quite everywhere – 'This gives us
hope, all views of town to shun' (l. 139) – but even there the sea is in
possession, filling the interior with mementoes of the sailor-son.

Anticipating Letter IX ('Amusements'), Crabbe hints briefly that for
some there are natural beauties to be found among the fens, bogs and
crag-pits, but for most there is only the inn, which is scarcely a change,
for although the people are free for a day, they have only 'allotted
hours' and come mechanically once a week. Only in the sea is there a
variety comparable with the friend's countryside: 'various and vast . . .
horrid now, and now serene'. But the variety ranges from the 'limpid
blue', not to the pleasantly 'lively', but to the 'foggy banks' which
recall both the smoke on the shore and, through the repeated allusion
to Pope, the treachery common to men and sea. The direct quotation of
the third *Moral Essay* (l. 339) in the description of man's ambushes of
trap and gun –

> Or yon broad board, which guards each tempting prize,
> 'Like a tall bully, lifts its head and lies' –   (ll.133–4)

is echoed in the description of the sea:

> And oft the foggy banks on ocean lie,
> Lift the fair sail, and cheat th'experienced eye.   (ll. 171–2)

In a semi-Thomsonian way, but with more economy, Crabbe contrasts
a summer calm with a winter storm. In the first, everything is so still
that the shimmer from the hot pebbles is almost the only movement,
and all that 'contends' is the warmed air rising against the cooler
falling. The movement of the sea itself is finely described so as to suggest
both its present gentleness and its latent power:

> Then the broad bosom of the ocean keeps
> An equal motion; swelling as it sleeps,
> Then slowly sinking,   (ll. 179–81)

with the ships seeming not to move, but in fact being urged on by the
ceaseless tide. In the storm it becomes mere 'restless change', meaningless aggression, with the waves 'As if contending in their watery chase'
(l. 207), rushing forward and then, like the river, 're-flowing' in an
endless rhythm,

Raking the rounded flints, which ages past
Roll'd by their rage, and shall to ages last.   (ll. 212–13)

The monotony is reflected by the 'level line' of ducks migrating 'day after day, flight after flight'. At this point the reader of Thomson would expect a pathetic girl, but here we are given another twist of the irony as the would-be predator of wrecks, aligned with the waves of the sea when he runs 'As if he fear'd companion in the chase' (l. 236, cf. l. 207 quoted above), finds that a fellow-man is the prey. Only the women's cries are 'piercing like the squall'; their 'kinds of power', however varied, are all puny, and the best that can be done is to shine lights which will give false hope.

After a clumsy transition, Crabbe concludes the letter with a description of evening, when 'business sleeps' and the recreation is escapist: 'To pass off one dread portion of the night' (l. 278). 'Show and song and luxury' are combined in an attempt to 'Lift off from man this burthen of mankind' (l. 280); but even before the drunken sailor has staggered home, business starts again: 'the jingling bells betray/How business rises with the closing day' (ll. 287–8). The river, too, reasserts itself through the silence, and its 'rippling' tide is again echoed by the 'measured cadence of the lads who tow/Some enter'd hoy', and associated with the parting-bell.

It is not a flawless piece of writing by any means: the last eight lines would be irritatingly pedestrian even if consigned to a prose footnote, and there are lapses, such as the picturesque lines on the moon in the storm, which are more serious because more difficult to mentally cross out. But the spirit of place evoked by the vivid sensuous descriptions and the intense vision of the interrelation of man and nature, focused by certain recurrent ironies, and understood as a complex structure of dependencies, antagonisms and resemblances, required the powers of a major poet. It is a capacious imagination which can add to the bustle and business of the quay, the boys paddling in a stolen boat, and even though the following four lines (91–4) about British seamen have the curious flatness and irrelevance for which Crabbe is notorious, it is an imagination which is more disciplined than is commonly allowed even by his admirers. The 'stifling smoke' impresses us more vividly because of the verbal contrast of '*fresh*-filled lime-kilns'; and in the visual, tactile and aural description of the lines,

Faint, lazy waves o'ercreep the ridgy sand,
Or tap the tarry boat with gentle blow,
And back return in silence, smooth and slow,   (ll. 182–4)

which have much less than average poetic tension in them, there remains present the monotonous ebb and flow which informs the letter and the lives it depicts.

Unfortunately, considered as portrayal of an early nineteenth-century town, *The Borough* as a whole does not maintain this vividness and control: almost all the strength goes into the narratives, which represent individual lives but, in some cases, at the same time give insights into the feel of contemporary provincial life. The most outstanding exception is the description of the Club of Smokers in Letter x, which engages the full vigour of Crabbe's imagination. The question, 'Dare you come/To that close ... room?' is a real one, for there is a nightmare horror in the way the objects have absorbed the attributes of the men: 'the very candles seem/Dying for air', 'the poor ventilating vane ... is now grown drowsy too'. The inspiration is clearly from Hogarth, of whose *Gin Lane* Lamb was to write a year later: 'the very houses, as I heard a friend of mine express it, tumbling all about in various directions, seem drunk – seem absolutely reeling from the effect of the diabolical spirit of phrenzy which goes forth over the whole composition.' With extraordinary economy Crabbe makes us not only experience the suffocating fantasies and hot drowsiness of the smokers, 'half-sleeping by the sleepy fire' and suddenly roused by the shock of the 'sweet, cold, clammy punch', but also note from an exterior perspective the comic sight as 'prosing topers rub their winking eyes' and attempt vainly to make their conversation flow like their punch. Hogarth's comedy is there as well as his grotesque imagination, and not so much by translation of picture into words as in earlier works: the opening question, the brief use of past tenses, the feel of the punch, and above all the dialogue, show that Crabbe has fully assimilated Hogarth into his different medium. The dialogue captures very precisely and amusingly the nature of drunken conversation, with its foolish repetitions to gain self-confidence and an illusory sense of control ('as I said', 'as I say', 'I spoke my thought – you take me – what I think'), its second-hand aggressiveness ('I spoke my thought', 'And sir, said I') and its pseudo-collusiveness ('mind me', 'Ay, there you posed him', 'here are none but friends'). The opinions which emerge from all these clichés are convincingly self-contradictory. The man who says, 'It is my bounden duty to be free' (l. 257), complains later that 'they're all contending for their private ends' (l. 263), and only just manages to deflect a dangerously revealing nostalgia for the days when votes could be sold ('once a vote would bring ...') into the contradictory cliché, 'It made a man to serve his country and his king' (l. 266). Meanwhile his companion has moved from complicity to quite another line of thought concerning his own 'private ends':

'But man is man, although the man's a mayor;
If Muggins live – no, no! – if Muggins die,
He'll quit his office – neighbour shall I try?'   (ll. 259–61)

Unfortunately the rest of the letter has none of the quality of this
passage. Crabbe's imagination is rarely at full stretch in the descriptive
parts of *The Borough*.

It was implied earlier that the theme of some letters has only an
indirect relevance to the ostensible subject. The Church, in Letter II,
serves as a focus for a preliminary sketch of a proper attitude towards
time and mortality. Man cannot conquer time in any way, but although
he must submit, he must not allow his imagination to be made morbid
by it: it must be used to gain a more proper perspective on life. The
church itself is subject to time: it, like the builders, 'will in time decay'.
But time is not merely destructive: it has softened the appearance of the
tower which was harsh when new. Man's attempts to forestall time by
painting stains on the stone to look like lichen are swept away by rain
and frost, but the same natural forces help to make the real lichens
grow. The monuments which were intended to defeat time have been
made half illegible; the statues of the Lord and Lady reclining on their
tomb are 'Mangled and wounded in their war with time' (l. 102). Death
levels all, both in the sense that all are reduced to dust and in the ironic
sense that all monuments bear panegyrics regardless of the merits of the
deceased. But the forgetting of animosities is not necessarily hypocrisy:
the perspective of death makes one remember the best in people.

The concluding tale of the girl whose sailor-fiancé dies of fever is a
little too long to serve merely as *exemplum* and insufficiently imagined
to work well as a narrative, but the intention is clearly to represent a
grief which is even a little beneficent, yet not allowed to fade as much
as a fully mature attitude to time and death should make it. Death has
sanctified her relationship to the people her fiancé named on the day he
died. On the other hand, there is a possessiveness in her attitude over
the gravestone and a degree of indulgence in her grief which we are
invited to regard steadily more severely. It is not good to shun human
contact in order to keep company with the dead. She has not allowed
time to perform fully its beneficent function.

The paradoxes of freedom preoccupied Crabbe's imagination almost
as much as time. The letter of *The Borough* in which they most dominate
the argument is the fifth, on 'The Election'. The freedom to riot is
obviously incompatible with the basic civil liberty of passing unhurt
through the streets. In the description of electioneering the language
enforces the irony in detail: '*take* a liberty to come', 'Friends *should* be
free'. Crabbe's election has none of the violence and broad comedy of

Hogarth's, but it does show the dreary and debasing range of canvassing
techniques, from the ingratiating use of the candidate's Christian name
to the caller who retails scandal as blackmail in a way which deprives
one of the liberty of throwing him out. The system as a whole
encourages flattery, slander, bribery and hypocrisy. Despite the ideal of
freedom, the political operators are 'bribed, bought, and bound'. The
precious freedom is sold for advancement.

To the Mayor profit has, in a completion of the irony, become the
reason for a more real freedom based on civil order. Naturally he now
wants peace, since he has already gained the seat he wants. From the
start money had power over him, but he learns that it gives him power
over others: the man whose land is mortgaged to him is 'bound'. When
he has taken the next step of seeing that interest in the sense of power
is related to interest in the financial sense, his political machine is set
up. The ironies seem to deny the reality of political freedom so sharply
that it is puzzling to find Crabbe in the final paragraphs referring to the
abuses he has described as mere excrescences on the sacred tree of
Liberty.

It has often been said, justly, that there is insufficient structure to
The Borough, but it seems particularly puzzling that Crabbe chose to
end it with the letter on schools. It is not very distinguished in
execution, but the intention would seem to have been to bring together
the two major recurring preoccupations, with time and with freedom
and power, relating both to the poet himself. The 'busy wives' at the
beginning buy their own 'freedom' which restricts their children, who
cannot escape and who dread the matron's power. Higher up the
educational scale, learning remains, with differing degrees of seriousness,
a process of restriction. We are asked to pity the teacher Leonard who is
'Confined for ever to the pen and slate' (l. 120), but only to give, with
some satirical overtone, 'one soft sigh' to the boarding-school miss who
feels 'The spirit's bondage and the body's pains' (l. 189). The sympathy
for the scholar who is at the extreme end of the scale owes something to
Johnson's *Vanity of Human Wishes*: after years of labour and anxiety
he may find that he has 'just lost the object he would gain' because a
rival has beaten him to it. But Crabbe's main point is that even if the
scholar is successful, 'The honour too is to the place confined' (l. 384).
His power and freedom are limited by his very success:

> What is a monarch in a crowd of kings?
> Like other sovereigns he's by forms address'd,
> By statutes govern'd and with rules oppress'd . . .   (ll. 391–3)

The only real freedom lies in the exercise of the 'powers' of the mind which provide a pleasure that can be augmented by gain or praise, but cannot be taken away by their absence. The poet, tracing the modes of men's minds and the shapes of their passions, is the specific case: ''Tis good to know ...'

But all power can be abused. The first day-school master uses his power as a kind of fence against the domestic worries which rush upon him as soon as his pupils leave. The other major abuse of power is by the boy-tyrants, who cause fear in the present and have even more serious influences on their victims' future lives:

> these young ruffians in the soul will sow
> Seeds of all vices that on weakness grow.   (ll. 302–3)

One function of these two portraits is to define by contrast the poet's use of the 'powers of rhyme', based on the explicit emphasis: 'Who am myself attainted and afraid' (l. 463). He is not proud, like Pope, to make men afraid of him, but, having shared his knowledge of 'Man as he is', anxious to leave the individual to 'GOD and his conscience'.

The preparatory-school mistress is able through her experience to anticipate the effect of time: she 'knows what parts will wear and what will waste'. As educator it is her role to 'check' such things as pride; but as disinterested observer of the truth, she sees how limited her powers are. The Burgess who was 'Cold, selfish, dull, inanimate, unkind' (l. 51), has acquired only a veneer of softness in order to get on in the world: beneath he remains the same. The length of her experience – 'Long has she lived, and much she loves to trace' (l. 45) – enables her to fear and hope for what time has not yet revealed, but may reveal in the future: she

> oft retains her fears
> For him, who now with name unstain'd appears;
> Nor hope relinquishes, for one who yet
> Is lost in error and involved in debt.   (ll. 61–4)

Similarly, it is the aim of the poet who 'loves the mind, in all its modes, to trace', to 'make distinct the latent and the faint'. He has the obvious advantage that he can project his characters through as much time as he chooses.

The arguments of the three letters just discussed are interesting in so far as they relate to Crabbe's central concerns, but as treatments of the subjects of the letters, they, like the others, are not very adequate. Crabbe did not rise to the opportunity of writing a discursive description of the life of the Borough in its various aspects.

So long as contrast and likeness between juxtaposed character-sketches remained Crabbe's primary structural technique, as it was in *The Parish Register*, it was not possible for a more developed narrative form to emerge. The characteristic structure of the letters of *The Borough*, resembling that of the periodical essays of the preceding century, with a discursive thesis followed by a narrative *exemplum*, is not very successful since Crabbe has little of Dryden's capacity to deploy an interesting argument in verse. But although some of the illustrative narratives remain merely illustrations of not very interesting arguments, this form exerted only one pressure on the narrative, instead of the various pressures of a range of contrasts, thus allowing it to develop more freely. The rest of this chapter will deal with the most successful parts of *The Borough*, the narratives.

An extreme case of mere illustration is Neddy in Letter VII. He is treated in the simple 'progress' form: the pattern of his adult behaviour is easily recognisable in his schoolboy pranks, and little else is told about him, except his extreme ignorance and his success as a quack. There is no interest in him as a feeling person and his motivation is given in the most perfunctory terms. He does not even add to the abstract argument: his portrait contains nothing which is not assumed in the mere word 'quack'.

The 'progress' of Frederick Thomson in 'Players' (Letter XII) is very melodramatic, and despite the overt pathos he is not sufficiently alive for the reader to feel any human engagement in his suffering. But the relationship between his history and the letter as a whole is much less inert than in Neddy's case. Crabbe's view of the players in general is that they are rootless yet restricted: 'Slaves though ye be, your wandering freedom seems'. Forced as they often are to act comic roles when feeling pain, or tragic roles when feeling cheerful, they will naturally have 'varying views and restless schemes'. Frederick's parents have differing opinions about his future which they do not resolve, and he is still 'a neglected case' when they send him to college, where they hope the problem will disappear: 'he/Might choose his station'. All he can choose is freedom from imposed discipline: 'He could not descend/ To pedant-laws'. After Frederick's attempt to confine himself to an office, his father unhelpfully tells him, 'My son, you're free': that is his problem. After further disgrace the parents are still indulging a 'secret fondness' which helps to maintain the ignominy. They share the ambivalence of the players: the father says dramatically that he will abandon him, 'Yet left him not'; the mother hears of her 'desponding boy' with 'a kind of joy'; and a younger sister is taught to give Frederick some money 'with feign'd affright'. When he falls ill the better side of their indulgence shows: he has 'pardon, comfort, kindness'. But now it is too late:

Headstrong, determined in his own career . . .
He made his shame his glory – 'I'll be free.'   (ll. 261, 266)

The pun on 'determined' makes the point sufficiently: the lines which
Crabbe deleted from the first edition were too dogmatically deterministic.
Like the players, he is 'determined' to be 'free'. But he needs more
rapidly 'changing scenes' than even the players' life can provide, and
so is left totally free, totally rootless – 'He to himself, unhappy guide!
was left' (l. 302). The writing at the end becomes extremely bad, but
the reference to the Prodigal Son makes the point fairly clear: the father
would have pitied and accepted him back, but the sinner has not the
strength to reach him.

Although the lawyer Swallow has a metaphorical name, referring
both to the devouring of his clients' fortunes and to his method of
softening them up by feeding them well, he is treated much more
realistically than Frederick Thomson. The relation to the main thesis
of the letter (VI) is neatly and humorously made when Swallow's father
does not wish his son to set up on his own:

But, taught by habit, he the truth suppress'd,
Forced a frank look, and said he 'thought it best.'

(ll. 218–19)

Swallow's basic method is very simple, but very effective and credible:
by treating his clients with lavish hospitality, he can claim demonstrated goodwill in the event of failure, and meanwhile give a false sense
of security based on assumed superiority: 'subtle avarice look'd like
thoughtless waste'. He has found a legal way of achieving something
very like the aim of Edmund in *King Lear*, except that the property
ends in his hands and not those of the young men he casts in Edmund's
role. The deception is not just stated but given, with life and with
humour, when he mocks the heir as he flatters him: 'did you ever see/
Limbs better turn'd? a prettier boy than he?' (ll. 286–7) When no more
fish can be caught like this, he does not feign complete religious
conversion, but carefully retains a few irrelevant vices and merely
confesses 'the need' – 'The more the praise to the converting sect'
(l. 341). Their sense of superiority thus boosted, they think they can
manipulate him. When they are disabused, the comic tone is sustained
in the gratuitous consolation he offers them: 'The Lord would help
them', and temporarily he is left, like Jonson's Face, unbeaten. The
sudden shift of focus at the end is effective, chopping his success down
to size:

But lives the man by whom such deeds are done?
Yes, many such – but Swallow's race is run.   (ll. 371–2)

It is a pity Crabbe thought it necessary to elaborate.

The relation between the main thesis of 'Prisons' (Letter XXIII) and the dream of the condemned highwayman at the end is ironic. The opening theory is that the mind accommodates itself to any conditions, including prison: that 'hope and mere want of feeling' help to induce some form of insensibility. In the highwayman, 'Each sense was palsied', but because his feeling of despair was so acute. His nightmare about the hanging is vividly imagined, with the heartless shout from among the mixed crowd of spectators and the thirst he will feel; and it preserves the quality of dreams in the way the priest with him on the cart turns into the one he knew as a child, bringing about a transition into a dream about the childhood itself. On looking back now he knows that he will never again experience such delight, though at the time much of the pleasure lay in dreaming about the future with his Fanny, a future which never materialised. The touch of irony adds to the poignancy of his attempt to re-live the scenes. As the dream continues, we, like him, have our attention fully occupied by the details of the scene, the flowing crimson seaweed and the pellucid jelly-fish. With a realism that achieves an unsentimentalised pathos, the dream is shattered first in its own terms by a wave threatening his Fanny, and then, with appropriate blank brevity, by the truth, the watchman waking him to 'the day'.

Of the narratives which are used to conclude letters based on a theme, as opposed to those which spread so as to fill the whole letter, the best two are on William and Walter in 'Trades' (VIII) and on Juliet Hart in 'Inns' (XI). In the first, William is only used to point contrasts and the interest is primarily in the lonely egoism of Walter; in the second the main interest is in the representation of a dramatic scene involving several separate consciousnesses. Of the two brothers, Walter succeeds and William enjoys. At an early stage they agree to dissolve their business partnership. William tells Walter then, 'take your due'; the cause of his unhappiness is that he gets it. His history takes one of Crabbe's most ironic forms: he is cursed by getting precisely what he wanted. 'Let one mind one, and all are minded then' (l. 125) is arithmetically true but shows a crippling incapacity to glimpse what might make life worth living. His only conception of relationship with others is making sure 'That all about him were of him afraid' (l. 132), so that he will be 'obey'd'. 'He never thought or felt for other men' (l. 124), and while his energies are fully occupied in money-making, he has no reason to want others to think or feel for him. William, conversely, puts personal relationships before money – 'To please his child he let a bargain slip' (l. 140) – which makes him a poor businessman, though he does not find that 'want of wealth could make him poor'. The principle in his family is pointedly opposite from 'Let one mind one': 'Their common comforts they had all in view' (l. 165).

When he has achieved his fortune, Walter finds that he has been too successful in making himself feared: when he seeks affection he receives instead 'fear undisguised'. When he wants love from his wife, she can only offer 'duty', and when he asks specifically for two parts of the marriage vow, love and honour, it is even clearer that he has only the one he once thought sufficient – obedience. In his desperate attempts to get at her 'inmost thought' all he can do is to try to bind her to the external sanction of the vow, and he is rapidly thrown by her silence into the third person – 'Why can't the woman speak?' The degree of his incomprehension is shown in his question, 'Have you not all things?' but he knows all too clearly what he is not being given: 'you evade; yes! 'tis as I suspect'. Again when he asks his child for love and is given only obedience, he knows what he lacks and what he gets – 'I require/Love, and they'll do whatever I desire' (ll. 189–90) – but the form in which he puts it – 'I require Love' – demonstrates the inability to change his own response from the exertion of power to the expression of love. The egoism is such that he slips easily from dialogue into soliloquy and then back into dialogue. Underlying the plain absurdity of trying to buy love, there is the basic selfish motivation of 'I would be happy': 'I would be happy – I have means to pay' (l. 193). He can see that they 'dread' him, yet cannot break the habit of extorting fear: when the second child trembles, he shouts, 'Idiot, leave the room!' Isolated in his egoism, he naturally but absurdly has paranoid suspicions that his wife is making the children hate him, and falls back on indulged self-pity: 'I've not a friend in all the world'. In the confusion of anger, frustration and self-pity, he can so far forget his principle, 'Let one mind one', that he can represent himself as having worked for his family, whom he can then blame for preferring the company of William, while 'I, who gain you fortunes, have your hate'. At the beginning of this self-torture he was dismayed to find that he was feared, but his confusion is such that he is now enraged when he is not feared: 'No awe, no fear, no duty, no control!/Away! away!' (ll. 216–17) He is trapped between the awareness that money cannot give him what he needs and the fact that only money can now give him the one thing he still has – power:

> 'What's wealth to me? – yes, yes! it gives me sway,
> And you shall feel it – Go! begone, I say.'   (ll. 219–20)

Yet the final, sad irony is that the power itself has become an illusion: he has driven them from his presence, but that is, as he has already perceived and only temporarily forgotten, precisely what makes them 'glad'.

The mock-heroic muse invoked at the beginning of 'Inns' lets Crabbe down in the laboured descriptions of the inn-signs which make up most of the letter, but she maintains a carefully modulated comedy in the passage on Juliet and her reluctant Romeo, James. The tone is very light throughout, and it is with a sense of comedy far more than with disapprobation that we note the debasement of language. 'They'd seen the play, and thought it vastly sweet' (l. 237) empties the ominous content of 'evil' in 'James in an evil hour went forth to woo' (l. 235). 'Gentle' and 'generous' are debased by 'Ev'n at a word': The nymph was gentle, of her favours free, Ev'n at a word...(ll. 239–40). The nature of James's 'repentance' is defined by 'he reason'd and he ran'; and his capacities for serious thought about the implications of his position are not extensive: 'The thoughtful Romeo trembled for his purse' (l. 249). The funniest part is the central scene. The father's curses are undermined in an established mock-heroic way by his 'wicker throne', but more dramatically when Juliet retaliates by reminding him when his own son was born. Her mother jumps up to justify her own 'frailty', but at that moment James arrives, so she switches immediately to the obligations of a man who 'breaks the laws'. As her speech lengthens, she manages to work back to proving that 'what came to pass/Was no reflection on a loving lass' (ll. 271–2), but then changing tack again, she veers too near the conscience of the father:

> 'The rogue who ruins, – here the father found
> His spouse was treading on forbidden ground.
> 'That's not the point,' quoth he . . .   (ll. 287–9)

He rescues his dignity by redefining the terms of the discussion: instead of 'villainy and crime', he wants to use such language as 'What's done amiss' and 'my misfortune'. He has his daughter's generosity (when two lasses wanted him, 'I would with all my soul/Have wedded both') but tries to demonstrate from his own case that none the less 'law is our control', not apparently realising that his own former *ménage à trois* does not provide very safe ground for such an argument, however much emphasis he puts on the 'conscience' which distinguishes him from the 'rogue who ruins'. When Juliet herself is at last given an opportunity to speak, she does not threaten like her mother or reduce moral behaviour to enlightened self-interest like her father, but goes a considerable way towards restoring the content of the words earlier debased. She speaks to the best in him – 'My loving James' – even though fear of the law was the stronger motive for his return, and provides him with an opportunity of realigning the 'reason' previously linked with running. Her own generosity becomes a quality of human warmth as she defines its nature against the cold manipulation of the traditional sexual game in which chastity is bartered for marriage. There is just a little of her parents' tendency to reinterpret the past in her use of the word 'forbore' – 'Bonds and conditions I forbore to ask' (l. 306) – but it is true, and genuinely to her credit, that 'I laid no traps for thee, no plots or plans' (l. 307). By refusing to blackmail him even now, and just silently holding up the child to make the direct human appeal of son to father, she leaves room for James himself to feel the reconciliation as a 'triumph' and to make a 'proud speech' in which his word is, with no mock-heroic resonance, 'worthy'. In the restored relationship there is neither the forced legalism of the mother's conception of how to 'make a woman honest', nor the father's gallop through the formalities to allay the smart of conscience – 'A ring, a licence, and the thing is done' (l. 296) – but something which is worthy of ceremony, 'Three times at church our banns shall publish'd be . . .' (l. 315) and which can even assimilate so solemn a word as 'grace'.

Crabbe's control over direct speech is now such that the horror of Walter's self-constructed prison emerges vividly from the shifting tones and implications of his dialogue and monologue. The achievement of the Juliet passage is equal in quality though very different in kind. The range of Crabbe's imagination at this stage of his development is conveniently indicated by the contrast between the pathetic introversion of Walter and the genial, expansive comedy of Juliet's family scenes.

The group of letters on the Alms-house and its inhabitants (XIII–XVI) can be seen as belonging to a transitional phase between the thesis-and-illustration form and the self-sufficient tale. Blaney, Clelia and Benbow each have a letter to themselves, but they also help us 'still more to understand/The moral feelings of Sir Denys Brand' (ll. 338–9), who thought them worthy of a place in the almshouse. The first letter, of the group, on the trustees, is in the old form of contrasted sketches, of the Founder, Sir Denys and Laughton. Sir Denys is dead: it is important to the group of letters as a whole that his choices should be seen in the perspective of death. His conception of magnanimity is ostentatious public benefaction; such simple deeds as feeding the hungry and housing the homeless can be left to meaner minds. Crabbe, like Johnson writing in *Rambler* 60 about biography, regards the 'private act' as more revealing of essential character. Sir Denys imitates aspects of the Founder's asceticism, but in order to be seen and admired. The servant's hall is maintained lavishly both to show off his real wealth and to provide a ready-made contrast with his own ostentatious temperance. But there is not only hypocrisy in himself. He forces it on his servants, for if they had obeyed when he told them to be temperate he would have dismissed them. The just irony is that the hypocrisy he forces on others is very easily deployed against himself: the idle boy who crudely mimics his false humility immediately gains his patronage.

The effect of the letters on Blaney, Clelia and Benbow depends largely on our seeing in the perspective of time three people who have totally failed to face its implications. They are now old and they have never heeded the exhortation of Rasselas, 'Let us live as men who are sometime to grow old', which in Chapter XVII is met by the young men he is addressing with 'a general chorus of continued laughter'. Johnson's word 'continued' makes the point so lightly that it is barely noticeable. In Blaney the laughter has become more explicitly forced:

> Hark to that laughter! – 'tis the way he takes
> To force applause for each vile jest he makes.   (ll. 9–10)

At his most degraded stage, when he is 'with laughing, leering eye' trying to corrupt the young and hawk pornography, he is, in his different way, like Sir Denys in projecting his own pattern of behaviour on to others:

> And many a youth has turn'd him half aside,
> And laugh'd aloud, the sign of shame to hide.   (ll. 181–2)

So although it is natural for Sir Denys, despite his rhetorical concession, 'the fellow's quite a brute', to be crucially blind to his nature ('with all his sin,/He has a manner – let the devil in', ll. 197–8) we are made so clearly aware of the real character of the 'manner'–

> Show not that manner, and these features all,
> The serpent's cunning and the sinner's fall? –   (ll. 7–8)

that some zest in the verse can reflect his forced gaiety without qualifying our moral response at all. His first ruin is undistinguished, 'in the common road', and when he gets more money his conception of 'loftier flights of vice' is merely a more ostentatious version of the same thing: 'singing harlots of enormous price'. The emotional poverty of his life is only hinted at indirectly:

> Cruel he was not. – If he left his wife,
> He left her to her own pursuits in life.   (ll. 29–30)

His only relationship with his wife is one of similarity: they both 'laugh'd at Time till he had turn'd them grey' (l. 56). But time also makes 'common pleasures' cease to please; private vice has to be 'season'd' with the subtler thrill of corrupting others. He is now most pleased 'When a fair dame her husband's honour sold' (l. 73). Death does not change the lights for him – 'Nor ceased the laughter when his lady died' (l. 99) – and he puts a mocking epitaph on her tomb: 'A tender wife, respected, and so forth' (l. 102). The emotional vacuity becomes more definite –

> A father's feelings he has never known,
> His joys, his sorrows, have been all his own –   (ll. 106–7)

and he vainly attempts to fill the void with 'ramblings of the brain' and 'Taste'. The gesture of comic defiance with which he gives his last guinea to 'an opera-bird to hum an air' shows again the habitual attempt to evade feeling, in this case despair, through forced gaiety.

In lines clearly echoing the first sentence of *Rasselas*, Crabbe explicitly asks the reader to look at what Blaney now is, through the perspective of time:

> Come, ye! who live for Pleasure, come, behold
> A man of pleasure when he's poor and old.   (ll. 128–9)

In the final state before admission to the almshouse, he has become 'a useful, needy thing', a 'grey seducer' not of women for himself, but of 'Unbearded folly into acts of vice' (l. 153). When Sir Denys admits him, he still remains immature, 'an old licentious boy'. Ironically, Sir Denys has inflicted on him the worst possible punishment: to such a man nothing could be worse than to be put where he 'must live alone and think'. The 'partial favour' referred to at the beginning means not only that Sir Denys was biased in choosing him but that it is a very mixed blessing for such a man to be sent to a place where he is expected to 'ponder and repent'.

As the basic form is very clearly established with Blaney, Crabbe can allow Clelia a greater degree of zest which makes her more attractive. Despite its stupidity there is something we are drawn to admire in her resilience, the way she takes up time's challenge, resisting its implications at every stage. The word 'spirit' recurs throughout the letter. She is a sprightly nymph who decides that twenty-five is the age where she belongs and where in 'Time's despite' she will remain. On the other hand, the steady passage of time is insisted on more firmly by the division of her history into phases of regular, ten-year length. Her particular skill is in manipulating people, but, adroit as she is, she is out-manoeuvred in the battle of the sexes. Encouraged to think that it becomes her to be gentle, her gentleness finally leads, with an unexpectedness enacted in the verse, to giving more than her hand.

Ten years later, as mistress of an attorney, she brings knowing smiles on herself when she brags of her former upper-class acquaintances, but can ride them out easily enough. Another decade sees her the spirited landlady of the Griffin, but this time she cannot submit to the new situation and can only re-enact her past patterns of behaviour. In the last ten years, her habit of manipulating has become very crude in the attempts to capture the softened hearts of widowers, and the failure to respond creatively to time is now crippling. Her tears are of self-pity, not self-knowledge, and all she can do is to haunt the places where her honour died. But unlike Blaney she commands some pity. With characteristic moral obtuseness, Sir Denys chooses to praise one of her chief surviving vices. Her 'wounded pride' still

> Among the poor, for poor distinctions sigh'd;   (l. 177)

> 'With all her faults,' he said, 'the woman knew
> How to distinguish . . .'   (ll. 204–5)

His crassness indicates that the scale of values on which we registered some approval of Clelia's 'spirit' was itself somewhat awry. Despite her superiority in some respects, she and Blaney make good companions in that they are both living wholly in the past, both (like Sir Denys) taking pride in their follies. As they dilate on their past, the reader is implicitly invited to think of, for example, Jeremy Taylor: 'Let old men be very careful that they never tell the story of their sins with any pleasure or delight . . . lest they be found to laugh at their own damnation.'[2] Blaney and Clelia have learnt nothing about time – 'Hour after hour they sit'; and they conceive their fall to have been due to an external fate which it makes sense to curse.

The best letter of this group is the one on Benbow, a man resembling Collett of *The Parish Register*, but developed with much greater imaginative sympathy. The source of Crabbe's inspiration is clearly given in the opening comparison of Benbow's face to Bardolph's, but the Falstaff experience has been creatively translated into an eighteenth-century context.[3] As with Falstaff, we respond with a double moral code: we all fall for his vivacity and sense of humour, yet we remain aware that in a man whose age is continually emphasised other qualities are crucially lacking. In Crabbe's time Falstaff had already become senti-mentalised: between 1746 and 1788, the emphasis had shifted from, 'Tho' Falstaff is a fardle of low vices, a lyar, a coward, a thief; yet his good-humour makes him a pleasant companion', to 'his alacrity bears him above all disgust; and in the gay wit we forget the contemptible coward'.[4] By 1810, the year of *The Borough*, a writer in the *Monthly Magazine* goes as far as to say that 'in a full view of the character of Falstaff, his vices seem completely in the back-ground. There is a charm, which withholds the spectator from the contemplation of them.'[5] For this reason Crabbe cannot leave his allusion to make the contrary point

by itself. Falstaff's comments on Bardolph's face, in *Henry IV Part 1*, III,
iii, in fact include the frivolously meant but unintentionally suggestive
remark, 'I make as good use of it as many a man doth of a death's-head,
or a *memento mori*. I never see thy face but I think upon hell-fire.' There
is as much pity as for Clelia: Benbow is essentially isolated – '(as he
thought) beloved' – and our response is explicitly guided by the 'reasoning few' who 'His feelings pitied and his faults reproved' (l. 20). But
emphasis is put on the absurdity when 'Vast sums were paid, and many
years were past' (l. 3) on the cultivation of a 'glowing face'; and he is
aligned with the stupidity of the other two when 'with some grey beads-
men, he regrets/His former feasting.' What he 'regrets' is not his
former indulgence but his inability to continue to indulge. We are also
prepared for the debasement of language which runs through his monologue, qualifying our response to it. 'Worth and honour', 'truth' and
'friend' are only relative terms in Benbow's vocabulary:

> Worthy, and why? – that o'er the midnight bowl
> He made his friend the partner of his soul,
> And any man his friend: – then thus in glee,
> 'I speak my mind, I love the truth,' quoth he.　　(ll. 38–41)

But with these guidelines established, the best part of the monologue
can hold in precise balance the vivacity and the blindness. He begins by
cashing in on the Merrie England legend – 'Our bold forefathers loved to
fight and drink' (l. 64) – but it quickly becomes clear that his beloved
Squire Asgill confined himself to the second of these activities:

> 'He bravely thought it best became his rank
> That all his tenants and his tradesmen drank.'　　(ll. 67–8)

There is a very strong emotional attraction in Asgill's magnanimity:

> 'Of Heaven's free gifts he took no special care . . .
> He never planted nor enclosed – his trees
> Grew like himself, untroubled and at ease:
> Bounds of all kinds he hated . . .'　　(ll. 76, 80–2)

It is left entirely to us to note that planting does not necessarily involve
enclosure. He is clearly 'one of the boys' with his poaching 'at other
game', and the tone of genial, expansive comedy is sustained in the
description of the borough-damsels who 'stray'd to gather flowers'.
Asgill's amours are comically justified as a means of broadening social
contact:

> ''Twas schooling pride to see the footman wait,
> Smile on his sister and receive her plate.'　　(ll. 94–5)

Perhaps so, but whose pride was schooled, and whose needed to be? Benbow sees it as big of Asgill to tolerate the priest's talk of vice – 'he only swore and smiled.' It is not only two men's false scale of values we see, but a phase of social history, in the assumption that the relationship between squire and priest is that of patron and dependent. Benbow briefly widens his scope as he warns other rectors and curates to remember 'Who are your friends, and at their frailties wink' (l. 113). After all, it is foolish to lose the most influential men in what he describes as the priest's 'audience'.

Benbow's criticisms of Asgill's son are allowed even freer play. The rent-day visits contrast with the former geniality of communal life, 'And if there's love, they have it all at home' (l. 125). To Benbow, this last line is a dirty joke, and though there is possibly a kind of love there which Asgill senior did not know – the son has married – this remains only a possibility: the explicit emphasis is on the powerfully felt conviviality,

> 'Where a huge pollard on the winter-fire,
> At a huge distance made them all retire',   (ll. 132–3)

against the deeply imaginative representation of the old hag's 'stinginess' – 'Who carves the meat, as if the flesh could feel' (l. 138). The reader is left entirely to draw his own conclusions when Benbow's self-identification with old Asgill's ghost begins to obtrude:

> ''Twould cause among them lassitude and fear;
> Then wait to see – where he delight has seen –
> The dire effect of fretfulness and spleen.'   (ll. 147–9)

''Twould cause . . .' lightly indicates Benbow's emotional identification with the ghost, but there is nothing explicit against him.

Asgill senior is seen in his prime, Captain Dowling in his decline and up to his death, and Dolly Murrey at her death. For Dowling, the value-word is 'man' – 'He was a man, and man-like all his joys' (l. 154). Benbow is 'led to question was he ever boy'; we are led to question whether he ever grew up. His qualifications as 'man' are the beef he eats for breakfast, preferably with salt and its associations, and his capacity for drink. His illness, gravel, gout and shortness of breath, is emphasised twice, and he is 'flannel'd every limb'. Like Asgill he prefers drinking to fighting, despite attempts to assimilate the two activities: 'Man after man they from the trial shrank' (l. 170). The line, 'He did not drop a dotard to his grave' (l. 181), is comically undermined in the mock-heroic manner:

'Still to the last, his feet upon the chair,
With rattling lungs now gone beyond repair.'   (ll. 182–3)

He chooses to die 'as a man', and not 'sneak away'; but when 'death
looks ugly' there are motives other than bravado for taking another
glass.

Dowling was trapped in time, 'every hour the same'; in Dolly
Murrey the image is more obviously physical: she is lame and has to be
placed in her chair. Like Blaney, Clelia and Benbow, she is essentially
isolated: 'Love never made impression on her mind' (l. 208). In her case
it is in the cause of freedom:

'She suffer'd no man her free soul to vex,
Free from the weakness of her gentle sex;
One with whom ours unmoved conversing sate.'   (ll. 210–12)

'Unmoved' is aptly ambiguous: she could not move, being lame, but
also she was incapable of moving or being moved sexually. She is
allowed to die triumphing in her own terms and apparently as one
'practised how to die'. But her lameness reminds one of Clifford
Chatterly's: she is not given the free run of her values. The strongest
part of the letter is clearly the central paragraphs on the Asgills, where
despite the criticisms made through various ironies, our sympathies are
drawn powerfully towards Benbow's and the elder Asgill's values, for
they seem to be the values of life against death: 'I survive,/To breathe
in pain among the dead-alive' (ll. 228–9). 'In pain' there reminds us,
with the portrait of Dowling behind it, that Benbow himself belongs
among the 'dead-alive', however much he may attempt to drown the
suggestions of the bell, which tolls every day, in memories of the life he
led. But in the Asgill passages the hints are so light that even when we
have taken them, we can read through again and love the old rogue and
his hero – until we reflect that, like Falstaff, he is an old rogue and his
values involve a crucial failure to come to terms with the fact of time.

The sequence of letters on the Alms-house is good not only because
Blaney, Clelia and Benbow are each allowed the full length of a letter,
but because Crabbe's imagination was particularly engaged by the
theme of time, which is central to all three. They are set in a gradation
from the clearly repulsive Blaney, through the spirited but stupid
Clelia, to the barely criticised zest of Benbow. Each has failed gravely
in not coming to terms with the facts of time and ageing, but Crabbe's
overt criticism of them can become less each time as the general point
is established. The letter on Benbow is the most delicately poised
between criticism and imaginative sympathy, but its effect depends
partly on the context of the other two.

The four letters on the Poor of the Borough are very unequal in value. 'Abel Keene' and 'Ellen Orford' are interesting in conception, but hardly at all in performance, whereas 'The Parish Clerk' and 'Peter Grimes' are clearly the best achieved work in Crabbe before the *Tales* of 1812. The reference to Dives at the end of Abel's suicide note shows the intention to make his history specifically a warning from the perspective of death: 'if one went unto them from the dead, they will repent' (*St Luke* 16. 30); Abel's age is emphasised throughout. But there is no imagination in the rendering of the struggle between his orthodoxy and his new beliefs, and the 'psychological landscape' of his declining state is part cliché and part irrelevance.

The long introductory passage of 'Ellen Orford' provides Crabbe with an opportunity for further criticism of contemporary fiction, but the tale itself does not achieve anything superior. There is a note of exasperation which shows that Crabbe is not merely echoing Johnson in his complaint,

> That books, which promise much of life to give,
> Should show so little how we truly live;   (ll. 15–16)

but Ellen's tale of woe, which includes her husband's suicide, one son's death by hanging and another's incest with her idiot daughter, is not really, to use Johnson's phrase, 'level with life'.

On the contrary, the story of Jachin, the Parish Clerk who steals from the collection box, is, as Leslie Stephen says in his essay on Crabbe in *Hours in a Library* (1876), 'almost audaciously trifling'. Falstaff lies very clearly behind Benbow, encouraging a two-sided response; Malvolio[6] lies less clearly behind Jachin, as Crabbe wants to tip the balance the opposite way from Shakespeare, but there is a similar complication of an initially comic response. The resemblances to Malvolio, in his formal manner, the enjoyment he gets from dramatising himself and the dislike of feasts and music, suggest one way of responding to his egoism. The narrative voice, too, at first strongly encourages us to mock – 'No wonder Satan took the thing amiss . . .' (l. 44) – but although the tone has not ostensibly changed, we find ourselves (as in *Twelfth Night*) in bad company when we laugh at 'one who, out of place,/Had volunteer'd upon the side of grace' (ll. 82–3). We do laugh, but we are laughing with 'Satan's friends'. We realise on reflection that we should have been more prepared for the formal rejection of the comic Muse: 'There is no jesting with distress and crime' (l. 121). Crabbe's strategy follows the rhetoric of *The Vanity of Human Wishes*, in which Johnson invokes the scorn of Democritus, the laughing philosopher, precisely in order to challenge him on 'how just that scorn' is.

Even before the shift of tone there is much which is seriously wrong about Jachin. He likes to distance sin from himself by attributing it to Satan. The ironical resemblance between what he attributes to Satan and what is later done by his own 'reason' – 'The flattering guide to make all prospects clear' (l. 24) – is not yet known, but should (we see on reflection) have been foreseen: when he professes 'Defiance stern, and hate that knew no rest' (l. 19), he is clearly copying his Foe. He tries to project onto others his own fear of women, and a repressed sexuality asserts itself in a mild sadism which is certainly not wholly comic. His arrogance is more sharply pointed in the allusion of his self-righteous abstention from watching theatrical performances with the vicar ('where my master goes forbear to go') to *St Matthew* 8. 19: 'Master I will follow thee whithersoever thou goest.'

The first temptation arranged by 'Satan's friends' is easily overcome: Jachin's reason is not to be defeated by anything so gross as alcohol. In the second they follow up our own observations about his fear of women, but he calmly rejects the surface temptation again. Satan's 'weak' friends have, however, achieved more than they realise. Jachin's pride and self-confidence are dangerously increased by his victory, and as time passes the pride grows. But although the emphasis at this stage is on his corruption, the words 'sad' and 'wounded' in the line, 'Raised sad commotion in his wounded mind' (139), prepare us for the careful introduction, in the description of his final temptation, of a first invitation to sympathise with him, in the ambiguous phrase, 'poor Jachin'.

The temptation itself is seen largely from an interior perspective. We have been given all the facts necessary to the crime, and before the temptation occurs we are taken right into the experience of the moment by the sound of the coins chinking. The first thought is merely factual: the congregation give money to the poor. The second also has a factual basis which we know: Jachin is poor. So we experience how easily the line of thought flows on, even though from our other, exterior perspective we see clearly that it is sophistry. Thoughts pour rapidly through his mind as he rationalises away his scruples. Law quickly comes to mean to him no more than what 'silence puts to sleep', and the main consideration becomes safety. He adopts the classic manoeuvre of the self-deceiver, pretending he is only putting a hypothetical case, while he gets on with planning the details. The adage, 'Fertile is evil in the soul of man' (l. 178), serves to remind us of Jachin's self-protective conception of evil as separate from himself. The next line tacitly modifies it: 'He paused, – said Jachin . . .'.[7] He knows quite well what is involved in the sort of egoistic utilitarianism he is indulging in, but he shrugs it off with an allusion to Pope's Sir Balaam (*Moral Essay* III, l. 367) which briefly revives the comic tone –

'But I'll be kind – the sick I'll visit twice,
When now but once, and freely give advice' –   (ll. 184–5)

and now that the pattern of thought has become established, reason has become wholly engaged in rationalisation:

'Yet let me think again:' – Again he tried,
For stronger reasons on his passion's side.   (ll. 186–7)

The description of his first actual theft is very delicately held on the verge of comedy. There is a definite mock-heroic tone it it, but the sound of the second coin chinking, which surprises the reader as much as it does Jachin, suddenly stops the tendency to smile, with a recognition of the reality of the danger and the state of mind of a man who could have forgotten one of the crucial details of his carefully laid plan. Subsequently, rationalisation remains necessary for a while – 'Oft was he forced his reasons to repeat' (l. 213) – but habit reduces him to total moral insentience.

As it is important that there should be no sense of triumph about the discovery that Jachin is the thief, the man who finds out is deliberately made very unsympathetic – 'A tyrant fond of power, loud, lewd and most severe' (l. 231). There is very little in Jachin to draw our sympathy: even though we have seen the major corruption taking place from within, he is a prig, a gross hypocrite and a very petty thief, the meanness of stealing money from the poor being emphasised by the touches of mock-heroic. But the insistence on the 'sly intent' and 'angry spirit' of the overseer when he is 'peering round' and when he calls out in triumph, 'Foul deeds are here!' alienate us sufficiently to prepare us for a fuller sympathy with Jachin. The potential significance of the fall to him is rendered at first chiefly through the witnesses and what is apparent to them: the awful absence of overt reaction ('not a groan, a look') and the unanimous decision that he obviously needs no other punishment than his own conscience. When even the harsh overseer agrees, the reader can clearly not dissent. We are not taken far into Jachin's own feelings because sheer numbness dominates – 'Let me withdraw' represents almost all he can feel – but from the repetition of 'all witness'd ... all had witness'd' there is a hint that he has not yet overcome his pride, and he can as yet still think, 'I owe to Satan this disgrace and shame' (l. 255).

As time passes, his attempt to reduce law to what 'silence puts to sleep' is felt to be painfully inadequate: 'he hourly saw/How much more fatal justice is than law' (ll. 262–3). All shun him, but to remove the last possibilities of feeling any satisfaction from this, Crabbe notes that it is only the 'simple' who smile. In the description of his decline there is some specific symbolism: the 'blind courts' in which he sits correspond to the dead-end his life has become. But there is greater power in the emotional suggestiveness of the contrast between his 'shrinking' form and the broad beach where he is exposed on the oppressively 'silent summer-day'. The experienced sense of shame and desolation hold our unsentimentalised sympathy. There is nothing of the sentimentality of Abel draped over his tombstone or of Ellen wallowing over the mole on her hanged son's neck. Nor is there any triumph in noting that the being alone which he formerly advised ('Go not with crowds') has become dreadful to him: we are not too easily to draw the easy moral, but to feel what it is like to have the moral drawn about oneself – 'Compell'd to hear the reasoning of the poor' (l. 284). *The Vanity of Human Wishes* (the Wolsey passage, l. 111) again comes to mind. There are unfortunately some rather plodding lines at the end. But the reality of his repentance is well registered by his ability to see the irony that a man who set out to be an example to others in the sense of 'guide' now is one in the sense of 'warning'; and the limitations of the repentance are suggested in the inability to face the vicar who has come to minister to him. The silence in which he dies is truly awful.

In 'The Parish Clerk', Crabbe has taken a tale of petty theft and deliberately drawn out comic aspects of it, yet by an extension of sympathy into the most unpromising material he has shown the pathos which underlies the progress of vice in a man of very little human stature indeed.

The Shakespearian experiences lying behind 'Peter Grimes' are clearly indicated by the epigraphs from *Richard III* and *Macbeth*. In one way the subject is more difficult than that of *Macbeth*, as Grimes has none of the profound moral imagination which retains our sympathy with Macbeth despite all his attempts to repress it; though conversely, of course, Grimes's moral obtuseness makes Crabbe unable to take us into the tragic experience of a murderer who knows the horror of what he is doing and has done. The quotation from *Richard III*, taken from the speech (v, iii, ll. 177–206) in which he registers the total moral bankruptcy and confusion of his egoism, is perhaps more precisely apposite, but on the other hand the rhetorical structure of the play, though strained to the limit by Shakespeare's imagination, does not allow us to be taken so deeply into what it felt like to be Richard as we are into what it felt like to be Grimes. Both Shakespearian protagonists are also unlike Grimes in that their histories involve the fates of kingdoms. John Moore's *Zeluco*, a late eighteenth-century study of a man equally depraved as Grimes, for whom pity is yet invited, does not have this advantage, but it has the excitements of an exotic plot and melodramatic machinery to hold the reader's attention between the passages of

detailed psychological analysis. Grimes is not only a dull, callous murderer, capable of understanding the moral implications of what he has
done only in the most self-centred terms, but his history is as trivial and
unexciting as a murderer's could be. In a different way from Macbeth,
he represents an extreme limit to the dramatic imagination. For a similar
sort of achievement, one has to think, for example, of George Eliot's
Casaubon.

He can usefully be termed a 'limit' in another sense also. In *Little
Dorrit* (Book II, ch. 33), Tattycoram says of the extreme reductive
egoism of Miss Wade: 'I have had Miss Wade before me all this time,
as if it was my own self grown ripe.' There is no counterpart to Tattycoram in 'Peter Grimes', though in some of the later tales Crabbe sets
up a comparable relationship, but Grimes himself stands as a classic case
of an egoism 'grown ripe', collapsed into the intolerable. As a suffering
man Grimes draws our pity: in Butler's words, 'There is an obligation to
[goodwill] . . . arising from his being a sensible creature; that is, capable
of happiness or misery. Now this obligation cannot be superseded by his
moral character.' But he stands at the extreme verge of what one would
consent to call human if one were using the word 'human' as a value-
term in critical discourse.

It is clear from the first paragraph that this is no case of social
determinism. Peter Grimes senior feels a 'love' and 'care' for his son
which are emphasised by the reference to physical contact: 'And took
young Peter in his hand to pray' (l. 7), and enough of his nature is
indicated – 'enjoy', 'quiet', 'civil' – to show that his son's stubborn
abuse and defiance are innate. The fact of the father's death is held back
till the last word of the paragraph with the effect of making us register
firstly Peter's drunkenness in itself, secondly the indecorum, and thirdly,
on reflection, the appropriateness of such a nature finding the release of
conscience only under the influence of alcohol. His drunken conscience
wanders between the general sense of shame and the partial memory of
actual incidents in the brief snatch of dialogue and sight of 'old Peter in
amazement' and the 'sacrilegious blow' with his father's response:
' "If thou art old," said he,/"And hast a son – thou wilt remember
me" ' (ll. 28–9). Grimes is remembering him before he is old, and
although it now seems that the father's words are implicitly mocked
when we shift from them straight back to the present 'maudlin' nature
of his son's grief and the ease with which it can be relieved by drink,
the irony is doubled in that he will again remember, in less comfortable
circumstances than 'on an Inn-settle'. The phrase 'tyranny of age'
recalls the letter with which Edmund deceives Gloucester and so,
together with the brief sketch of Grimes senior, emphasises the injustice
of the son's demand for 'freedom'. As in *King Lear*, freedom is con-

ceived of initially as the opposite to established relationships and social structures, but rapidly degenerates into wanton exertion of power. As well as taking us into the moral consciousness of this extraordinarily alien person, 'Peter Grimes' brings together Crabbe's two most characteristic themes, showing, to put it in abstract terms, what happens to the pursuit of freedom when it is projected through time.

Grimes's permanent state is already hinted at in the line, 'Now lived the youth in freedom, but debarr'd (34); the freedom imposes its own form of restriction. At first he is not even able to be a slave to his own desires: 'Hard that he could not every wish obey' (l. 36). Crime provides the only means of escaping the restrictions of a limited purse; but although it gives a new degree of power – 'On all he mark'd, he stretch'd his ready hand' (l. 42) – the following line mocks its range in the contrast between the nouns, which suggest a limitless inclusiveness, and the pettiness of the verbs: 'He fish'd by water and he filch'd by land' (l. 43). More importantly, it increases his isolation: 'The more he look'd on all men as his foes' (l. 50). The 'mud-wall'd' hovel', which is only a place to keep his hoard, is the outward expression of it, as his father's dwelling expressed his different sense of values: 'His wife he cabin'd with him and his boy' (l. 2). But silent expression is not enough: to feel the reality of his freedom he must see it registered by another consciousness. He needs to have 'A feeling creature subject to his power' (l. 58). The boy's misery is portrayed with powerful brevity, 'the bruise, that made the stripling stoop' and 'the ridges on his back'. At this stage the physical cruelty is an evil no greater than the general social acceptance of such outrageous exploitation of orphans, so the townspeople are appropriately uninterested. If they had put themselves to the trouble of asking questions, their emphasis would have been economic: 'He'll serve thee better if he's stroked and fed' (l. 76). 'Stroked and fed' suggests behaviour towards an animal rather than a boy. Those who do hear the boy's cries think them material for pleasantry: 'Grimes is at his exercise'. The bewildering whirl of pain which the boy's life consists of is made more vivid by the contrast between this calmly made remark and the sudden battery of past-participles: 'pinn'd, beaten, cold, pinch'd, threaten'd, and abused' (l. 79). His stunted, imprisoned life is suggested by the enclosing balance of the lines: 'Struck if he wept, and yet compell'd to weep' (l. 82). Meanwhile, Grimes becomes more dependent on the proof of his freedom: he now enjoys demonstrating his power, by violence, and by depriving the boy of his freedom. The result on the boy is ironically similar to Grimes's own pursuit of freedom on himself – 'Compell'd by fear to lie, by need to steal' (l. 91).

When there is a fact so uncomfortably blatant as a death, the people's social conscience is a little disturbed, but little enough for Peter to remain 'untroubled and unmoved'. At the second death they 'reason' clearly enough that his account must be false, yet let him off. When they briefly light on the truth, his conscience is hit, but his fears at this stage are confined to what a jury's verdict can set aside. Even when they begin to respond to the situation more humanely, the pity of the seamen's wives is ironically mis-focused. What concerns them is not the human outrage of Peter's behaviour or the practice of forced apprentice-ship in general, but the possibility that the third boy is 'Of gentle blood, some noble sinner's son' (l. 123). Their pity, like Grimes's own, is self-interested:

> in the town they gave
> Fire, food, and comfort, to the gentle slave;   (ll. 132–3)
>
> And his vile blows with selfish pity dealt.   (l. 137)

The death of the third boy is again handled with powerful, unsenti-mental brevity: enough is said when the boy is driven by terror of the sea to cling to *Grimes's* knee. Uncontaminated pity for the boy comes only now, when it is too late; and the judgement the mayor pronounces is at last sufficiently just to remind us of what Jachin found: 'How much more fatal justice is than law' (l. 263). Although ostensibly he is let off, the judgement is shot through with irony: Grimes's freedom is to be limited by having to employ a 'freeman'; he is now free of human attachment to a degree beyond his hopes; and the ghosts of the boys will abide with him instead. The judgement could not in fact be more severe: it is the full reflection of his soul.

He is now alone, so totally free of the restrictions of human obliga-tion that his characteristic activities – 'command', 'curse' – become pointless: there is no one to hear him. But it is now that we are taken most fully into what it felt like to be Grimes. The justly famous descrip-tion of his psychological landscape is at one, very important, level literally what Grimes sees. Because of his self-imposed isolation, his mind has nothing else to engage it. The whole first paragraph is a single sentence describing what he is 'compell'd ... each day ... for certain hours ... to see': the same dull views merely varying with the tide from water only to 'mud half-cover'd and half-dry'. The observation of the blistering tar and the 'uneven ranks' of stakes is aptly precise because his life has become little other than watching these things, and for the same reason the metaphorical reference of the words is both unobtru-sive and completely convincing: diseases in 'blighted tree' and 'blisters', imprisonment in the 'bounding marsh-bank', 'stakes' and 'impeded boat', decay in 'uneven ranks' and 'entangled weeds'. In the second paragraph the description is not of what Grimes was 'compell'd ... to see', but of what he 'chose from man to hide ... and view'. As the egoism is driven further in on itself by the surrounding monotony, as well as by its own momentum, he becomes addictively fascinated by the reflection of his own decay. The words 'nursed' and 'loved', which take their meaning from relationships between people, are fouled by intro-version:

> He nursed the feelings these dull scenes produce,
> And loved to stop ...
> Where all, presented to the eye or ear,
> Oppress'd the soul with misery, grief, and fear.
>
> (ll. 199–200, 203–4)

So again, we do not have Crabbe saying in effect, 'This is an image of Grimes's mind', as Tennyson says, for example, of Mariana: we are experiencing in imagination what Grimes did. It is an important stage of his development that he chose to wallow in images of himself, to gape at the 'gaping muscles' and look, 'dull and hopeless' at 'dull scenes' and listen to a 'dull, unvaried, sadd'ning sound'. If the narrative structure, which takes its meaning from the total narrative context of the tale, is not kept in mind, the distinctive achievement of the passage cannot be seen and it becomes mere Tennysonian evocation. Even within the scene he chooses, Grimes chooses to see only what reflects himself. A 'dark warm flood' running 'silently and slow' is to him 'the lazy tide/In its hot slimy channel', and where the small eels 'play' near the 'warm shore', it is the 'sidelong crabs' scrawling their 'crooked race' which draw his attention. At the same time as reproducing literally what Grimes's consciousness has been reduced to being aware of, the lines again comment metaphorically on the quality of the consciousness. At this level, it is perhaps a mistake to look for particular meanings – to think, for example, of the 'dark warm flood' as the life-force which Grimes has reduced to a 'hot slimy channel'; the effect is more an associative one, 'sultry' and 'lazy' suggesting exhaustion, 'gaping' vacuity, 'slimy' stagnation, and above all there is the sense of unnatural vileness lurking in the recesses of Grimes's mind, which hangs over the whole passage, evoked most particularly by the 'hot slimy channel', the eels, the mud and the 'sidelong crabs'.

At this stage, he can still whistle his way past the three places which he most dreads, but when the whole community, men, women and children, reject him, the only possible response he has left himself is a defiant wish for the solitude which is continuing his destruction. His remaining activity has become even more pointless: at his 'bootless labour' he can only swear at the fish. When the nightmares grow more terrible, he is driven for the first time to express his self-pity in terms of a desire for the human contact he has deprived himself of:

> he felt forsaken, grieved at heart,
> To think he lived from all mankind apart.   (ll. 229–30)

'Forsaken' is an outrageous misrepresentation of the facts, but there is
more to 'grieved' than the sense of 'aggrieved': the shutting of his self-
made trap is truly pitiful – 'Yet, if a man approach'd, in terrors he
would start' (l. 231). The incipient pity is emphasised by a rhetorical
manoeuvre, similar to the introduction of the overseer who catches
Jachin but less obvious: the summer lodgers' reduction of Grimes to an
object of idle curiosity provokes the reader by reaction to insist that he
is not a tourist attraction, but a man in a peculiarly awful spiritual cul-
de-sac. Some power has indeed 'chain'd' this man who wanted freedom,
but it is not 'for a time', and not in order to hold him in mystic stasis
for Wordsworthian contemplation, as one might think from:

> At certain stations he would view the stream,
> As if he stood bewilder'd in a dream.   (ll. 243–4)

When 'some curious, some in pity' go to him, it is clearly the latter we
are invited to identify with; and when they are joined by those who
'follow'd and cursed', Grimes has become wholly the victim, the hunted
– 'A lost, lone man, so harass'd and undone' (l. 256). For once 'our
gentle females, ever prompt to feel' respond rightly first time and perceive 'compassion on their anger steal'.

In Grimes's final monologues there is no repentance: he sees himself
self-pityingly as the victim and feels only hatred towards those he has
wronged. But although we are kept in mind of the moral stupidity, the
horror he has to experience compels pity. At first he is trying to defend
himself at an imaginary trial, re-enacting the past; but the 'chain' is
also a physical one to his delirious mind. He is particularly haunted by
the memory of his father, who represents most fully what he has cut
himself off from and therefore now has to hate. Even though he is half-
conscious that 'he wasn't there', he is afraid he will testify against him
as a kind of externalised conscience. The isolation is vividly suggested
by 'What, all agreed?' but it quickly becomes clear that he does not
really want 'time to pray': ''Twas part confession and the rest defence'
(l. 288). His dying speech is contaminated by the habits of concealment:
'He hid the knowledge, yet exposed his heart' (l. 287). He has reversed
the roles of his father and himself – 'he who always tried/To give me
trouble' – but in so doing has not realised that he is also exposing the
reality of the moral relationship: the meetings at which the ghost makes
Grimes watch, 'and so neglect my trade', remind us of the first paragraph, 'He left his trade upon the Sabbath-day' (l. 6). The setting of the
ghost scenes is as un-Gothic as possible: it is not a moonless night but a

'hot noon', and Grimes's quiet assertion, 'No living being had I lately seen' (l. 299), is not cliché but a fact we have every reason to credit. The authentic terrors of nightmare are conveyed by the impotence:

> 'I would have struck them, but they knew th'intent
> And smiled upon the oar, and down they went;' (ll. 312–13)

> 'To row away with all my strength I try'd.' (l. 325)

The paranoia which is the ironic culmination of his desire to see 'all men as his foes' is focused by the illusion that his father is preventing him from catching any fish, and again he is precisely reversing the roles:

> 'A father's pleasure, when his toil was done,
> To plague and torture thus an only son!' (ll. 302–3)

'Quiet Peter' has become 'the hard old man', partly through memory of his earlier misrepresentation of 'the tyranny of age', and partly through transference of his own characteristics. There is no real humility in 'I humbled me and pray'd/They would be gone': there is only fear, a fear he tries to conceal behind understatement – 'I was loth to die'. He transfers the guilt to the father – 'Fathers should pity' – although even in imagination it is Grimes who strikes, and all he can claim to have 'weaken'd all my frame' is the responding 'hollow groan' which comes through the water. Grimes is not even rendering his imaginings truthfully:

> ' "Father!" said I, "have mercy;" – he replied,
> I know not what – the angry spirit lied.' (ll. 332–3)

He does remember, but is suppressing the reply so that he can continue to represent his father as 'the angry spirit' and vindicate himself:

> 'I had pity and my arm withdrew . . .
> But he has no compassion in his grave.' (ll. 335, 337)

Grimes's version of the motionless phase of what the general Preface calls his 'progress' is comparatively feeble: the horror is not effectively dramatised, and the writing becomes repetitive, and positively bad in the phrase 'each little villain sprite'. The paragraph on the 'one fierce summer-day' is weakened by what immediately precedes it, but it is less Gothic than the 'glee' and the blood at first might make one think. The phrase 'father-foe' briefly summarises the demonstration of how this relationship has become the focus of his confused paranoia. The hand is the one which once led Grimes to pray, and the syntax shows his fixation: the line, 'He with his hand, the old man, scoop'd the flood' (l. 356), would have lost all its strength if it had been, more obviously, 'The

old man with his hand scoop'd up the flood'. The horror of Grimes's
nightmare is emphasised by the contrast of 'force' and 'rest': 'Still did
they force me on the oar to rest' (l. 354). The burning blood itself is not
mere machinery: it is fused with the actuality of the hot sun, and part
of its significance derives from the reference back to the drunken recollections of his conscience at the beginning, when he 'Gave the hot spirit
to his boiling blood' (l. 21). The last line, apparently flat – 'I thought the
demons would have turn'd my brain' (l. 361) – is authentic: Grimes is
at a degree of insanity corresponding to that in which a drunken man
tries to maintain that he is still substantially sober. The final state is a
vision of hell itself, 'all days alike'. He is in such a wretched state that
he is frightened of the 'frighten'd females'. There are no 'better
moments, for Grimes as there were for Jachin: the apparent 'rest' is only
exhaustion. The accumulated ironies of his egoism are lightly recalled in
'inward' and in the compelling need he now has to try to speak; but
the emphasis is on 'broken':

> Then with an inward, broken voice he cried
> 'Again they come!' and mutter'd as he died.   (ll. 374–5)

'Peter Grimes' has not the complexity of some of the best 1812 *Tales*,
but in one respect it remains at the height of Crabbe's achievement. As
the humane representation of a barely human consciousness it has few
rivals in English literature.

As an attempt to render the life of a community, *The Borough* must
be regarded as a failure: there is in its structure hardly any opportunity
to represent the inter-texture of lives and classes, which the capacious
form of a complex novel can contain. Its value as social document is also
limited: in most letters there is so overt an attempt to prove an argument that the representations cannot be taken as fair, and the arguments
themselves are not penetrating criticisms of contemporary society. The
laborious attack on quack doctors in Letter VII, for example, is far less
effective social criticism than the brief facts about the 'work-house
clearing men' in 'Peter Grimes', which are limited to what is necessary
to understand the narrative. It is the narratives which really live in the
mind, and it is chiefly in them, where the poet's imagination is most
engaged, that we find the best insights into social as well as individual
life, at the point where the two are inseparable.

4 *Tales*, 1812 (1)

In the 1812 Preface Crabbe, in answering what he took Jeffrey to have suggested in his review of *The Borough*, indicates that he found himself unable to achieve the large-scale articulation of an 'Epic Poem'. Despite this limitation, in the *Tales* he developed to its finest point his distinctive narrative form, in which both character and the more general insight that accompanies profound characterisation are embodied in a way nearer to the nineteenth-century novel than to the 'portrait' of the major eighteenth-century satirists. It is a form in which the verse and the restricted length encourage a verbal texture closer than in all but the best work of the greatest novelists, and an economy of incident which, in comparison with the diffuseness of novels below the stature of the best, can also be seen as a strength. One of the concomitant limitations was suggested at the end of Chapter 3; but another, which may seem equally serious, will be shown to be less so in the light of Crabbe's own remarks in the Preface. In a major novel, characters may be set in moral as well as narrative relationship, each illuminating the others. Little Dorrit, for example, is set at the centre of Dickens's novel between the two 'limits' of Miss Wade's reductive egoism and Mrs General's cultivation of surface; we see Fanny travelling along the 'way' which ends in the condition of Mrs Merdle; Clennam's self-pity is parodied by John Chivery's habit of composing pathetic epitaphs for himself, and his neurotic sense of guilt by the absurd accusations of Mr F.'s aunt. These and other forms of moral relationship run right through the book, giving aesthetic structure and enabling Dickens to express his moral, social and psychological insights with great complexity of qualification and of tone. Crabbe's best tales are, as John Speirs has noted (*Poetry towards Novel*, pp. 156–7), compact structures in which characters and episodes are set in a kind of relation to each other which at a verbal level we are accustomed to call wit; but they are too short to do so with a complexity approaching that of the mature Dickens. In admitting his own limitations in the Preface, however, Crabbe also suggested that the characters in his tales did not 'appear as an unconnected multitude': he described them as 'beings of whom might be formed groups and smaller societies, the relations of whose adventures and pursuits might bear that kind of similitude to an Heroic Poem, which these minor associations of men (as pilgrims on the way to their saint . . .) have in points of connexion and importance with a regular and disciplined army.' In the light of following remarks, it is clear that he has *The Canterbury Tales* in mind here. Crabbe's *Tales* do not fall into rigid groups from which a formal argument can be extracted, as used to be done with Chaucer's 'Marriage Group', but, as in *The Canterbury Tales*, there are certain recurring subjects, which are seen in different perspectives and contexts in different tales, in such a way that composite pictures gradually emerge, which are more than the sum of the individuals. One large group of tales can be seen as shaping a sense of what constitute the richer and the poorer forms of inter-sexual relationship, of which a subgroup is centred more particularly on marriage, and another raises various questions concerning moral and intellectual freedom; and in a few cases there are clear pairs, such as 'Procrastination' and 'The Parting Hour', which show in very different ways the effect of very long separation on a relationship between man and woman. But such groupings are neither mutually exclusive nor a sufficient means of describing the tales which fall into them. The interrelations are essentially fluid, so although there is no formal articulation such as in a great novel, there can be an accumulated complexity and an over-all sense of capaciousness impossible in the simple contrast and thesis-plus-illustration forms of Crabbe's earlier works. In order to do justice to both the unity Crabbe was able to achieve within particular tales and the unsystematic complexity of the whole collection, it is necessary to consider most tales in specific detail.

Of the tales which remain closest to the 'progress' form, the least interesting is 'The Patron'. There is a fundamental lack of control, the reason for which is indicated at line 321. 'Thou art religion's advocate', says the young poet's father. He is not; but Crabbe was when he was at Belvoir Castle, patronised by the Duke of Rutland. Crabbe has failed to transmute his personal experience into the balance between sympathy with the poet's feeling and detachment from his arrogant self-delusion, which seems to have been intended.

'Edward Shore', Tale XI, is a more successful treatment of a 'progress'. The beginning is clearly modelled on the lines on the scholar in *The Vanity of Human Wishes* (ll. 135–74: even if Genius survives external dangers such as the weakness of the body, poverty and the seduction of the passions, it remains subject to the danger of its own success. But whereas Johnson thinks in terms of a real achievement jeopardised by unjust response from others, Crabbe thinks of the false sense of security which renders a proud mind vulnerable to temptation. Consequently, Edward Shore's rationalist ethic cannot be given free play: the point of the tale is that it must break down. This renders Crabbe liable to the vulgarity of the father in 'The Patron', a common attitude in contemporary fiction, expressed tersely by Elizabeth Hamilton: 'genius is less valuable than virtue' (*Letters of a Hindoo Rajah* (1796) 5th ed., Vol. II, p. 103). On the other hand, comparing Shore with his most obvious forebears, Pertinax (of *Rambler* 95) and Opsinous (of *Adventurer* 12–14), it is clear that Crabbe has given him considerable scope. Unlike Pertinax, the sceptical Shore continues to argue for virtue even after he meets his friend, who does not, and his fall is by no means so easy as Opsinous's. One of the chief ironies, as in 'The Lover's Journey', is his ignorance of how far his conscious views depend on his subjective state. A man who 'felt his bosom light, his conscience clear' is naturally inclined to think that 'the pure prompting of the will within' is a sufficient moral guide, not in need of external sanctions. He cannot see that feeling can effect action in any way other than by force or by deliberate indulgence of 'wish':

> 'Unless it forces, call it as you will,
> It is but wish, and proneness to the ill.' (ll. 73–4)

In his rejection of trade, law, medicine and theology, there is a touch of Faustus's pride, but it is qualified by the upright motive for rejecting law and war ('he must the cause approve'). His 'good-nature', 'dignity and grace' are real. A sharper irony lies in the contrast between his friends' hopes of the 'progress he would make' and his own 'restless thoughts': his intellectual fastidiousness includes a moral rootlessness which ends in a different sort of 'progress'.

To a large extent this rootlessness is taken on its own terms: his rational doubts themselves expose the limits of his reason to an extent which requires only light allusion to the opening of Dryden's *Religio Laici*:

> Reason, his sovereign mistress, fail'd to show
> Light through the mazes of the world below. (ll. 87–8)

The irony is finely balanced in 'No passion's victim, and no system's slave' (l. 106). He thinks that he is no system's slave, but his emotional capacities for life are limited by the radical uncertainties of his professed scepticism; and in the same sentence we see that he is 'slave to fame' and victim of a passion which, although he remains *unconscious* of it, is revealed to us when we are told that he 'o'er each sense in conscious triumph reign'd'. Unfortunately, Crabbe does not leave it in these terms, but vulgarises the attitude to Shore when he tells us, as if from the safety of mediocrity, that Shore 'sought no common guide'. Shore looks down on the 'grosser herd' and 'vulgar crew', yet seeks aid from a group of doubters; but the irony of this only works if one already assumes that what he doubts is self-evidently true: otherwise it seems sensible to pursue truth with like-minded people. The question is begged again when he is described as one 'Who found no rest, nor took the means to find' (l. 102). But this is only a temporary lapse. The emotionally stunting effect of his fastidious scepticism is developed through allusion to *Rasselas* (Chapter VI), in which the inventor plans to 'trace the Nile through all his passage' and to survey the 'moving scene of land and ocean', commerce and war, 'with equal security':

> 'Tis thus a sanguine reader loves to trace
> The Nile forth rushing on his glorious race;
> Calm and secure the fancied traveller goes ...   (ll. 123–5)

Shore 'beheld life's shifting scene' from the safety of his own room: his 'visions were enjoy'd', but he is to a damaging degree 'lost to life'. His mind is, as we have seen earlier, 'lively', but it is 'abstracted' from the business of living, and its consequent sense of being 'still, serene' is a dangerous illusion. Thinking he is seeing in perspective 'all that crowds neglect, desire, pursue', he is in fact steadily making himself 'Still more unfitted for the world's affairs' (l. 143). This has developed very directly from the initial fastidiousness of

> He gave his restless thoughts to views refined,
> And shrank from worldly cares with wounded mind;
>
> (ll. 49–50)

and before the main action of the tale, the emotional impoverishment is shown more fully in the response to Anna. The sexual relationship only brings out a similar 'idly busy' activity, a 'pleasant trifling'. The answer to the question 'did he love?' can only be a catalogue of the actions of his feet, eyes, tongue and ears. But as well as showing how 'abstracted' he is from emotional engagement, the episode also shows him deceiving himself again about his feelings.

> Not rich himself, he saw the damsel poor;
> And he too wisely, nay, too kindly loved,
> To pain the being whom his soul approved.   (ll. 161–3)

Either he knows he doesn't love and is representing selfish prudence as magnanimity, or, more probably, despite his earlier confidence about the heart's deceptions, he really does not know he does not love her and so, genuinely but quite mistakenly, thinks he is being kind. Either way, the effect is to confirm the illusion that he has complete control over his feelings: the experience leaves him as emotionally callow as before. In the discussions with his Friend, he is just as unconscious as he was at the beginning that his reasonings are based on an emotional predisposition:

> from his feelings all his fire arose,
> And he had interest in the themes he chose.   (ll. 186–7)

The Friend represents a possible further step along the 'progress' of scepticism. He is outwardly serene but his underlying feelings are cruder than Shore's: 'His mind reposed not, for he hated rest' (l. 176); and he wants to make others as perplexed as himself. The contrast emphasises that Shore's feelings remain good, despite his continuing immaturity; and the comic suddenness of the Friend's marrying a young beauty after his condescending talk of 'men's delusions' sets off the pathos of Shore's fall. The wife is as callow as Shore: she is a 'child' who still has 'school-day dinners in her head' and her love can be represented in even more external terms than Shore's feeling towards Anna: her 'heart's content' is 'daintiest food', 'costly dress', and 'summer-visits'. But the distinctive achievement of the rendering of the adulterous relationship is the way it is seen as an entirely *natural* process: there is nothing of the hot-house melodrama of Opsinous's seduction of his friend's daughter. The two young people left alone sustain the mood of civilised decorum which prevails in the Friend's house – 'They calmly gazed on the declining sun' (l. 231) – and it is nature which threatens it, while they remain unaware:

> Till rose the moon, and on each youthful face
> Shed a soft beauty, and a dangerous grace.   (ll. 234–5)

The wife's comparison of her husband's 'grisly beard' and his appearance when asleep with the good looks of Edward reminds one of 'The Merchant's Tale', but unlike May's, her feelings are innocent enough not to have to be concealed by a Chaucerian claim not to know them, such as 'But God woot what that May thoughte in hir herte'. In his ignorance of human nature the Friend is clearly foolish, but he has good grounds for trusting them, 'For neither yet the guilt or danger knew' (l. 261). Pertinax's scepticism left him free to argue according to the inclination of the moment, 'inclining as occasion required to either side'; the combination of scepticism and the emotional immaturity derived from the consequent detachment leaves Shore more vulnerable than he himself realises to 'occasion'.

The fall itself, during the Friend's absence for a few days, is handled with great delicacy. The characteristic restlessness of Shore and the capriciousness of the wife are centred more particularly on their confused oscillation between attempts to behave normally and the growing,

constraining awareness of each other which they try to hide but each
perceive in the other:

> Within their room still restless they remain'd,
> And painfully they felt, and knew each other pain'd . . .
> And ever changed, and every change was seen.
>
> (ll. 267–8, 280)

Shore is trapped between his awareness of what is happening (his
'troubled eye') and his pride (he 'felt too brave, too daring to withdraw'), and the following lines render both the wife's forced behaviour
and the mutual awkwardness and embarrassment:

> While she, with tuneless hand the jarring keys
> Touching, was not one moment at her ease.   (ll. 273–4)

Although the adultery is seen as natural to the point of inevitability,
there is a triviality in it and an absence from it of anything approaching
joy or pleasure, which makes explicit moralising unnecessary. The
husband's response has some dignity in its acceptance, but it is cool to
the point of an emotive callousness he would not have liked to admit to,
when he writes of what he knows will paralyse Shore. Shore himself is
so decisively trapped by his own ethic that the verse sermon on his
situation is irritatingly superfluous: ' "The pure have fallen." – "Then
are pure no more." ' (l. 76) He cannot acknowledge his fall in the form
of repentance, for that would entail rejection of his belief in the purity
of the honourable man; but he knows all too clearly that he has fallen
and cannot forget it. Like many of Crabbe's fallen heroes, he seeks
escape from the sense of guilt in arguing for fatalism, but the particular
irony in his case is that he has moved from belief in the complete moral
freedom of the will to an opposite belief in predestination, remaining
equally ignorant that he acted, and is now thinking, in a way determined by his own feelings: 'We think our actions from ourselves pro-
ceed' (l. 358). They do, but from a part of ourselves Shore has still not
come to term with. He is 'ardent, and determined still', using his reason
only to defend his feelings.

Some of the remaining course of Shore's progress is done with a banal-
ity indicated by 'let me . . . hasten to the time/(Sure to arrive) when
misery waits on crime' (ll. 374–5). But it is interesting that what finally
deprives him of reason is the Friend's supererogatory kindness in anony-
mously bringing about his release from jail. The degree of kindness is
qualified by the contrast between his continuing to shun Shore and the
'mild religious pity' of the other person Shore wronged, Anna; but,
as John Speirs has noted (*Poetry towards Novel*, p. 185), the action shows
a characteristic fairness in Crabbe. There is not, this time, any callous-

ness involved – he could hardly be expected to want to resume friendship with Shore – but Shore cannot tolerate the kind of pity which
includes an implication of contempt. The course of his madness is very
carefully related to the earlier stages of his progress: Crabbe is not here
interested in an abnormal state of mind in itself. He 'now laugh'd loudly
at the clinking chain' as he had formerly scorned the 'law that binds';
secondly, the 'speech without aim' corresponds to the phase when he
could not 'firmly fix the vacillating mind'; and thirdly, his 'fantastic'
drawings on the wall – 'With brutal shape he join'd the human face' (l.
430) – refer to the time when his rationalising mind was confronted with
the fact that the brute body was part of itself. He only regains physical
freedom when it is clear that he has permanently lost the reason which
he once thought gave him moral freedom, and he remains emotionally
dependent on Anna and on his new 'approving friends'. His final state,
'The children's leader, and himself a child' (l. 463), both commands our
pity and represents the moral and emotional immaturity of his whole
history. The tale has taken a moral belief of some acknowledged nobility
– that a man should act justly without needing the sanction of external
laws – and shown by projecting it through time that it is not enough to
live by. Although there is some sermonising which reduces the impact,
most of it is in terms of what it is to be a man who holds such a view.
The line of thought reaches both backwards to the chapter of *Rasselas*
(XXXIV) in which Imlac persuades Nekayah, after the loss of Pekuah,
that standing by a moral law is one of the things which make life
tolerable to a sensitive person, and forwards to our own time, when
liberal theologians consider that man is now too adult to need law.

John Dighton, the hero of 'The Convert' (Tale XIX), is like Edward
Shore in that he has no centre on which to base a moral stability, but
for reasons opposite to Shore's. Whereas Shore thinks too highly of his
reason, Dighton does not use his sufficiently, remaining content with a
faith which affects his feelings only. Dighton's mind is morally as well
as intellectually uninquisitive. His illegitimacy is itself seen as predis-
posing him towards both a damaging self-sufficiency and a moral rootlessness. The degree to which he was not responsible for his development
draws our pity, but the consequences are serious. That he never tried to
find out who his parents were is the reflection of their lack of interest in
him; but the lack of inquisitiveness leads out also into a dangerous
moral and religious indifference.

It is feeling that makes him turn to religion – the immediate, compelling feeling of the fear of death. At this stage of his progress, the
Dissenters who become his religious mentors are unconcerned about his
passivity of mind as it makes him gratifyingly ductile. He allows them
to set him up as a stationer and even to choose a wife for him. But as his

business and his consequent sense of security grow, the fear on which his religion was based diminishes. As he becomes more self-sufficient again, he begins to sell questionable literature and to challenge his teachers' right to interfere. This can easily be justified to himself, for he has learnt to dissent from Dissenters. When they do interfere, he challenges their authority by indicating the resemblance of their behaviour to that of the Roman Catholic priests they taught him to despise. But although he thinks he has pinned them down ('Can you . . . condemn . . . who . . . resemble them?'), the irony has another edge, for he is condemning them and in the rejection of external authority he, as he was pleased to point out, resembles them.

For a long while the chief effect of time is to increase his trade, and the only sense he gives to the word 'consequence' is social distinction. But at the age of sixty-five another sense suddenly dawns on him; why continue to strive when he has no son and his name cannot survive him? He seeks comfort in books, but with characteristic aimlessness, so only increases his doubts. His wife merely derides 'fears she never felt', and the Dissenters unhelpfully deal out daily censures. In the confusion and isolation, the sad consequences of his rootlessness and self-sufficiency, he is confronted with the imminence of death. At first he tries to persuade himself that death is welcome: 'A life of doubt must be a life of pain' (l. 431). But as the consequence of a life of doubt begins to impinge on his thoughts, he fights off fear with self-justification: 'I'm sure my conduct has been just and fair' (l. 433). He cannot hold the line of thought: the emphasis wavers from a religious feeling – 'But I repented, and have sorrow still' (l. 435) – to a worldly regret for what he has lost – 'a growing trade/Gave greater pleasure than a fortune made' (ll. 436–7). It concludes with a self-pity which is not moving in a religious direction at all. The pathos of it is that he is as directionless as ever, at this moment when only one direction is left:

> 'Nor views, nor hopes, nor plans, nor taste have I;
> Yet sick of life, have no desire to die.'   (ll. 444–5)

'The Convert' is not one of the best of the *Tales*: there are several dull passages of sermonising in it, and the only really lively writing is in Dighton's last speech. It is in a conventional 'progress' form, with Dighton's moral faults being drawn out by the passage of time and reaching their climax in the confusion and isolation in which he dies. There is some ironic pathos in his history, but he is not dramatically alive enough for it to be very moving.

Fulham, whose 'Struggles of Conscience 'are portrayed in Tale XIV, is as unimaginative in moral and religious matters as Dighton, but his actions and choices are far more deliberate – so deliberate, in fact, that his Conscience can be represented as a dramatic figure with which he has an evolving relationship. His initial moral nature is defined by contrast against his Uncle, a 'serious Toyman'. The uncle's occupation (selling fashionable trifles and trinkets) mirrors his religious instability, but there is a real seriousness in his 'anxious pains', 'Collating creed with creed', to arrive at one in which he can rest. Fulham both lacks this integrity, being prepared to accept his 'truth ... without the toil' at second hand; and also, perceiving the degree to which 'his uncle was by fancy led', retains a measure of detachment which leads him even at the start to set his own limits to moral and religious demands:

> 'Though I the strictness of these men reject,
> Yet I determine to be circumspect.'   (ll. 38–9)

His competitive, quantitative conception of faith shows a far greater contamination by the values of commerce than his uncle's:

> 'my good uncle, by all teachers moved,
> Will be preferr'd to him who none approved; –
> Better to love amiss than nothing to have loved.'   (ll. 44–6)

The source of the allusion here makes tacit comment: Mrs Marwood says "'tis better to be left, than never to have been lov'd" in Act II, scene i of Congreve's *Way of the World*. Fulham thinks he has followed 'his uncle's way', but his motives are not other-worldly: when Conscience begins to trouble him, he finds 'The labour useful, for it brought him rest' (l. 59). He is against sin partly because it causes discomfort ('he fear'd the pain/Of sins committed') and partly because it is unprofitable:

> Desire of profit, idle habits check'd,
> (For Fulham's virtue was to be correct).   (ll. 66–7)

As the relationship with his Conscience develops, it becomes clearer that it is a parody of the relationship between man and wife, with a pre-marital discussion of the limits of each other's sovereignty, which the allusion to Congreve prepared us for, and an initial state of 'mutual love' disturbed only by 'Domestic strifes, preliminary wars' (l. 99). In the discussion, Fulham shows that he has already considered what to do if he should give way to temptation: he will regain repose for himself by buying it for the poor, or even, his imagination comfortably expatiates, 'build – who knows? – an hospital like Guy'. But on the whole he and his Conscience at first live at peace.

The first major conflict comes when the desire for profit urges him to the use of the lottery which is on a literal interpretation legal, but clearly not blameless. In the lively dialogue which represents his inward struggles, Conscience demonstrates his evasiveness:

> 'Still it may happen.' – 'I the sum must pay.'
> 'You know you cannot.' – 'I can run away.'
> 'That is dishonest.' – 'Nay, but you must wink...'
>
> (ll. 120–2)

Fulham wants his 'trifling errors' to be weighed in a moral balance against his virtues: 'Upon my conduct as a whole decide' (l. 124). That he does not consort with harlots seems obviously to outbalance the 'mere ideal things', which from the start he wanted Conscience not to trouble him about.[1] This time he finds it relatively easy to silence her, but his conception of the danger he is facing is perilously limited. Success, in his terms, confirms the limitation of his moral understanding:

> 'Still,' mutter'd Conscience, 'still it might have chanced.'
> 'Might!' said our hero; 'who is so exact
> As to inquire what might have been a fact?'   (ll. 139–41)

'Mere ideal things' have not, to him, the status of 'fact'.

The issue is pressed further when he abuses Conscience by saying to customers that she prevents him from asking more, when half the price would have been above the market value. Both are conscious that he is lying, but he excuses himself by comparison with the way of the world – 'he sold as others sell' – and by legalism – 'are men compell'd to buy?' 'There was no fraud' in an indictable sense. When Conscience refers to a law more 'ideal' than the laws of the land, Fulham adopts the classic manoeuvre diagnosed by Butler:

> 'Show me the chapter, let me see the text...
> And I shall feel it duty to obey.'   (ll. 173, 176)

As Butler puts it, 'there are numberless cases in which the vice and wickedness cannot be exactly defined.... This is the very province of self-deceit and self-partiality: here it governs without check or control. "For what commandment is here broken? Is there a transgression where there is no law? a vice which cannot be defined?"'[2] Conscience does not reply directly, but merely reminds him of his motive for entering on the compact with her, by putting the alternative: 'hear your passions as they rise.'[3] This makes Fulham thoughtful, but he cannot resolve the fundamental conflict in his view of Conscience, wanting its authority to protect him from the discomfort of sin and yet wanting also to set his own limits to the authority. So when it comes to action he merely falls back on the prevailing mores – ''tis thus that tradesmen live'.

When he exposes corruption in the Vestry accounts in order to gain an office himself, his own action of bringing hidden crimes to light is parodied by the response of his Conscience: 'You wear a mask'. His new 'bargain', exchanging silence for an office, is no longer the way most tradesmen live, but although Conscience does not rest, she makes less resistance than before. Fulham's Conscience is not seen as in Butler, but as a fallible aspect of Fulham himself. It is natural that when neglected she should grow less attentive. But the effect (as Conscience warned) is what he most wanted to avoid:

> he who felt some pain, and dreaded more,
> Gave a peace-offering to the angry poor.   (ll. 258–9)

To emphasise the fallibility of his Conscience, the temporary peace bought in this manner is disrupted by the necessity of taking the 'sacramental test': Conscience is more outraged by disloyalty to his sect than by the recent crime. When she gives way, wanting peace, the ensuing truce in their relationship 'rather proved/That both were weary, than that either loved' (ll. 298–9).

This reminder of the image of marriage between Fulham and his Conscience is carefully placed before his actual marriage to the wealthy maid, who is 'not quite an idiot'. Her Guardian knows how to sell her to Fulham – 'my ward would make an easy wife' – but Fulham is well equipped to haggle ('Yet not obey'); he knows much about the obstinacy of the weak. He no longer bothers to do arithmetic with his Conscience, but with flat hypocrisy calls the marriage 'an act of love'. Conscience is commensurately blunt:

> 'This is a fraud, a bargain for a wife;
> Expect my vengeance, or amend your life.'   (ll. 341–2)

It is the last bargain in his progress. The actual marriage is an ironic parody of the relationship between Fulham and his Conscience: the wife parodies Fulham and he is treated as he formerly treated his Conscience.

> The wife was pretty, trifling, childish, weak;
> She could not think, but would not cease to speak.   (ll. 343–4)

We are reminded of the 'trifling bickerings' of the period of 'mutual love' between Fulham and his Conscience, and of his repeated success in talking his way to victory: 'With idiot-cunning she would watch the hour' (l. 347). His cheating of his own Conscience was equally 'idiot-cunning'. He wanted peace, yet kept challenging the authority of Conscience; his wife now wants 'To vex and tease, without an open war' (l. 352). Both are 'callous to rebuke and shame'. Her final technique is, like Fulham's, to listen and ignore: 'Attend I will – but let me have my way' (l. 362). She gradually wears him down as he did his Conscience: from 'forbade' he is reduced to 'begg'd her to attend'. Conscience offers no rest as long as he fails to perceive the irony of

complaining he has 'To pass a life with one who will not mend' (l. 367);
and that he does fail to perceive it is clear from the sense in which he
uses the phrase 'vile bargain': 'All that I possess/From this vile bargain
adds to my distress' (ll. 365–6). The possibility of parting at the cost of
much of her money is one he will not seriously contemplate.

At the impulsive temptation to murder, his Conscience comes forward
in the role of true wife, 'faithful, fond and true', to save him from himself; but when he thinks more deliberately ('watchful as a lynx was he')
she can only warn ineffectually. As he plans to trap his wife into the
adultery which would enable him to divorce her, he thinks he is being
very cunning:

> 'Enraged with me, and near a favourite guest –
> Then will her vengeance prompt the daring deed,
> And I shall watch, detect her, and be freed.'   (ll. 403–5)

As he stands back congratulating himself on his powers of manipulation,
we see him manipulated by the moral force which stands back one stage
further. In taking his revenge by making his wife act in revenge, he
enables Conscience to take her revenge on him, as previously threatened.
From now on, she remains as watchful of him as he is of his wife. So
far from freeing him, his putative revenge traps him in a condition of
remorse from which there is no escape: like Macbeth, he finds there is no
way out for the evil-doer who retains possession of what he has wrong-
fully gained. But the allusions to Macbeth in the epigraphs and concluding paragraphs are not altogether apt: Fulham has nothing of Macbeth's
stature and his tale has not the intensity of 'Peter Grimes'. Out of context, the epigraph from *The Merchant of Venice* seems more apposite:
'My conscience is but a kind of hard conscience. . . . The fiend gives the
more friendly counsel.' Fulham sold his soul not to the devil but to his
Conscience and she now takes possession of him: 'Conscience, roused,
sat boldly on her throne'. The imagery of bargaining used throughout is
given a final twist. He can no longer buy peace with alms: 'Give what
he would, to him the comfort came no more' (l. 438); and 'Avarice
grieved' at the price he gives for the servant who becomes his mistress.
There is considerable imagination in the rendering of his attempts to
escape the 'watchful foe';

> Soon as the morning came, there met his eyes
> Accounts of wealth, that he might reading rise.   (ll. 460–1)

But the shocks he gets from reading the newspaper, and the flat tone of
'The hurrying day, the conscious night the same' (l. 481), are more
appropriate to the shallow mind and trivial experience of Fulham than
the dreams of 'grim men' and laboured allusions to *Macbeth*.

In 'The Struggles of Conscience' the basic 'progress' form is greatly enlivened by the dramatisation of the figure of Conscience and the ironic parallel between Fulham's relationship with his Conscience and his relationship with his wife. The steady gradation of his actions towards increasing evil is accompanied by gradual and not over-schematised shifts in the attitudes between him and his Conscience. But the ironies operating in the body of the tale are not of a kind which bring out any pathos: they only show up Fulham's folly and the punishment which is justly dealt out to it. The pathos at the end involves a rather too sudden shift of mood, which is insecurely handled.

In 'The Learned Boy' the tone is insecure almost throughout. One reason for its failure as a tale is that a routine 'progress' form is allowed to distort what might have been an interesting subject. The contrast between the father's strength of mind, in resisting the women who have designs on him after his wife's death, and the boy's pusillanimity, shown in his over-persuasion by his religious grandmother as well as by the free-thinking clerk, might have been developed interestingly. But the emphasis shifts from this contrast to the progress of the boy, Stephen, which is handled in a cursory, pedestrian manner. A second major failing is the loss of control at the end. The words 'boy' and 'man' are frequently repeated throughout the tale, emphasising Stephen's immaturity, so that a whipping might possibly have been made to seem an appropriate response to his continued childishness, though the tone would have been hard to control.[4] As it is, Crabbe's attention is concentrated too fully on his own animus against free-thinking. The potential comedy of the concluding scene is ruined by Crabbe's excessive sympathy with the father and his emotional pleasure in the whipping of a free-thinker.

As in *The Borough*, various paradoxes concerning freedom recur throughout the *Tales*. The basic form is constant: claimed freedom is shown, usually by means of projection through time, to be an illusion or a self-set trap. But the variety of ways in which this happens accumulates into a very wide-ranging analysis of a fundamental pattern of human life. Edward Shore wants freedom from law in order to act according to 'the pure prompting' of his reason. John Dighton wants freedom from authority in order to achieve his material 'consequence'. Fulham wants freedom from the nagging of his Conscience, though he finds her useful in reducing the discomfort which results from evil. Stephen imitates the freedom of the London clerks, but so closely that he merely substitutes rote-learned freethinking for rote-learned scriptural jargon. In 'The Gentleman Farmer' (Tale III), the kind of freedom Gwyn most wants is from dependence on other people. His name, which means 'innocent', perhaps suggests Godwin, who valued freedom so much at one time that he regarded co-habitation as an evil in so far as it inhibited individual development (*Enquiry*, ed. cit., p. 302). But Rousseau is equally in mind: 'There is only one man who gets his own way – he who can get it single-handed; therefore freedom, not power, is the greatest good.'[5] Crabbe shows that freedom of this kind is more dependent on power than Rousseau sees, that as soon as one starts to live one ceases to be 'single-handed'. Shore, Dighton and Fulham achieve in varying degrees the kind of freedom they want, and find it is not what they wanted at all. 'The Gentleman Farmer' is one of Crabbe's most considerable variations of the 'progress' form. Gwyn finds that his kind of freedom is not so much undesirable as impossible, and as R. L. Chamberlain has pointed out (*George Crabbe* (1965), p. 129), he does this through a kind of reverse progress, in which the despiser of law and religion is eventually not only respectably married and a convert, but fully content to be so. Poor Gwyn becomes the victim of 'power, conceit, and avarice', but the comic side of it is that as far as he knows he is better off than when independent.

The introductory paragraphs are not well focused, but Gwyn emerges from them as lacking in moral experience – 'no child or wife/Cross'd the still tenour of his chosen life' (ll. 43–4) – preferring the shallows to the deeper waters of the world he has withdrawn from and needing to exhibit his superiority to the 'dull plodding tribe' he has chosen to live among. He likes to hide his 'powers', but in order to show them when unexpected, and he likes the powers in themselves:

> As with his friends he pass'd the social hours,
> His generous spirit scorn'd to hide its powers;
> Powers unexpected, for his eye and air
> Gave no sure signs that eloquence was there.   (ll. 65–8)

At this stage we scarcely notice the presence of the friends. He clearly intends the suddenness of his speech[6] to contrast with the 'step by step' caution of 'shackled minds'. He is not a rationalist like Shore: he wants freedom for his feelings as well as his reason – 'I resolve to live/By rules my reason and my feelings give' (ll. 164–5). What matters to him is that he should be free from interference in the conduct of his life from the kinds of control exercised by doctors, lawyers and priests. Some of the irony in the long speech expounding his views operates on his present rather than his future state: taken in a sense other than what he intends, the line, 'You have no safety in your innocence' (l. 110), applies bluntly to himself. But most of the irony lies in his unwitting prophecy of his own future life, when human need and circumstance have made him dependent on others:

'In pain, in sickness, we for cure apply
To them we know not, and we know not why.'   (ll. 87–8)

'In all that most confines them they confide.'   (l. 158)

When he scoffs at the notion of legalising feeling in the form of
marriage – 'Forced to be kind! compell'd to be sincere!' (l. 136) – we
think forward to his own marriage where he is so sincerely ignorant of
the coercion brought to bear that he attributes it to genuine love for
him, and so is glad to bind himself. Gwyn claims that it is the priests
who keep men's fears alive and vex their souls. As yet there is nothing
explicit to connect this with the parenthesis with which he introduces
his attack on them, '(friends alone are round)'; but the case accumulates
when we find that he keeps his free-thinking books behind a curtain,

> Then when his friends were present, for their use
> He would the riches he had stored produce.   (ll. 210–11)

When he takes Rebecca as his mistress, she seems only an extension of
his furniture: 'the pleasant mansion graced/With a fair damsel – his
no vulgar taste' (ll. 220–1). But although she is shrewdly 'still', 'Watching his eye, and waiting on his will' (l. 223), her mere presence has
altered the conditions of his life. He is no longer producing unexpected
displays of 'power' to impress his friends: he is committed to a social
stance. He has already lost his freedom: those who stand by conventional
moral values can now adopt a more specific attitude towards him than
vague admiration, so that he is emotionally committed to defending this
stance. When the local wives pointedly ignore Rebecca,

> He despised their rudeness, and would prove
> Theirs was compulsion and distrust, not love.   (ll. 234–5)

But he too, though he doesn't know it, is under compulsion – to produce
a proof in support of his adopted position. Since it is a position which
puts him at considerable social disadvantage, there is also a need to prove
he really wants to hold it:

> Brave as he was, our hero felt a dread
> Lest those who saw him kind should think him led.
>
> (ll. 243–4)

To demonstrate his own freedom adequately he is forced to deprive the
rest of the household of theirs:

> Hence sprang his orders; not that he desired
> The things when done: obedience he required.   (ll. 247–8)

It is a power based on fear, the fear 'lest he should be supposed afraid', which ironically reflects back on his view of the power of priests. In response to these antics, Rebecca need only remain 'still', simply rousing his contempt for the vulgar herd a little when it flags. She is perfectly content to see no other women at Gwyn's table.

But Gwyn's troubles go further, for Rebecca is no more just a focus for social attitudes than just an object of taste. Gwyn shows half-conscious awareness of her existence as a person in the slight hesitation which enters his manner for the first time – 'And in her presence thought of what he said' (l. 266). But he does not think far enough to perceive her motive for going to church and honouring the priesthood. He thinks he can accommodate such perversity within the magnanimity he reassumes in the company of his friends:

> Gwyn to his friends would smile, and sometimes say,
> ''Tis a kind fool, why vex her in her way?'   (ll. 277–8)

She is planning to make him take her way also, but time is on her side and she does not need to exert power crudely, for he is also undermined from within. The deep-lying insecurity, which needed to impress by unexpected power and to attribute its own fears to the malice of doctors, lawyers and priests, expresses itself, now that his independence is threatened by Rebecca's power, in a much more immediate though only half-realised way, in the form of hypochondria. One of the major ironies is that this makes him peculiarly vulnerable to quacks in a way he foresaw: 'Gwyn something felt – he knew not what – was wrong' (l. 288). A second is that it makes him more dependent on Rebecca as audience for his anxieties: 'She must perceive, of late he could not eat . . .' (l. 291). Rebecca at first fears that some of her power may be lost to a quack, but after some thought finds a means of strengthening it which she can put in terms which will please Gwyn: Mollet is her own cousin, so he can be to Gwyn 'a friend'. Gwyn's views on freedom depended more than he knew on the 'mirrors in gilded frames' in his house reflecting only the furniture which he had selected according to his own taste: 'The sofas rose in bold elastic swell' (l. 60). To complete the irony, Mollet fully establishes himself in the household by manipulating the response of Gwyn's nervous mind to the sharp east wind. As Gwyn sits comically projecting his hypochondria – 'And Gwyn sat pitying every bird that flew' (l. 350) – Mollet need only pretend to be leaving to stimulate Gwyn's fears to the point of begging him to stay. 'Make me thy friend', says Gwyn.

Gwyn now has two people on whom he can depend. As Rousseau emphasised, dependence entails loss of freedom – Rebecca's eye is now the one to be watched, and Mollet strictly regulates Gwyn's daily life –

but they are 'friends' so he is perfectly happy. The final change occurs when the further passage of time brings out Gwyn's spiritual malaise at a deeper level than the hypochondria:

> When wint'ry winds with leaves bestrew'd the ground . . .
> Then came fresh terrors on our hero's mind –
> Fears unforeseen, and feelings undefined.   (ll. 388, 394–5)

The pride he imputes to the priest is his own: unlike Cornelius (of *Acts* 10), with whom he aligns himself, he thinks he is equipped to assess for himself the credentials of his spiritual adviser, and consequently lays himself open to the third of his rulers. Gwyn's own taste installed Rebecca as his mistress; Mollet manipulated his fears to secure his footing in the house; Wisp's position is decided in negotiations between Mollet and Wisp in which Gwyn has no active role at all. Before he meets Wisp, Gwyn is on the verge of self-knowledge: when he expresses 'the freedom of his mind' to Mollet at this stage, it is not in the old terms, but to acknowledge that he is 'to ills and errors prone'; and he does seek light, even though he puts comfort first: 'to my soul the pious man may bring/Comfort and light'. But Wisp is an *ignis fatuus* whose power of manipulating people is based both on a self-blindness, for the hypocrisy includes self-deceit ('He thought it prudent then, and felt it just', l. 468) and on keeping blind those he offers to guide. Gwyn has a new set of friends,

> No friends beside he needs, and none attend –
> Soul, body, and estate, has each a friend . . .   (l. 515–16)

and is as glad as he could be. But even a peasant can see that Gwyn is the victim of 'power, conceit, and avarice'; so the final description of Rebecca as virtuous is not altogether comic:

> And fair Rebecca leads a virtuous life –
> She rules a mistress, and she reigns a wife.   (ll. 517–18)

The basic form of the tale is comic, the man who boasted his freedom being totally and gladly controlled by people he has invited into his house willingly and in order to protect himself from his own fears. But only a cynic could laugh without reservation at the way Gwyn has substituted one form of self-delusion for another, learning nothing, even though he does, despite himself, become happier and more 'respectable'.

Gwyn's tale shows a radical change in the 'progress' form. In 'The Mother' (Tale VIII), the major effect is achieved through arousing expectations of a conventional 'progress' and not fulfilling them. Dorothea as a child is rich, beautiful and spoilt, and seems destined for a fall. She is cold by nature, and as the first stage in a 'progress' her parents make

her worse by treating her with indulgence. Her marriage seems the
second downward step of a 'progress': her husband complies so spine-
lessly with her capriciousness that he ends in an early grave. This leaves
her free to pursue with her elder and more beautiful daughter her one
real source of pleasure:

> Beauty to keep, adorn, increase, and guard,
> Was their sole care, and had its full reward.   (ll. 81–2)

In the daughter's case, these lines are simply ironic: she dies prema-
turely. In the mother's case the irony develops more slowly. She seeks
solace for her daughter's death in the mirror and in attempting to persuade her younger, plainer daughter, Lucy, to marry her dead sister's
socially distinguished lover.

Lucy is one kind of conventional novel heroine, the plain girl whose
virtue is more beautiful than beauty, and there is some sentimentality
in the handling of her, which mars the tale. Her response to her sister's
death and to her mother's reaction to it is rendered well. There is a
sense of alienation from her mother in the presence of death, which is
clearly disturbing, but difficult to stabilise into an attitude. Her mother
would not be able to understand if she did speak, but silence makes her
vulnerable to misinterpretation. But in making Lucy die of love, Crabbe
runs dangerously close to a convention of third-rate sentimental novels.
The function of her dying visions is to emphasise by contrast the spiritual poverty of the mother. The first vision, for example, is of the
woman who touched Christ's garment in *St Luke* 8. 43 ff. The woman
tried to hide, in her humility, in the crowd, and against her will was
perceived by Christ; the mother buys people to listen to her memories of

> How from her carriage as she stepp'd to pray,
> Divided ranks would humbly make her way.   (ll. 347–8)

But the tone of the visions seems false in a naturalistic tale.

Crabbe is not, on the whole, very good at conclusions. His tales quite
often end with a lame paragraph of summary or moralising. But
although 'The Mother' as a whole is not among his most notable poems,
the last paragraph of it belongs with the best of his work. The mother's
spiritual poverty is such that Crabbe has no need to complete her
progress. Having lost her husband and both daughters, she is again
alone, and the horror of her case is that she has not changed. As we last
see her, she is comparing a picture of herself when young with her
reflection in the mirror. What we might expect is a contrast between a
youth of beauty and an old age of paint. But in fact she is 'still coldly
fair', and as she compares the two images she can say, referring to the
picture first:

> 'This, as a likeness, is correct and true,
> But there alone the living grace we view.'   (ll. 357–8)

Her concern with her beauty still has 'its full reward': the beauty
remains, and the good fortune she has had throughout has left her with
enough money to buy praise which is all she needs from other people.
But as we contemplate the line in which the beauty in the mirror is
described, the force of the word 'alone' strikes home: the mother is
content to see her 'living grace' reflected in the mirror rather than in
the fulfilled life, the 'speaking grace', of her children. In the last line,
'And, gazing, slowly from the glass retired' (l. 360), there lies, behind the
physical action and the grotesque narcissism it signifies, the suggestion
of another slow movement, of which she has taken no account. But she
can be left in her moment of victory over time.

In 'Arabella' (Tale IX), the mutation of the 'progress' form is more
subtle than in either 'The Gentleman Farmer' or 'The Mother'. The
intellectual, over-fastidious girl who has eventually to lower her sights
more than she need have done is a type who recurs in contemporary
minor fiction.[7] Crabbe keeps the basic form, but greatly sophisticates
the moral reflections arising from it: Arabella truly matures, and the
degree of self-deception which is also involved is not so baldly comic as
Gwyn's.

Our preliminary attitude towards her is carefully kept open-minded.
Various possible weaknesses are suggested but negated. She is 'the boast
and pride' of her father, but 'willing to obey'. She may be hard if she is
'like a bright and polish'd brilliant', but she shows love to her father in
his illness. Her prudence makes her rivals think her a prig, but she has
'with her prudence, all that youth admires'. To her intellectual inferiors,
she is a freak:

> ... strangers coming, all were taught t'admire
> The learned lady, and the lofty spire;   (ll. 35–6)

but her reading is so respectable[8] that their shock registers their limitations, not hers. Her discretion in relationships with men is explicitly
distinguished from neurotic fear and from coquetry. The only real vulnerability is in the list of virtues she lays down as necessary in the man
she expects to marry: for example,

> He at all times his passions must command,
> And yet possess – or be refused her hand.   (ll. 69–70)

'Possess' also reaches forwards to 'her hand': if the passions at this
man's command include his love for her, the possession of her hand
might be abused. But even here, the most explicit criticism, made by
those who

                          began to weigh the rector's gold;
            To ask what sum a prudent man might gain,
            Who had such store of virtues to maintain,   (ll. 72–4)

reflects more on their debasement of the meaning of 'prudent' than on
her idealism.

   The first two suitors she rejects also provide means of undercutting
unjust criticism of her. Unlike Dr Campbell, she does not acquire from
her learning a sense of superiority to the 'vulgar' people's need of religious forms and the hypocrisy of a condescending observance of them.
The irony of her rejecting 'A man who own'd, nay gloried in deceit' (l.
100) is not yet apparent. Vicar Holmes more quickly finds that her
prudence is not one of the kinds which opt for an old man as husband.
With the third man she is more coldly calculating, but, on the evidence
given, right to reject him. It is not until she tries to impose her will on
Edward Huntly by maintaining that he is obeying 'not the maid he
woos, but his own will', that she becomes confused enough to be vulnerable to deception:

            Young Edward grieved, but let not grief be seen;
            He knew obedience pleased his fancy's queen.   (ll. 135–6)

Her behaviour becomes unnatural: she turns colder as the year turns
warmer. When the appearance of the woman Edward had seduced and
abandoned vindicates her delay, she in turn grieves but can firmly reject
him. When his mother interferes, however, she creates much greater
difficulties by making appeal to Arabella's reason:

            His mother fondly laid her grief aside,
            And to the reason of the nymph applied.   (ll. 155–6)

She makes a bad start by suggesting that Arabella should deceive people:

            'It well becomes thee, lady, to appear,
            But not to be, in very truth, severe',   (ll. 157–8)

and she only produces arguments which Arabella had already dismissed
in her list of required virtues, and most of which could be simply restated
as reasons why Edward should marry the girl he seduced. The main
point is that Arabella does not make this obvious rejoinder, but rationalises on her own motivation. When she says 'Forgiving woman is
deceived and spurn'd' (l. 164), her mind is on what might happen to
herself, not what has happened to the seduced girl, who is brushed aside
as 'a weak woman'. Her feelings include a good deal of pride:

            'Say that the crime is common – shall I take
            A common man my wedded lord to make?'   (ll. 165–6)

She calls it 'virtuous pride', but she is very confused between virtuous
reasoning and rationalised feeling. Pride becomes 'virtuous', love
'vicious'; and it clearly matters too much to her that 'He must despise
me, were he not denied' (l. 176). Dr Campbell, she could say, 'might
despise her'. To argue that

> 'The way from vice the erring mind to win
> Is with presuming sinners to begin,
> And show, by scorning them, a just contempt for sin'
>
> (ll. 177–9)

is reasonable if one is thinking in terms of public justice, as Angelo is in
Act II, scene ii of *Measure for Measure* (ll. 37–41); but it leads to dead-
lock if one is thinking, as Arabella is, of personal behaviour to an individual sinner. She is merely finding a reason for the scorn she already
feels. Unlike Lucy of 'The Mother', Edward is propelled by the
momentum of his own pride towards a marriage on the rebound from
which he can smile at Arabella; Arabella in turn is driven to harden
her attitude, 'remorseless in her pride'. She has thus reached a state
which can draw the admiration of the spinster friend whose rationalisation has arrived at a comic limit:

> Much she preferr'd, she cried, the single state,
> 'It was her choice' – it surely was her fate.   (ll. 186–7)

In the central paragraphs of the tale, Crabbe makes a major qualification to his more usual conceptions of the moral effect of time: the
passage of time may have a beneficent effect, softening instead of
hardening:

> Man, stubborn man, is like the growing tree,
> That, longer standing, still will harder be;
> And like its fruit, the virgin, first austere,
> Then kindly softening with the ripening year.   (ll. 246–9)

In Arabella's case, this natural process is clearly opposed to her
unnatural delay with Edward, and in general it is seen as a good: 'The
pride will soften, and the scorn will die' (l. 197). In the short portraits of
Captain Grove, Ellen and Zelinda, which illustrate the argument without having narrative connection with each other, Crabbe is using an
Augustan method to challenge an Augustan commonplace: the incon-
sistencies they show, ''tis folly to condemn'. Tolerance, if 'virtue yields
not', is clearly better than proud scorn. But in so far as it is *merely* an
effect of time, Crabbe indicates that it is a limited good. The change in
Ellen's attitude to Belinda cannot be attributed with glib cynicism to a
subsequent need for an abortion herself; but the word 'No' also answers

the question, 'Was it the lady her mistake had seen?' (l. 210) Similarly, although it may be a gain in tolerance through experience and self-knowledge if those who when young felt 'wrath for trifles',

> Now find those trifles all the mind engage,
> To soothe dull hours, and cheat the cares of age,   (ll. 218–19)

it remains foolish to cheat the cares of age. More obviously, Zelinda's youthful disdain for fashion is merely changed into a more blatant vanity, when old Zelinda is 'Pleased in rich silks and orient gems to blaze' (l. 223). So the major qualification registered by the paragraph is itself qualified: it is foolish to laugh at this softening effect of time, for it is usually harmless and sometimes an improvement; but it may be manifested in motives less than the highest.

   That Arabella's decision to marry the merchant at the end is natural and good, is emphasised by the contrast with the mean-minded envy of the entrenched spinster friend, the kind of person who misrepresents 'native woods and groves,/As scenes of dangerous joys and naughty loves' (ll. 274–5). In reaction against the friend we warm towards Arabella. But the friend stands as a limit not only of prudishness, against which the healthiness of Arabella's decision can be contrasted, but of rationalisation, which can bring out and put in perspective Arabella's vindication of her acceptance of a man who has several half-caste bastard children. Her 'anger, shame and fear' clearly precede her attempts to find weakness and frailty in the merchant, so that to represent herself as saving a 'victim from a man so base' carries rationalisation to the point of hypocrisy. Arabella can perceive this. When the friend invites her to 'dwell in virgin-state, and walk to heav'n with me', she notes with some asperity that there is no necessary connection between virtue and spinsterhood: wives

> 'Could walk as well, and lead as holy lives,
> As angry prudes who scorn'd the marriage-chain,
> Or luckless maids who sought it still in vain.'   (ll. 291–3)

It is in this context that we watch Arabella pause before replying, in a way which recalls Butler's observation that in common cases the first view is usually right and that self-deception requires deliberation: 'Intent she cast her eyes upon the floor' (l. 308). We know from the perception lying behind her recent acerbic remark that she begins with a lie: 'I question not your motive, zeal, or love' (l. 310). Instead of drawing out the irony of the friend's words, 'not all our care and art/ Can tread the maze of man's deceitful heart' (ll. 284–5), she exploits them for her own purpose: 'who can guess/Those deeds of darkness men with care suppress?' (ll. 312–13) But although there is a certain out-

rageousness in her claim to 'Christian love', the tone is dominated by
the gentle comedy of her attempts to enlist patriotism –

> 'He brought a slave perhaps to England's coast,
> And made her free; it is our country's boast' –   (ll. 314–15)

and the parable of the wheat and the tares: 'good and ill/Were sown at
first, and grow together still' (ll. 316–17), and the precise reversal,
emphasised by the repeated rhyme-words, of the argument she used the
first time she rationalised her feelings:

> 'The noblest way,' she judged, 'a soul to win,
> Was with an act of kindness to begin,
> To make the sinner sure, and then t'attack the sin.'
>
> (ll. 335–7)

Unlike Gwyn, she has really learnt something; and it is clearly better to
act as she does than as her friend advises and does. Her marriage is
scarcely 'holy work' but at least it will not perpetuate scorn and pride.
On the other hand, she *is* rationalising: 'Christian love' is something
better than this. Her tolerance is not charity: it comes of recognising the
lonely consequences of remaining a fastidious spinster. Crabbe's prose
note makes the point by indicating that the scale of values by which we
approve Arabella's behaviour is itself a little awry: the more important
judgement is not according to consequences, but according to motive.

But the final reflection is suggested by his use of the first person
plural: 'we often take credit to our virtue for actions which spring
originally from our tempers, inclinations, or our indifference.' The second
epigraph is spoken by Isabella, a character uncompromising perhaps to a
fault, who can yet say,

> To have what we would have, we speak not what we mean.
> I something do excuse the thing I hate
> For his advantage that I dearly love . . .   (II, iv, ll. 118–20)

to which Angelo can only reply, 'We are all frail.' As George Eliot put
it in *Middlemarch* (ch. 61), 'If this be hypocrisy, it is a process which
shows itself occasionally in us all.' In the third paragraph of the tale,
Crabbe has already 'placed' those who are inclined to feel superior to
Arabella:

> A hundred arrows came with vengeance keen,
> From tongues envenom'd, and from arms unseen.   (ll. 39–40)

They belong with those who, in Johnson's great poem, are 'with safer
Pride content' to note the fall of Wolsey. The tale as a whole thus stands
as an embodied qualification of the implicit request in all Crabbe's

work, that the quality of his characters' lives be assessed by the reader, with a view to recognising what attitudes in life are enriching and what attitudes impoverishing. If judgement is not made, we surrender to, for example, the 'thoughtless vengeance' of the girl seduced by Edward, or to the prevailing mores, regardless of their worth. On the other hand, it would be 'folly to condemn' Arabella. The judgement must constantly interact with self-knowledge.

In 'The Dumb Orators' (Tale 1), Crabbe has entirely laid aside the machinery of the 'progress', concentrating, as Hawkesworth had advised, on a minimum of incident. But the intention is not, as Jeffrey supposed, merely 'to show, that a man's fluency and force and intrepidity of speech depend very much upon his confidence of the approbation of his auditors': it is to express in a less obvious form the perception, which most deeply drew Crabbe to the 'progress', that character partly creates itself by its own choices. Writing of biography in *Rambler* 60, Johnson had observed that it is not always in actions of obvious outward importance that a person's intellectual or moral character will most significantly manifest itself. In this tale Crabbe, with his interest in the moral significance of time, goes further: the two events on which it turns are outwardly trvial, but the first thrusts on Justice Bolt an insight which could lead to radical redefinition of his moral nature, and the second shows him decisively rejecting that insight and hardening, probably permanently, his established character.

While travelling some distance from his home, Bolt comes across a learned club, at which he thinks he will be able to exhibit the powers of oratory he prides himself on. At first he is coolly confident of his technique: he will remain silent for a while before making a decisive contribution to the discussion. But when he decides to break the silence, we follow the rapid shift of his mood from disappointment to perplexity as he realises he is among a gathering of free-thinkers, unable to judge the right style of reply and so remaining silent perforce. As soon as he wonders why he can be so affected by the presence of men he despises, his conscience gives the correct reply: he needs the support of applause in order to speak effectively. The perception leads on to a self-criticism of his whole settled character. Now that for once he is himself the unwilling listener to long harangues, to which he cannot reply, he learns from experience how inconsiderate his own previous habits of domineering argument have been. For this particular situation he convinces himself that flight is the best course of action, and he rushes out to relieve himself of his victorious reply in the safety of his own closet. But although he manages to reconcile himself to the particular failure, the general inference his conscience drew from it remains with him: he knows that because of his cowardice then, he has, when no longer surrounded by enemies, no right to hold forth so confidently without consideration for his listeners. Although time reduces the discomforting effect of this knowledge, he remains aware of it:

> Some years had pass'd, and he perceived his fears
> Yield to the spirit of his earlier years.   (ll. 279–80)

But this gradual shift is gathered into a flood of feeling when by chance the roles are reversed and Hammond, the leading free-thinker, is alone among Bolt's friends. The capacity for self-criticism is drowned by it: Bolt simplifies the situation into himself as man of law and Hammond as foe of order. The courage arising in the old fashion from the support of a friendly audience brings with it a dangerous emotionality which submerges the memory of his own fear in the fantasy of what he will inflict. Bolt's failure of sympathy is emphasised by the contrast with Hammond's ability to connect his present feelings with what he must have inflicted on Bolt. With considerable generosity of mind Crabbe gives the genuine conscience not to the Christian but to the free-thinker. Completely oblivious both to what Hammond must be feeling and to his former insight into himself, Bolt launches into a diatribe on his church and country which sweeps him into a totally false version of the previous encounter. The inference drawn by his conscience is completely forgotten and he attributes his former silence to demonic power. Right at the climax of his rhetoric, when our view of him has been for some time an exterior one, Crabbe suddenly takes us inside him to register an unexpected feeling of pity. At this second moment of crisis, Bolt briefly feels a pity derived from the first experience. But he rejects it, and in doing so recreates his former self. By the end he has rooted out of himself the ability to register anything more than his own victory and the resulting loss of all sense of shame. As we leave him, he is discoursing in total self-delusion on the victory of his cause, implying that only those who oppose it could tremble as Hammond has done. The more tolerant man created by the first experience is lost in the resumption of his former self.

'The Dumb Orators' is not one of the more obviously outstanding of Crabbe's tales, but in its unassuming form it expresses a perception close to the centre of his understanding of man.

Like 'The Dumb Orators', 'The Lover's Journey' (Tale x) is based on experiences of very little ostensible importance or obvious narrative interest. But whereas Bolt's insensitivity derives from a hardening of character, Orlando's derives from the instability of immaturity. The general statement of the opening paragraph on the subjectivity of the mind is less directly derived from the views of Locke, popularised by Addison, Young and others, than it may seem. Locke thought that the 'secondary qualities' of matter, such as colour, smell and sound, could not be said to exist in objects in the way we perceive them (*An Essay concerning Human Understanding* (1690) Book II, ch. viii), and Addison popularised Locke and other men whose work encouraged similar ideas in a famous image in *Spectator* 413:

> In short, our Souls are at present delightfully lost and bewildered in a pleasing Delusion, and we walk about like the Enchanted Hero of a Romance, who sees beautiful Castles, Woods, and Meadows; and at the same time hears the warbling of Birds, and the purling of Streams; but upon the finishing of some secret Spell, the fantastick Scene breaks up, and the disconsolate Knight finds himself on a barren Heath, or in a solitary Desart.

Crabbe, on the other hand, assumes that the senses perceive reality as it is – 'the outward eyes/Present the object' – and that the distortion occurs when the mind, influenced by its own feelings, interprets what the senses present. Orlando's barren heath is not transformed into a landscape of castles and woods: his state of mind simply makes him peculiarly alive to the beautiful aspects of what is actually there. His eyes supply the facts; his feelings supply the categories and the associations. Stunted furze is seen as 'neat low gorse'; and despite the fierce heat and rising clouds of dust, he can describe the spray of dog-rose as 'dew-press'd' and say with more originality but equal anomaly, 'snow-white bloom falls flaky from the thorn'.[9] Crabbe also assumes that normally a correction can be easily made:

> Sorrow and joy are in their influence sure,
> Long as the passion reigns th'effects endure.   (ll. 12–13)

It is only love which is so extremely unpredictable, constantly changing in mood and clothing 'each object with the change he takes'; and in the genial humour which runs through the tale one can sense the perspective of an older man on what is essentially the behaviour of a *young* lover. Laura's choice of Orlando as her name for John is perceptive.

The humour is present, for example, in Crabbe's attributing to Orlando a fantasy about village life which clearly evokes *The Deserted Village*. The village maidens of his imagination are very unlike the gypsy girl he is soon to meet: 'Nor know they what disguise or flattery mean' (l. 83); and their love, even on his own account, scarcely seems the kind which 'long endures': 'Easy their service, and their love is free' (l. 85). We see as much through Crabbe's eyes as through Orlando's. A very characteristic passage on the fens, in which the key-words emphasise a sense of restriction ('confined', 'narrow', 'straiten'd'), intractable hostility ('resists', 'frets', 'sharp', 'wiry', 'rigid') and desolation –

No hedge nor tree conceals the glowing sun,
Birds, save a wat'ry tribe, the district shun,
Nor chirp among the reeds where bitter waters run –

(ll. 126–8)

is ludicrously followed by Orlando's optimism expressed in pious cliché:

'Various as beauteous, Nature, is thy face . . .
All are appropriate . . .'   (ll. 129, 131)

– appropriate to 'bog and marsh, and fen'. There is a genial fatuity in his patronising remark on his rose-tinted view of 'some scatter'd hovels' –'"Ay, this is Nature," said the gentle 'squire' (l. 74) – and in the touch of pride with which he observes that the things he can appreciate 'Are only poor to undiscerning men' (l. 132).

As in some of the novels mentioned in Chapter 1, the 'progress' in the usual sense of the word is confined in this tale to the single short episode of the gypsies. Crabbe's debt to Hogarth is particularly clear here. According to a letter written to Scott, the passage was actually based on a picture by Crabbe's son John,[10] but John must have been imitating Hogarth, for the methods of introducing a time-perspective into a pictorial design are essentially his. The grandfather contemplating the younger generations with 'sadness in his face', traces 'the progress of their future years' with an actuality before him which parodies his wife's fortune-telling, 'tracing the lines of life': he can read the lines 'assumed through years' rather than the life-lines of the palm. We move through the generations in sequence, tracing the progress of gypsy life. The twelve-year-old girl can look demure and give a 'light laugh'; her mother is 'negligently dress'd' but has still 'some touch of grace'; her grandmother has only a 'solemn and dull' expression. She can get a seductive 'look of languor' into her eyes; her mother's eyes are 'bloodshot'; her grandmother has a 'hard and savage eye'. From the 'roguish leer' we move through the 'wild face' to 'Each feature now the steady falsehood wears' (l. 179). The girl's brother comes forth to act out the stale routine of the pimp, 'Who seem'd offended, yet forbore to blame' (l. 160); her father merely stands 'dejected' and 'unheeding' towards his wife; her grandfather sits 'Neglected, lost, and living but by fits' (l. 183). One of the functions of the passage is obviously to deflate Orlando's vision of the idyllic life of the land: envy is clearly a predominant feeling and they are so far from merry-making that even their mutual animosity is sullenly silent. They are not natural: the girl is 'train'd' and her grandmother's false expression is 'assumed'. It also emphasises Orlando's naïvety, harmless though it is: his pence are in his hand, but not given till after their sly manoeuvre, which he has clearly

not understood. But, equally important, the reality of their progress puts
into perspective Orlando's pampered vacillation of mood. 'Change in
every state' there may be, but the kinds are very different. Placed as it is
just before his discovery that Laura has gone to visit other friends, it
brings out in particular the posturing of his address to his 'dumb companion':

> 'Still art thou doom'd to travel and to pine,
> For my vexation – What a fate is mine!'   (ll. 222–3)

The contrast is pointed by the mock-heroic diction, 'doom'd', 'vexation'
and 'fate'.

The beautiful countryside, to which he is now blind, obviously contrasts with the barren heath, but it also sustains the mock-heroic note:

> Forth rode Orlando by a river's side . . .
> That roll'd majestic on, in one soft-flowing tide.   (ll. 232, 234)

His emotional correlatives to 'many a devious stream that reach'd the
nobler flood' are clear. He is proud of his superiority to the materialism
of the 'proud farmers', and his moral sensibility, previously impervious
to the reality of the gypsies, becomes exquisite as it blends into a self-
pity made ludicrous by the rhyme:

> . . . it shocks
> One's feelings there to see the grazing ox; –
> For slaughter fatted, as a lady's smile
> Rejoices man, and means his death the while.   (ll. 252–5)

With Pope's fourth *Moral Essay* behind it, the estate of Loddon Hall can
emerge as truly natural. The cattle, horses and deer are fed by those
they serve: man and nature collaborate in a way the purely predatory
attitude of the gypsies, indicated in the father's theft of fences for fuel,
makes impossible. The children not only enjoy, but give back 'new
beauty to the day'. The 'moving picture' created by the whole scene is
one of grace and of active life. The happy parents watching from indoors
represent the second generation of a very different progress; but the
vision of the gypsy grandfather is paralleled by Orlando who is the only
one who can interpret such a scene as a 'cheat'. His misrepresentation
of the daughters of the house, 'Form'd to seduce, encouraged to beguile'
(l. 283), recalls the gypsy girl, trained in the use of her 'early powers';
and his view of the boys, 'Sure to be tempted, sure to take the bait' (l.
285), both leads back into his self-pity and reflects on his gullible response to the gypsies. The married couple he next sees provide another
means of extending the parallel progress: 'And spleen beheld them with

prophetic view' (l. 297). They too are 'alert, alive' in a way Orlando can only register as 'noise'. They are 'Bound by strong ties', and the bride's 'soft languid air' is real, unlike the gypsy girl's. Orlando's mixture of self-martyrdom and condescension is lightly sustained in: 'Our trav'ller, lab'ring up a hill, look'd down' (l. 288). But his magnanimity ('I spare you – go, unhappy pair!') blends in an undignified manner into pleasure at the anticipated reunion with the offending Laura. Scorn dwindles to resentment; the resentment itself melts away; and before he meets her, he is able to see his 'selfish sorrows' for what they are, not letting them contaminate the meeting. The concluding paragraphs skilfully condense the return journey into a series of jumbled impressions whose sequence only makes sense in the memory; and like Orlando, we scarcely notice that on the second stage of it he is alone. The syntax of the repeated last phrase, 'that but appear'd to die', seems clumsy if one takes it to mean only that the views disappeared from Orlando's preoccupied mind immediately he passed them. It should also recall the grandfather's vision of the gypsy children approaching 'their latter end' like himself, 'Without a hope, a comfort, or a friend' (l. 195).

> the vacant eye
> Wander'd o'er viewless scenes, that but appear'd to die.
>
> (ll. 358–9)

Orlando's little anguish is the experience of a young man.

In 'Advice; or, the 'Squire and the Priest' (Tale xv), the strength of the tale again goes into the two major episodes, the giving of the advice and the dramatic rejection of it, and the perspective of time is only hinted at in the conclusion. The mood is predominantly comic, but the conclusion is not comfortably so, as the older man finds his habits disturbed but not easy to break, and the younger man experiences some of the consequences of a young man's behaviour.

The prevailing tone of the opening description of the squire is one of genial comedy. For example, having ceased to trouble priests with such things as wedding ceremonies, he regards it as ungrateful of them that they should continue to trouble him. When he has his nephew trained as a more complaisant successor to the rector who disturbs his peace, the situation seems set for pleasant mutual convenience. The squire will no longer be bothered by irritating moral criticisms, and the young priest will have a sinecure. But ironically the very pliancy the squire wanted makes the priest vulnerable to an evangelical Simeonite preacher. Primarily the influence is good, leading him both to more self-awareness and to more care for others; but as Crabbe suggests in the image of ignited sulphur, the situation becomes potentially explosive.

The main effect of the squire's attack of gout is to increase the comedy by building up his anticipation of having the kind of rector he wanted: when he hears of the young man's first three successes, he assumes a share of the praise himself for having patronised him. It also emphasises his obduracy: the confrontation with death has no effect on his moral attitudes, even though the pain lingers to remind him.

Much of the comedy of the scene in which the squire gives his advice derives from his inability to register what the young priest is thinking. The simple integrity which leaves the youth unable to say anything except that he is feeling unwell is interpreted as nervousness about when he will preach before the observant eye of the squire; but while the mistress's eye insults the priest and the priest's is angry in return, it is the squire's which remains essentially shut. He casts himself in the role of magnanimous patron who will soothe his nervous protégé, whose excuse about not feeling well he thinks he has seen through. The advice itself is given in the style of a formal sermon, divided into sections (First, of the first . . .') and with an introduction and conclusion which summarise the chief points. It becomes clear that his conception of moral accounts resembles Fulham's: a faith which weighs sins alone, without counterbalancing alms and charities, will not do. When he moves on to the second of his headings, how to ensure friends, he shifts towards an even more blatant expression of his own interests: the illustration of the folly of preaching about sins to the sinner's face is drawn pointedly from his own gout. He would feel pain if someone's hand seized his painful limb, but anger if the hand were that of the doctor whose job is to cure it. To show the extent of the magnanimity, the squire concedes that it is sometimes necessary to speak of sin, but he offers various palliative procedures. In one of these Crabbe wrily parodies the rhetoric of the second book of *The Village*: the poor must be consoled by the fact that they are without the responsibilities of the rich. In another he parodies the end of *The Borough*: the attack on vice must be in the abstract, sparing individual sinners – such as the squire. As he has already pointed out, it is a priest's charitable office not to hurt but to heal. But that the situation is not merely comic is registered by the sudden shift of mood from the drunken rhetoric of the squire to the priest's response, a silent sigh and sorrowful expression.

The sermon in which the priest shows himself to be uncompromisingly, and for the squire uncomfortably, evangelical is again handled in a prevailingly comic manner. The squire is at first able to channel his alarm into magnanimous sympathy for the lad who begins his sermon with such a strange air and accent, but very quickly it has to turn to self-protective scorn. The comedy is increased by our view of the priest's mannerisms through the squire's eyes and by the squire's own gesticu-

lation as he attempts to relieve his sense of frustration under the con-
straint imposed on him by the surroundings. The priest's feelings
naturally cannot be rendered in comic terms, but his integrity, exhaustion and anxiety, although conveyed, are not allowed to disturb the
comedy, as, without being debased at all, they are brought down to
earth by the more worldly reflection that whatever the future attitude
of the squire the tithe of ten good farms remains his own.

But the final situation is not accurately represented by John Speirs'
remarks, 'The Squire and the Priest have both modified and moderated
their attitudes. The comedy comes to rest at a balance. Good sense and
virtue are reconciled.' (*Poetry towards Novel*, p. 193) The prevailing
tone ceases to be comic, and the final note is one of sustained discord.
The squire's drinking companion stands as a parody of his own confusion, but not a predominantly comic one. He is vaguely convinced that
something must be wrong, but remains subject to his craving palate.
There is a little comedy in the contradictions and repetitions of his
drunken speech, but it represents a gross vulgarisation of the squire's
main speech of advice. The squire's mistress attempts more blatant
manipulation in trying to contrive a marriage. She does not succeed in
her own aims but merely increases the anger which causes her to withdraw. Despite his mixture of contempt and pain at his drinking companion's behaviour, the squire is in much the same position. He has
acquired enough inner light to disturb him but not enough to do much
about it. In his old fashion, he tries to find 'some ease from easy virtues',
but really he knows that he cannot compound with conscience and falls
back on the self-pity of 'ah! how weak am I!'

The priest is equally divided and dismayed by the division in the
parish caused by his own behaviour. He does not just learn to temper
his zeal with some good sense:

> With pain he hears his simple friends relate
> Their week's experience . . .
> His native sense is hurt . . .   (ll. 404–5, 408)

Unlike the squire he cannot channel any of this pain into easy contempt, for he knows he is responsible for the religious extremism which
has absurd effect on some of his parishioners. He is left in the situation
of having cultivated in them the material on which the scorn he
wanted to combat feeds. He cannot condone their behaviour yet
knows it would be inconsistent to condemn them for it. He is even so
far divided against himself as to be 'compell'd to smile' despite his own
moral sense and his recognition that he is the source of the absurdity.

Both men are trapped and it is not easy to see how they could escape or how, being what they were, they could have avoided their situation. The previous rector was not, on the squire's own account, a bigot, but made no better success of relations with the squire; and the priest has not only alienated his uncle, but divided the whole parish into two camps by his method of preaching. Crabbe certainly maintains a delicately balanced attitude towards both men, but there is no reconciliation in either of them. As well as portraying the two characters with great fairness, he has, without any heavy plot-machinery, created a situation which, as far as can be foreseen, will remain as dramatically tense as the two major episodes on which the tale turns. It is characteristic of the generosity of Crabbe's imagination that he is capable of leaving the situation unresolved in this way. Normally one would expect such an effect only from a professed sceptic, but it is a measure of Crabbe's secure possession of his Christian values that he is able to leave the priest in as divided a state as the squire.

Another conspicuous merit of the tale lies in his dramatisation of a particular historical phase, when the squire could regard himself as the patron of the local priest and when the priest had the courage to oppose the man on whom to some extent he was financially dependent. With their greater imaginative strength, the *Tales* of 1812 are more successful than *The Borough* in representing the spirit of the age as well as individual life-histories.

In the tales discussed in this chapter, Crabbe has been dealing primarily with single figures in a way which originally derived from the 'progress' form. The order of the chapter is based on critical considerations: as the order of composition is unknown, it must not be taken to represent a chronological development. In the tales discussed first, he keeps fairly close to the basic form: 'Edward Shore', for example, has a strong similarity, despite its great superiority, to Hawkesworth's Opsinous. In the case of 'The Learned Boy', the 'progress' form is clumsily imposed on unsuitable material. But in the tales discussed in the central part of the chapter, Crabbe plays considerable variations on the form in order to achieve more subtle effects. Gwyn's progress in 'The Gentleman Farmer', for example, is ironic in that, although there are serious implications, he is in some respects in a better state at the end than at the beginning; and the horror of 'The Mother' is precisely that she makes *no* progress in the conventional manner. In 'The Dumb Orators', Crabbe has laid aside the form of the 'progress' altogether, choosing instead to express his fundamental interest in the behaviour of character through time by concentrating intensely on two specific incidents of particular significance; and in 'The Lover's Journey', the 'progress' is confined to the gypsy scene and Orlando's comic attempts to impose on the people he sees subsequently the pattern he fails to perceive in the gypsies. In 'Advice', Crabbe is again independent of the formal machinery of the 'progress', concentrating on two major episodes and leaving the situation dramatically unresolved. He has also begun to develop his art beyond the treatment of a single central figure: the squire and the priest are equally important.

5 *Tales,* 1812 (2)

Most of the tales discussed in the preceding chapter are concerned with
single figures either changing or hardening their character through time
or in certain particularly significant actions or events. The tales discussed
in this chapter are primarily about relationship. Some of them are concerned with exploring what kinds of relationship are or are not good;
others are concerned with the influence of one person on another within
a relationship, for Crabbe saw that characters become what they are not
only in response to events or through what they do, but in response to
other people. Through other people men may perceive what they would
otherwise not have perceived, or they may become contaminated. These
categories are not exclusive and not exhaustive: as in the other tales,
there is much overlapping, so that although each tale is an aesthetic
whole, needing to be comprehended *as* a whole, one of the most important effects is that a composite picture is gradually accumulated, of what
qualities of relationship make for health and what for moral disease.

In 'The Brothers' (Tale XX), the opening contrast between George and
Isaac is too laboured and unspecific. It gives the impression that George
is a Tom Jones, warm, spontaneous, straight, imprudent, and Isaac a
Blifil, weak, calculating and actually 'crooked'. In fact Isaac is not deliberately evil in the manner of Blifil. The basic contrast is really that George
is prepared to subordinate all material considerations to his love for his
brother; whereas Isaac essentially uses relationships in order to secure
something else, something more tangible. George is not wholly blind:
'He saw his brother was of spirit low' (l. 25). But he is not interested in
exploiting his perception:

> ... the kind sailor could not boast the art
> Of looking deeply in the human heart.   (ll. 29–30)

Isaac, on the other hand, sees that Burgess Steel may be exploited and
so 'bow'd and bent the neck to Burgess Steel': he only serves him with
a view to securing a 'port-place'. Similarly, he prudently focuses his
love on the maid of a wealthy spinster, tailoring it to her 'spare and
grave' taste:

> Not an outrageous love, a scorching fire ...
> In present favour and in fortune's way.   (ll. 55, 58)

When war is declared and George's service as a sailor needed he begins at once 'To think what part became a useful man' (l. 64): his conception of 'use' is of what he can do to help others, his obligations as he sees them. Despite Isaac's repulsively hypocritical weeping, George instinctively gives half his pay to him. When Isaac is no longer in need of George's money, having gained his port-place and married prudently, he nonetheless writes a letter, ostensibly to warn his brother against the snare of marriage and its financial difficulties, but actually a vile mixture of self-abasement, self-pity, flattery, jealousy and begging. The deviousness is partly suggested by putting half into indirect speech and half into direct, but the full quality of it could only be conveyed by complete quotation, giving the various aspects of what is a very finely apprehended unity of tone. The forthright dignity of George's reply is effectively opposite:

> 'Forbear repining, and expel distrust.'
> He added, 'Marriage was the joy of life,'
> And gave his service to his brother's wife.   (ll. 129–31)

Isaac is uninterested in service of such kind, but in the renewal of George's commitment to send money he has all he wanted – 'This creature is a child.' Whereas George conceives 'use' in terms of obligation, Issac conceives it in terms of utility.

The little family scene before George loses his limb is not at all laboured. The hypocrisy is not made too blatant: 'Isaac half fainted in the fond embrace' (l. 143), but that is in character with his weakness as well as his hypocrisy, and the behaviour of his wife and children is natural enough not to make George seem foolish in saying, 'what to this is wealth?' There is enough manifest joy to justify his judgement. The loss of his leg suddenly deprives him of use in both senses: he is no use to his country as an invalid, and no use to Isaac as a pauper. But he does not repine: he can joke in his letter to Isaac about 'All of his brother that the foe might leave' (l. 161). Isaac is distressed, not at his brother's misfortune, but at having 't'admit so poor a guest'. The only counterweighing consideration which occurs to him is: 'Perhaps his pension ... may the man maintain.' Like a weak man he appeals to his wife for support in his decision, and her reply is 'kind' only in the sense that it resembles his own views. George is to her an object, a 'crazy building', which 'may be propp'd for years'. She naturally recognises no obligation to assist in the propping. To Isaac and his wife the relationship of the brothers is not something of substance:

> ... all the care, the kindness [George] had shown,
> Were from his brother's heart, if not his memory, flown:

> All swept away to be perceived no more,
> Like idle structures on the sandy shore.   (ll. 191–4)

But although swept away from his heart, traces remain in his memory. Although George is loath to face the truth, he has it brought home to him that he is a social as well as an economic encumbrance. The grog is 'to Isaac an expense' and the pipe-smoke offends the delicate nostrils of Burgess Steel and their lady patron:

> 'Could they associate or converse with him –
> A loud rough sailor with a timber limb?'   (ll. 205–6)

The off-handedness of the dismissive description is as horrifying as the more direct cruelty. Isaac is too weak to be openly cold: he does not feel warm, but is somehow afraid of what he is doing:

> Cold as he grew, still Isaac strove to show,
> By well-feign'd care, that cold he could not grow.   (ll. 207–8)

In his weakness he tries to fix the blame on his wife, yet not all the blame, for he leaves it deliberately unclear whether he is blaming her in pretended fellow-feeling – 'He too was chidden when her rules he broke' (l. 213) – or excusing her – 'she sicken'd at the scent of smoke'. He has not the courage to lay the blame solely on his wife, but only hints at it and then retracts, excusing it as 'a woman's way'.

George struggles hard to find some consolation in this degree of concern, still striving to see the best possible side of his brother, and there is no self-pity in him: the observation that no one cares about the sea leads not into repining but outwards to the nephew who is the exception. Isaac's wife is worried that the boy will be contaminated by the coarse sailor, and, as usual, 'So judged the father'. When the facts become so blatant that George has to say something about going, Isaac again exposes his priorities:

> 'I
> Am fond of peace, and my repose would buy
> On any terms – in short, we must comply:
> My spouse had money – she must have her will;   (ll. 235–8)

and he simpers in a self-pity which is not even honest, 'Ah! brother – marriage is a bitter pill.' (l. 239) The wife mixes her corresponding cowardice with a veiled threat: 'watch your brother's way,/Whom I, like you, must study and obey' (l. 242–3). As the strong man sadly gives ground, the weak man gains courage: when George retreats to the kitchen, Isaac becomes brave enough to say haltingly, after self-contradiction in his self-excuse ('The little freedom I'm compell'd to use',

l. 255) and lame attempts to blame his wife's relations, 'Brother – I wish – do go upon the loft!' (l. 259) We have seen George's reluctance to respond to maltreatment in kind, so that when he at last reacts to this outrage there is a sense of climax – 'He grew rebellious – at the vestry spoke/ For weekly aid –' (ll. 266–7) which meets with the kind of raw shock he would himself have experienced in the anti-climax of: 'they heard it as a joke'.

George's nephew is 'attentive' like his father, but his values are the same as his uncle's: he listens to his uncle's stories at some cost to himself, at a time when he might be playing. More strikingly, he is less concerned whether the food he takes up to the loft is 'purloin'd or purchased' than he is with the brute fact of the shame of treating an ill dependant thus. The crime against the possessions is insignificant beside the crime against the person. Against this, Isaac's wife reasserts their ethic – 'she saw no value in his life' – and has to lie about him to justify her attitude: 'your complaining friend'. But the boy instinctively knows that he is right, even though the word 'stealing' registers the dislocation of moral order:

> No! he would go, but softly to the room,
> Stealing in silence – for he knew his doom.   (ll. 298–9)

Isaac's own state at this stage is more one of self-deception than of hypocrisy. He hurries away from George,

> Yet to his wife would on their duties dwell
> And often cry, 'Do use my brother well.'   (ll. 302–3)

He has to verbalise about his moral obligations to the woman who is helping him deny them, intending at some buried level of his conscience 'something kind' and taking 'vast credit for the vague intent'. Seeing his son actually doing what he should do himself, his response is, for him, a violent one ('swearing – yes, the man in office swore') and it ends in vulgar threatening: 'Proud as you are, your bread depends on me' (l. 317). Isaac and his wife are more adept at 'stealing' than the boy. The wife notes that he 'watch'd his time' and then 'betray'd a something' and tells Isaac to retaliate: 'do watch them and detect'. There is a relish in Isaac's trap – 'The careful father caught him in the fact' (l. 338) – which captures the meanness of a man who could behave thus, and compels the question, 'Is *this* what he should be careful of?' The whole episode has arisen with great naturalness out of the preceding events, but Crabbe has achieved a moral resonance which makes Isaac's questions re-echo on his own behaviour as a summary of what he has become: 'Is this your conduct? – Is it thus you plan?' (l. 343) Characteristically he sends the boy back to his mother and stays

himself to rail at the helpless man. The repressed sense of guilt which
issued in the hasty blow at the boy, having nothing to seize on because
of the dead man's silence, is whipped up into a frenzy of violence, moving from 'do learn to know your friends' to 'Speak, you villain speak!'
and finally to 'I'll shake you from the bed,/You stubborn dog.' Of the
sudden realisation and its impact we are appropriately told nothing
except the bare exclamation, 'Oh God! my brother's dead!'

The quiet moral reflections which follow –

> Timid was Isaac, and in all the past
> He felt a purpose to be kind at last –   (ll. 356–7)

cut both ways. In part he is excused – kindness was intended – but the
first word gives the reason: the kindness was not very pure. Being kind
was always future; the dominant present reality was always 'av'rice,
peevishness, or pride'. His conscience will not be appeased with a stone
monument, apt though that is as a memorial of his coldness, and appropriately he is attacked by ague, for he always 'Shrank from the cold, and
shudder'd at the storm' (l. 18). He tries to align himself with the
brother he has abused: he retires 'to sigh and think alone'. But he is not
allowed by his more perceptive son to indulge in the self-pity of
identification with George –

> '. . . shall I like him expire.'
> 'No! you have physic and a cheerful fire' –   (ll. 368–9)

so he is driven back on confrontation with what he did, what 'my cold
heart denied'. He can now see George not just as one who vexed his
wife or as possessor of wooden limb and odious pipe, but as a generous,
true, kind brother, whose worth he can appreciate in a sense unknown
to him before. His wife, like Macbeth's, sees this conscience as a folly,
but Isaac cannot: 'my folly cost my brother's life'. It is not clear how far
he follows his son's advice to pray, but although the word 'repenting'
(not remorse) is used, he clearly does not develop very far. His tears are
'ready' now, as they once were not, but perhaps they are a little too
ready: as the tears fall, he is 'soothed' as well as 'grieved'. His understanding of George is limited if he can still ask, 'Did he not curse me,
child?' He has learnt that his old sense of values made him 'cold to
nature, dead to love', but his present attitude is indiscriminate:

> He takes no joy in home, but sighing, sees
> A son in sorrow, and a wife at ease.   (ll. 402–3)

All is reduced to the 'one sad train of gloomy thoughts' which possesses
him. His moral life is now in the past, as formerly it was in the future:
he considers himself 'without a hope in life', which implies among

other things that he does not feel for his son much more than he felt for his brother. Isaac remains deep in self-pity. He has discovered life's priorities too late. In 'The Brothers', Crabbe has taken opposing moral attitudes towards brotherly love and shown by projection through time that Isaac's utilitarian conception of relationship, though not initially evil, culminates in the sub-human.

One of the main centres of interest in 'Squire Thomas; or the Precipitate Choice' (Tale XII) is, as in a group of tales discussed in the last chapter, in freedom. Thomas, his wife, and her brother all sacrifice an important degree of freedom in order to gain money. In this particular case, there is no political dimension involved: Crabbe's interest in true and false freedoms was not merely a backwash from the French Revolution and associated English programmes and fears. That he values very highly the true freedom of a sound and mature relationship, can be seen from this black comedy of self-imprisonment. The second focus of interest is in the way the characters become contaminated by those they think they are manipulating. For ten years Thomas fawns on his aunt, accepting insults to himself and his parents for the sake of securing her money. When she dies and he inherits, he thinks he can brush off the thwarted legacy-hunters with hypocritical clichés. Their threats would be empty but for the fact that Thomas has been radically twisted by his ten years' experience: he has flattered so long that he now thinks flattery is owed to him. He has incapacitated himself for normal relationship and also made himself vulnerable to the same kind of exploitation as he practised over his aunt. Such exploitation begins almost immediately by one of the legacy-hunters, who becomes his servant.

The narrative section of the tale, the visit to the race-meeting, the apparent loss of direction on the way back in the dark, and the engineered meeting of Thomas and his servant's attractive sister, Harriot, is handled with economy and vigour. Thomas does not seem too stupid in being gulled, nor are the others made too villainous. Characteristically and justly it is the kind of toadying he would have shown to his aunt which finally convinces him that it is Fate which has brought Harriot and himself together. We know that he has a very dim apprehension of what he is doing in marrying her, but we also have much to discover ourselves after their marriage.

Harriot's tirade is clearly an attempt to precipitate a complete breach: after some wild attacks on life with Thomas, she quickly refers to withdrawing to her father's house, still believing that if not happy she is still free. She puts emphasis on the irony of Thomas's position: he has no right to accuse her of craft when he owes all his own wealth to deception. The biter is bit. But when she goes on to spell out the details for him, she has to admit that, although her family has its revenge for being

cut out of his aunt's will, she is having to pay a dreadful price for it.
They have their revenge in that Thomas is hooked; but so is she. The
second biter is bit. Like Thomas, Harriot has some capacity for self-pity
and she wants peace; but Thomas is not prepared to divide the spoil as
she suggests. Torn between avarice and fear, it is very natural that he
should settle for a course which enables him to keep the money and get
some revenge. But his revenge on her is also a revenge on himself: they
are trapped in a relationship of mutual hatred. The only progress they
can make is in refining methods of hurting each other. Both thought
that the selling of themselves was only temporary: Thomas thought his
trial past when his aunt died, and Harriot expected to be able to return
to her family with half the spoil. But for both the temporarily adopted
role has permanent effect. What they took to be a means, which could
be discarded, has radically contaminated the whole nature of the rest of
their lives. Through using people as objects they have made themselves
ironically vulnerable to sadistic manipulation at the expense of all possibility of a richer form of relationship. As in 'Advice', the prevailingly
and successfully comic tone gives way to an extreme seriousness at the
end, which is made all the more effective by the sudden change of mood.

Although 'Resentment' (Tale XVII) is centred on the relationship
between a man and his wife, it is resentment rather than the marriage
relationship as such which is the main subject. The word had a stronger
sense in Crabbe's time than it has kept. He was following one common
usage in assimilating it to revenge in one of the Chicago sermons:
'resent not, nor revenge whatever Advantage may be taken of thy
Gentleness.'[1] One effect of the tale is to strengthen the word by providing such a vivid embodiment of what Crabbe means by it.

At the beginning, our sympathies are with Paul. He has come to the
town to get away from the place where he was bereaved of his children,
and has since lost his wife also. Our predisposition towards pity is
strengthened by the false 'pity' of the 'female friends' who have designs
on him. The vulgarity of lavish hospitality – 'As if to prove how much
he could afford' (l. 44) – is offset by the generosity of it, later to be
contrasted with his wife's parsimony: 'he loved to see ... his neighbours free'. It is not until later that we learn why, like Merdle in *Little
Dorrit*, he is so quiet. The lady (she is called throughout by the term
which distances her), on the other hand, is not long allowed to seem
unambiguously 'discreet'. From 'maiden modesty' we rapidly move to
'by nature cool'; and discretion is quickly reduced to 'a virgin's dread'.
Lovers are to her merely 'deceivers, rakes, and libertines' who, through
the perspective of some self-pity, make 'harmless beauty their pursuit
and prey'. 'Pious habits' in practice are automatic fears – 'Soon as she
heard ... At once she fled ...' The coldness is unnatural ('turn'd to

stone the breathing flesh and blood') and a financial concern is already
clear: one unfortunate lover is told that 'He came to rob her, and she
scorn'd his art' (l. 76). So although the first word of the next paragraph
is important in registering Paul's willingness to manipulate, she is fair
game, and we do not condemn him:

> Hence, our grave lover, though he liked the face,
> Praised not a feature – dwelt not on a grace.   (ll. 84–5)

He appeals to her as a 'virtuous mate', hinting incidentally at her probable fears ('fear'd neglect') and the extent of his wealth, and she is
hooked enough not to notice that although he has not flattered her
appearance, he has flattered her prudence. What she values in him is the
reflection of herself, her 'cool prudence' and 'her own mild virtues',
and his money. Once they are married it is clear that for both the prudence was merely a convenient counter in the bargaining:

> In his engagements she had no concern;
> He taught her not, nor had she wish to learn.   (ll. 118–19)

Her interest is exclusively in social ostentation, 'In costly raiment, and
with kind parade' (l. 125).

The tone hitherto has not led us to expect, any more than she does,
that Paul will cheat her of her money. At the event we, like her, are at
first caught up in the vivid surface details, her 'measured step', the
sudden appearance of an unknown man in black, and the contrast
between Paul's customarily simple terms and the jargon of the lawyer.
She is so involved by what she has come to call her duty ('robed to
grace it in a rich array') that all prudence has gone. She is being badly
abused – 'I've no distrust,/For he that asks it is discreet and just' (ll.
140–1) – but on the other hand her absorption in the celebration is not
the kind of help she thought her prudence could contribute to Paul's
economy: 'joyful was the night'. Crabbe anticipates the probable response the reader has when he has assimilated the new situation – that
Paul is a knave and his wife a fool. Firstly, without minimising Paul's
offence ('deceit', 'crime', 'guilt'), he emphasises the accompanying
suffering ('troubled look', 'dreaded hour', 'sorrows', 'uneasy time').
Secondly our sympathy for the lady's folly is reduced both as she acts
up to her role of abused innocent (her 'guileless breast' is the extension
of her earlier fantasy, 'harmless beauty'), and as she refuses to see him
in any other light than as 'guilty wretch', even though he confesses in
tears and acts as justly as he now can – 'To legal claims he yielded all his
worth' (l. 172). She casts herself in the role of martyr, in which solitude
becomes a euphemism for lack of charity: 'I feel the misery, and will
feel alone' (l. 179). Our sympathies are not yet drawn strongly towards

Paul: he is clearly lying when he says, 'He would turn servant for her sake ... To show his love'. But his egocentric hypocrisy seems comparatively healthy beside her revelling in self-pity:

> 'Welcome this low thatch'd roof, this shatter'd door ...
> Welcome my envied neighbours ...'   (ll. 188, 192)

She does not really envy them – their familiarity with the 'loathsome meal' has merely bred the 'coarse feelings' she is delicately superior to – but the whole rhetorical movement gives more scope for self-pity: 'all to me is new ... Disgusts my taste, and poisons every sense' (ll. 193, 198). Her virgin fantasies will be relived:

> 'Daily shall I your sad relations hear
> Of wanton women ...'   (ll. 199–200)

The rhetoric which culminates in 'Hard is my fate!' has established such a prospect of woe that one wonders how she can think she is safer amid 'Mirth that disgusts, and quarrels that degrade/The human mind' (ll. 205–6), than with her husband. It is not safer: it is only, as she at first admits, easier. In contrast, we learn of Paul's suffering in quiet, measured words from the narrator:

> Pining in grief, beset with constant care,
> Wandering he went, to rest he knew not where.   (ll. 219–20)

The lady does not have to suffer long: a rich relative soon shows 'a kindness she disdain'd to crave'. Although she is too proud to crave the kindness, she is ready enough to secure it by tailoring her character to his:

> Frugal and rich the man, and frugal grew
> The sister-mind, without a selfish view.   (ll. 227–8)

The degree of unselfishness is shown by her ensuring that the money he leaves her cannot, by law, go to her husband. The precise nature of the Lady Bountiful role she subsequently adopts is unexpected. One expects the egoistic filter: 'She heard all tales that injured wives relate' (l. 245). The virgin prurience is tempered with a self-pity deriving from more recent experience. But one does not expect the degree of personal involvement:

> With her own hands she dress'd the savoury meat,
> With her own fingers wrote the choice receipt.   (ll. 243–4)

She now resembles Paul as he was before she met him, wanting to exhibit 'free bounty', yet keeping only a 'decent table', a comparison from which she emerges as unhealthily devious beside his naïve confusion. On the other hand, Crabbe is fair: she is prepared to give more than money, and that is much to her credit.[2] He also notes that it gives her pleasure to see signs of revelry among the stone-masons: she is not a caricatured prudish do-gooder. Our response is not allowed to simplify into premature condemnation. But in the course of the extended contrast with Susan, it becomes clear that she has not escaped fraud by deserting her husband:

> No practised villain could a victim find,
> Than this stern lady more completely blind.   (ll. 253–4)

The main purpose of the contrast is to sketch a richer way of life. The reflection is much the same as Johnson's in *Rambler* 79: 'He that suffers by imposture has too often his virtue more impaired than his fortune . . . it is our duty not to suppress tenderness by suspicion; it is better to suffer wrong than to do it, and happier to be sometimes cheated than not to trust.'[3]

When Paul reappears, 'patient and still', among the stone-masons, there is enough resemblance to the man who 'sat in solemn style' and rarely smiled, for the contrast with the 'merry' masons not to seem contrived; but Crabbe's apology for his reappearance is very flat-footed. The intention, presumably, was to make us anticipate a happy ending ('Our favourites . . . cannot die'). Paul's progress is foreshortened: the emphasis is on his present state, though his life has been much more eventful than his wife's. His penitence is qualified only by a healthy degree of self-respect – 'Feeling her wrongs, and fearing her disdain' (l. 322) – and whereas he can fight down the perception which prompts this fear and has the courage to apply for charity, her view of him is superfluously harsh: he 'wants the courage, not the will, to steal' (l. 350). No comment is needed other than juxtaposition with the quiet, urgent information: 'A dreadful winter came, each day severe . . .' (l. 351). In the long, penetrating dialogue between the lady and Susan, the lady's eye is on the just retribution for the past, and Susan's is on the present reality of the suffering:

> '. . . his fate appears
> To suit his crime' – 'Yes, lady, not his years.'   (ll. 357–8)

Immediately, the lady is put on the defensive: 'You must the vileness of his acts allow' (l. 361). When Susan replies that he feels the vileness himself, she again shifts the focus back to the past, not allowing him to escape it:

> 'When such dissemblers on their deeds reflect,
> Can they the pity they refused expect?'   (ll. 363–4)

As yet she sees no irony in this last line. The tale as a whole stands as
one qualification to Crabbe's view of time: if man forestalls the judgement of time with the wrong tone of voice, his arrogance is very ugly.
Refusing to face the present, the lady can only repeat, 'Think on his
crime'; and when pressed harder she is driven back to the underlying
egoism, expressed in a clipped tone as she fights down emotion: 'Brought
me to shame'. Driven one stage further back, she is reduced by 'He
cannot live' to the grotesquely comic limit of her Pharisaism: 'But is he
fit to die?' Susan's softly muttered reply is an apt allusion to Dives, but
aloud she makes yet another appeal to pity and an attempt to provide
some sort of restrained answer to the lady's hideous question: 'He tried
to pray . . . But the fierce wind . . .'

At the same time as constructing this dialogue, Crabbe builds up a
vivid description of the man's suffering, his tramping through the snow
and his attempts to set light to some gathered thorn-wood and 'straw
collected in a putrid state', the activity of trying to light it warming
him more than the dull smoky glow eventually will. As G. R. Hibbard
has noted,[4] there is an allusion to Goneril's words about Lear at the end
of Act II, scene iv

> 'Wilful was rich, and he the storm defied;
> Wilful is poor, and must the storm abide,'
> Said the stern lady – "Tis in vain to feel.'   (ll. 417–19)

The lines are ironically almost as applicable to herself: the lady is more
wilful than Paul ever was, so wilful that she does not notice that she
has undermined her own ethic. It is indeed 'in vain' for Paul to feel
further suffering now. Susan's 'soft and ever-yielding heart' is allowed
to become rather sentimentalised as Crabbe's attention is absorbed by
the lady. A simplification of her attitude is again forestalled: in an ugly
paraphrase of the Lord's Prayer, she does recognise her vulnerability:

> 'she too err'd, and must of Heaven expect
> To be rejected, him should she reject.'   (ll. 433–4)

But she does so in terms which retain the attitude of distaste and refine
the pride: 'she found within/A fair acquittal from so foul a sin' as to
spurn him; yet at the same time, 'No more the wretch would she receive
again' (l. 427). What she says is almost right: it is right, 'Foe to his sins,
to be his sorrow's friend.' What is wrong is partly the attitude with
which it is said, the tone of 'Go to the creature . . .', and partly that con-
taminating prurience which has become her habit:

> 'mark his feelings at this act of mine:
> Observe if shame be o'er his features spread.'   (ll. 440–1)

When she 'loved the objects of her alms to see', she was in a way following his example ('he loved to see/His table plenteous, and his neighbours free', ll. 45–6), but 'sorrow's friend' is ill employed in observing shame. As she continues, a note of triumph enters – 'By his own victim to be soothed and fed' (l. 442) – a subtle refinement of revenge, which carries the implication, 'Look how far I have come from resentment', and at the same time 'How completely defeated he is!'

> 'But, this inform him, that it is not love
> That prompts my heart . . .'   (ll. 443–4)

she means conjugal love, but the word implies more than she knows. How completely she has lost sight of him as an individual is shown by her conceiving it possible that he should send 'grov'ling thanks' or 'high-flown praise': to her he is simply 'a man so vile'. By the time she has reached the end of her little homily, it is clear that the resentment is not so refined as it seemed: 'there is one that he must not forget'.

While Susan is absent on her mission of putative mercy, the lady feels 'disposed to look,/ As self-approving, on a pious book' (ll. 461–2). Oscillating between feeling herself too merciful and thinking she ought to feel some pity, she is more concerned with defining her own rectitude than imagining Paul's suffering, even though the recent scene has epitomised 'The man's whole misery in a single view' (l. 467). 'Thus fix'd' in self-preoccupation, she does not hear Susan's return until the very words are spoken, 'He is dead!' Appropriately, we are not taken far into the lady's recognition of what she has done. Her first reactions are emotionally reined-in matters of fact – 'Expired he then, good Heaven! for want of food?' (l. 477) – and we only glimpse her realisation of her guilt in the fine stroke of her misunderstanding of Susan's self-accusation:

> 'To have this plenty, and to wait so long . . .'
> 'Blame me not, child; I tremble at the news.'
> ''Tis my own heart,' said Susan, 'I accuse . . .'   (ll. 479, 483–4)

The silence which Susan's words have to fill is terrible.

'Unlike 'Resentment', 'Procrastination' (Tale IV) does not indicate the central concern of the tale. The first paragraph states explicitly that love will expire between those who marry early as frequently as between those who delay. One interest is in the hardening of the character of Dinah in a way which has less obviously dramatic results than in 'Resentment', and another in the contamination of Dinah by her aunt. But although his love is finally destroyed by Dinah, Rupert remains loyal long enough to demonstrate that the sudden reversal of the easy

cynicism of the first lines, by the word 'esteem', indicates a real possibility that Dinah's progress is not an inevitable one:

> Love will expire, the gay, the happy dream
> Will turn to scorn, indiff'rence, or esteem.   (ll. 1–2)

The tale is one of a series of studies of the shape of the marriage relationship.

The first time it is used of Dinah, the word 'prudent' is not a criticism: we feel sorry that the 'poor virgin lived in dread and awe' since
she has an aunt who is exploiting her 'anxious looks', prevailing on her
to delay marriage by playing on the fact that 'she was yet a child'.
Dinah's reading-matter seems in the circumstances to be justified:

> Meantime the nymph her tender tales perused,
> Where cruel aunts impatient girls refused.   (ll. 30–1)

So we scarcely notice that already there is a resemblance despite the
difference between aunt and niece:

> While hers, though teasing, boasted to be kind,
> And she, resenting, to be all resign'd.   (ll. 32–3)

Beside the gross emotional blackmail of the aunt, who

> Talk'd of departing, and again her breath
> Drew hard, and cough'd, and talk'd again of death,   (ll. 36–7)

the relationship of the young people is shown to be extremely healthy:

> So long they now each other's thoughts had known,
> That nothing seem'd exclusively their own.   (ll. 46–7)

There is something of real value to be lost in Dinah, as well as Rupert,
and part of the feeling of the tale as a whole is a sadness at her transformation. When a prospect opens (the words 'view' and 'prospect'
recur throughout the tale), despite the pious cant of 'The kind must
suffer, and the best must die' (l. 59), the aunt's view is clearly in terms
of possessions – 'Dinah's care, what I bequeath will pay' – and as her
cough gives signs 'Of holding long contention with the grave' (l. 61),
the aunt's conception of 'Dinah's care' plainly already includes a care
for her (which will be repaid) as well as sorrow at what she dismisses as
'this brief delay'. After Rupert has gone, the manipulation gains both
subtlety, when 'She wonder'd much why one so happy sigh'd' (l. 73),
and blatancy, when she produces her possessions 'With the kind notice
– "They will be your own"' (l. 79). Her emphasis has tacitly shifted
from the earlier promise, 'the boy/And you together my estate enjoy'
(ll. 38–9).

But although the aunt is to blame in cultivating the 'poison-tree' of an ugly materialism in Dinah, it is Dinah's heart in which the feeling grows. Her view becomes restricted to the aunt's possessions, rather than the 'pleasant views and hopes' she shared with Rupert: 'she loved the hoards to view'. The word 'loved' itself has become debased. 'Care' has similarly ceased altogether to represent her sorrow at the delay:

> With lively joy those comforts she survey'd,
> And love grew languid in the careful maid.   (ll. 90–1)

'Languid' has its roots in the aunt's subtle insinuations – 'She wonder'd much why one so happy sigh'd' – but it is Dinah who is becoming more 'careful' of the 'comforts'. The cant becomes mutual: 'Now the grave niece partook the widow's cares' (l. 92) is their way of expressing such concerns as cleaning the plate and arranging the china. 'Loved' and 'bonds' assume very limited meanings in her vocabulary: 'She loved the value of her bonds to tell' (l. 98). The aunt's indulgence is no longer merely self-indulgence, but is changing the range of Dinah's emotions: 'Th' indulgent aunt increased the maid's delight' (l. 96). Dinah's vocabulary also begins to redefine the relationship with Rupert: the old feelings are reduced to 'romantic notions' and in her letters to him she now describes herself as Rupert's 'friend'. She is so contaminated by the aunt's values that she adopts the excuse of the cough for her own purposes:

> Seldom she wrote, and then the widow's cough,
> And constant call, excused her breaking off.   (ll. 106–7)

When the aunt dies, a veneer of 'correct' reflection barely covers the sigh of relief: "'tis comfort to reflect,/When all is over, there was no neglect;/And all was over' (ll. 114–16). In reality, it is not all over: the aunt's bones are in the churchyard, but her spirit lives on in Dinah. The 'love of hoarding' is masked by a hypocritical representation of it as a 'care', a 'duty': 'she resolved to take/Th'important duty for the donor's sake' (ll. 122–3). It is precisely the aunt's note of self-martyrdom: 'The kind must suffer, and the best must die' (l. 59). Thoughts of the past sometimes still press themselves on her consciousness –

> Sometimes the past would on her mind intrude,
> And then a conflict full of care ensued –   (ll. 126–7)

but the conflict full of care is translated into a materialist one: 'His worth she knew, but doubted his success' (l. 129). As John Lucas has pointed out,[5] the ostensibly balanced judgement here is quite irrelevant, since Rupert's success is no longer necessary to them now that Dinah is rich: it is merely an attempt to deceive herself about the nature of her conflict, an attempt which is evidently successful as her reflections

end with the thought that, although a broken vow is indefensible,
'Heav'n, perhaps, might yet enrich her friend.' She has reached the
point where a moral obligation has to be underwritten by a financial
consideration. Her conception of enjoyment is now defined by the
relation to the word 'save', in 'what the boy/Forebore to save, the man
would not enjoy' (ll. 130–1); and suffering is something which afflicts
only those outside the walls of her 'pleasant dwelling':

> She knew that mothers grieved, and widows wept,
> And she was sorry, said her prayers, and slept.   (ll. 140–1)

She even seems insulated from the passage of time:

> Thus pass'd the seasons, and to Dinah's board
> Gave what the seasons to the rich afford.   (ll. 142–3)

Her 'view' has now become fully self-contained:

> In small but splendid room she loved to see
> That all was placed in view and harmony.   (ll. 152–3)

The role of religion is merely to obstruct any dangerous degree of
spontaneity:

> books devout were near her – to destroy,
> Should it arise, an overflow of joy.   (ll. 156–7)

Yet, as Howard Mills has suggested,[6] there is clearly an indulged
repressed sexuality in:

> Silky and soft upon the floor below,
> Th'elastic carpet rose with crimson glow.   (ll. 162–3)

The climax of the description of the room, in which she has insulated
herself from all normal human activities, is the clock, a symbol of her
spinsterly hardness and a reminder, however obscured by decoration,
of the passage of time:

> And while on brilliants moved the hands of steel,
> It click'd from pray'r to pray'r, from meal to meal.
>   (ll. 178–9)

With its hands, feet, crest and face, the clock stands as the presiding
idol over this woman's materialist idolatry:

> Above her head, all gorgeous to behold,
> A time-piece stood on feet of burnish'd gold;
> A stag's-head crest adorn'd the pictured case,
> Through the pure crystal shone th'enamell'd face.   (ll. 174–7)

A conspicuous excellence in Crabbe's art is his ability suddenly to change the focus of attention. An example was given in the discussion of 'Peter Grimes' above. Here, in a masterly transition, Crabbe moves from the general description of the room, which embodies all that Dinah has become, to a specific occasion when her now established character manifests itself in a particular action which takes place in the room. Two friends have come 't'admire the view' and exchange spinsterly exclamations, on

> How tender damsels sail'd in tilted boats,
> And laugh'd with wicked men in scarlet coats.   (ll. 184–5)

Romantic relationship is now reduced to the level of 'naughty' fiction, a kind of fiction which respectable spinsters should not perhaps have read, but which associates itself naturally enough with the 'crimson glow' from which comfortable comments on 'such degen'rate times' are made. With great skill, Crabbe makes the conversation naturally take a turn which will arouse painful reflections in Dinah: '... what was once our pride is now our shame' (l. 189). The effect is immediate: there is no time to obstruct them with rationalisations before

> Thoughts of the past within her bosom press'd
> And there a change was felt, and was confess'd.   (ll. 194–5)

But the 'painful views' remain interior and she merely sinks into self-preoccupation: 'Still she was silent, nothing seem'd to see' (l. 198).

The inability of her maid, Susannah, to conceal her anger beneath decorum gives Dinah sufficient preparation for the abrupt entrance of Rupert for her to be able to rationalise away the impact of her sudden confrontation with her own change:

> Meantime the prudent Dinah had contrived
> Her soul to question, and she then revived.   (ll. 218–19)

This second time it is used, 'prudent' has come to mean merely self-interested. In contrast, the two lines in which Rupert's response is registered show, with great brevity, a frank manner, a confession of his own failure, and a concern for Dinah:

> 'Revive, my love!' said he, 'I've done thee harm,
> Give me thy pardon,' and he look'd alarm.   (ll. 216–17)

In reply, Dinah immediately distances him – 'See! my good friend ...' – and, vulgarising Crabbe's favourite text from *Hebrews* (12. 1), attempts to undermine his masculine vigour with religious cant:

'happier they whose race is nearly run,
Their troubles over, and their duties done.'   (ll. 227–8)

Rupert cuts straight through the cant, emphasising the positive possibilities of life: 'we are not girl and boy,/But time has left us something
to enjoy' (ll. 229–30). Grotesquely, Dinah takes him to refer to money –
'What! thou hast learn'd my fortune?' – and, while maintaining the
general drift of 'wealth is come too late', adroitly raises the question of
Rupert's wealth. The gruff honesty of Rupert's reply is so well caught in
the verse that it is clearly magnanimity and no sort of greed that makes
him prepared to share her money despite the obvious blow to masculine
self-respect. Naïvely, he has in mind the idea that it is 'more blessed to
give than to receive'. The purity of his feeling is emphasised by the
contrast with her casual blasphemy ('"Heavens!" return'd the maid')
and the vulgarisation of the *Song of Solomon* (4. 8), 'all my care is now
to fit my mind/For other spousal.' Her 'views' have become a peculiarly
nasty religiose version of her spinsterly voyeurism – 'Guides and spectators in each other's fate' (l. 248); and the word 'mutual', once used of
their 'common wish, the mutual fear', jars all the more strongly
because of the cant of 'pious love' and 'fellow pilgrims': 'The mutual
prayer that arms us for the grave' (l. 250). The sickening decorum,
which unlike that other 'maiden starch', Susannah, she can so easily
maintain, is made to seem even more repulsive by Rupert's partial incomprehension – 'What spousal mean'st thou? – thou art Rupert's spouse'
(l. 254). Her view must, he thinks, be wider than it seems: 'Something
thou hast – I know not what – in view' (l. 259). But all she has in mind
is the hypocritical self-martyrdom of her aunt: 'to its feelings leave my
wounded heart', a heart in which Rupert's own sufferings can clearly
find no place. Although it maintains the tone of an 'untamed' sailor,
his speech is complex enough to contain a damning perspective on her
– he cannot believe 'That God accepts her who will man deceive' (l. 268);
shame at his financial failure, not for its own sake but for her:

'It touch'd me deeply, for I felt a pride
In gaining riches for my destined bride;   (ll. 277–8)

and the physical weight of present griefs he tries to suppress, which
contrasts with the aunt's use of her cough – 'my very throat they
swell;/They stop the breath'. In response to such hardly to be expressed
feeling, Dinah sighs 'as if afraid to speak', and easily exudes more cant.
His gaze passes right through her, 'with steady glance, as if to see/The
very root of this hypocrisy'; and the stature of his humanity compared
with hers is rendered in a beautiful image in which the expression of
feeling strains the couplet metre almost to breaking:

> He her small fingers moulded in his hard
> And bronzed broad hand. (ll. 293–4)

Much of the conclusion is handled in visual terms, in the opposition of 'his plain artless look with her sharp meaning face', his 'thickset coat' and her 'shaded silk of changeful hue'. But just as Crabbe seems settled into an extended contrast, he suddenly shifts the tone to the brooding, deeply sad reflectiveness of a memory of time past:

> It might some wonder in a stranger move,
> How these together could have talk'd of love. (ll. 317–18)

As a comment on the pathos of human infidelity, its quiet authority rivals the moment of Henryson's Troilus half-recognising the leprous face of the woman he once loved and was betrayed by. Finally, we enter into the state of mind of each. Rupert knows what Dinah has become but remains bewildered that it has happened, 'His eyes on her intent'. Dinah too has 'observed' Rupert in front of her in the street, and Crabbe, not exaggerating her hardness, allows her to feel some pity, and even 'Some feeling touch of ancient tenderness' (l. 339). But immediately, she begins to overlay the feeling with cant – 'Religion, duty urged the maid to speak' (l. 340) – which gives time for pride to become engaged on the opposite side. She is trapped between a shame which she, unlike him, has not the magnanimity to acknowledge – 'She felt the shame of his neglected love' (l. 343) – and a fear that people will blame her for not showing the pity she herself knows she should show – 'Each eye should see her, and each heart upbraid' (l. 345). As a matter of practical expediency in the physical situation of having to get past him in the street, she is with great naturalism forced to adopt the course which makes the perfect symbol of her attitude: 'She cross'd and pass'd him on the other side' (l. 349).

In only 349 lines, with no heavy plot-machinery, but with masterly handling of point-of-view, of descriptive detail, particularly of Dinah's room, and of dramatic potentiality in the episodes natural to the development of the story, Crabbe has presented the gradual progress of Dinah from the unfortunate lover of a man to the hardened lover of possessions, with Rupert standing against her as an example of constancy and true humanity. The degree to which he has developed since *The Parish Register* is conveniently apparent in the contrast between 'Procrastination' and the sketch of Catherine Lloyd. Catherine, a similar type to Dinah, is presented almost wholly through description of her possessions, some of which is superfluous. In 'Procrastination' the development of the characters and of the relationship between them is rendered in much more dramatic ways as well as, where appropriate, in descriptive terms, and scarcely a line could be omitted without spoiling its careful structure. It is one of Crabbe's most fully accomplished tales.

'The Wager' (Tale XVIII) is like 'The Dumb Orators' in that an apparently trifling narrative raises issues of profound significance. Clubb and Counter succeed equally in trade, but have different ideas of marriage. Counter wants and gets a pliant wife; Clubb wants and gets an equal rather than a slave. After they are married, Counter keeps boasting of his freedom until Clubb is goaded into betting he will find it easier than Counter to ride off to Newmarket for a few days. He wins and Counter holds his peace in future. That is all, and the tale is short and light in tone. Mrs Haddakin described it as attaining 'competence without any special significance', and Fitzgerald thought it 'Very uninteresting'.[7] But Crabbe is probing deeply the question of freedom within marriage: what kind of freedom is worth retaining and what is not.

At the beginning, Counter's attitude is pseudo-magnanimous: his wife will be allowed to rule her own province, but that province does not include any of his own activities. Clubb's answer is very full. He sees at once that what Counter wants can easily be counterfeited, and that his certainty is misplaced. At first he puts this in terms of a comic reversal: the wife might pretend to obey until she is ready to rule. But as he goes on, he points out that submission is not love, that a woman in relationship with a wholly dominating husband may not give him her heart, and that a heart withheld might turn to anger or even towards another man. In this case he would not only lose his dominance, but also not know the truth, since she is likely to conceal her intentions; so his expected certainty would be broken by jealousy, and his male pride would be seriously wounded. With what he wants, in fact, Clubb is much less vulnerable despite less power: if he treats his wife as an equal, even if she is false to him, the only disgrace is hers, and his own dignity remains secure.

A man so easy-going as Clubb does not find it hard to get a suitable wife, a human being with plain faults, quick-tempered and more interested in governing than obeying, yet who deeply feels the force of the marriage vows. Counter's search for a wife, on the other hand, is a misdirection of his commercial activities, which reduces the woman to an object, who can have the neuter pronoun used of 'it' twice. She is just the woman to boost superficial male pride, who will obligingly shake when Counter raises his voice, feeding his egoism and relaxing his underlying fears. But we also receive hints of the weakness she will later use as a weapon: if left alone she feels a thousand fears. As soon as he starts to boast about his choice, Counter begins to show the precariousness of his power, the vacuity of the relationship – his wife is always silent when he parts from her – and his vulnerability to emotional blackmail, though he represents this as an aspect of his magnanimity: his heart is pained at the thought of upsetting her. Clubb is not so insecure as to have to answer and can simply reject the whole basis of his friend's boasts: better a woman to rule his house than one unfit to rule. Clubb in fact is secure enough in himself to feel more anxious about Counter: the need to boast must show a fundamental uneasiness, for if he felt pleasure he would wish to please, not to laugh at Clubb. Counter certainly has a very onerous time: he has not only to make all his own moral decisions, but also to rule his house. This scarcely makes him free, so the joke backfires when he says that Clubb laughs at liberty: he can afford to because in reality he has more of it, having resigned the absolute power Counter wants yet has only nominally. But the words are Counter's: Clubb does not feel the emotional need to laugh at the advocate of liberty.

When, under the influence of alcohol, the bet is laid, Clubb speaks squarely to his wife, admitting blame first and offering excuses later. His speech is direct and captures his mood well with the frequent parentheses showing his embarrasment and his not quite controlled sense of honour. His wife's reply is equally direct. Counter, on the other hand, speaks with an indirectness indicated by the use of the third person pronoun instead of Clubb's direct first and second persons. He is clearly contaminated by the techniques his wife has already used on him: he prepares his way with soft and winning words. Whereas Clubb ended with a direct question about whether his wife consented, Counter ends with an arm-twisting sigh which ironically recalls the declaration in his first speech that it was not in him to sigh like a suppliant lover, and which he has learnt from his wife's use of sighs to blackmail her way to what she wants. Her speech too is within quotation marks but in the third person, indicating her indirectness. She attempts to conceal the selfishness by expressing concern for him, but the emphasis is on herself: she would die of fear. The language captures the authentic note of self-martyrdom which parallels Counter's own blackmailing sigh. The effect on Counter is to set up a conflict – 'I know your honour must outweigh your wife' (l. 220) – whereas Mrs Clubb removed the conflict her husband felt: 'The husband's honour is the woman's pride' (l. 178). When Mrs Counter talks further about dying, in response to such escalation Counter exaggerates the stake from one hundred to one thousand pounds, and in counter-response she faints. Clubb's first speech on the dangers of a marriage of the kind envisaged by Counter puts the present antics in perspective. Mrs Counter is, as she says, true: although she is abusing her truth, she is not unfaithful, so the situation retains a basically comic nature. But Crabbe can now make fuller use of the third-person usage: the lines, 'Oh! she loved so well,/And who th'affect of tenderness could tell' (ll. 239–40), might be spoken by either the husband or the wife, might be real anxiety or more blackmail. His terror at what he might have done to her is largely, but not wholly, comic.

In his letter of contrition to Clubb, Counter shows himself to have come to resemble the wife he wanted to fear him: his heart is, he says, too tender for such strife. His magnanimity does not extend to a simple admission that Clubb has won, only that submission and control in marriage are no 'theme for wit'; and he ends his letter in self-delusion: let each, he says, guard against domestic strife. Clubb has no need to, and Counter will have little success. So the emphasis of the last paragraph is that, as Clubb is capable of seeing, 'such things are not a jest'. The pain is not so great as Clubb's first speech showed it might be, but even so Counter can no longer conceal under boasting the truth which pains him. Kindness in his relationship became a weapon ("twere cruel but to seem unkind'); whereas Clubb and his wife have sufficient real kindness to agree to spare some for Counter ('your friend's offer let us kindly take'). They realise that not only has Counter found, but 'through his life will find' that he has made a grave, irreparable mistake.

Counter has discovered that having a pliant wife, so far from ensuring his freedom, has led to a situation where mutual emotional blackmail acts as a continual impediment to liberty. It has also changed his own nature, making him use emotional blackmail in response to hers. On the other hand, the terms of equality in the marriage of the Clubbs have left each free to develop a particular moral character and at the same time have led to an agreement in practice which cements the relationship. The sex war has been treated with the comic tone appropriate to it, but the underlying perception is that 'such things are not a jest'. A response of laughter alone is the response of the insecure.

Most of the tales discussed so far in this chapter concern relationships which are not well grounded or fail to withstand the test of time. But in 'The Wager' attention is divided between the Counters' failure and the Clubbs' success, and in the tales which remain to be discussed the emphasis is on success. Crabbe is by no means always preoccupied with degeneration. 'The Parting Hour' (Tale II) is less tightly written than the best of the *Tales*, but it stands as a particularly striking example of a relationship which is not destroyed by time. Although the opening paragraphs both emphasise Crabbe's fascination with the effect of time and point to the structure of the tale, they are deliberately premature in reducing the inference to the observation of decay. Against all odds, Allen and Judith triumph over time. Yet it is not one of the obvious triumphs of sentiment. The third paragraph already makes it clear that they are not reunited in marriage, even though the quality of the relationship is such that few are capable of achieving it. The epigraph from *Cymbeline* adduces a contrasting example of a relationship restored in a sentimental fashion. Tennyson's *Enoch Arden*, which, as has often been noted, was probably suggested by Crabbe's poem, provides an example of an alternative sentimentalism in Enoch's tear-jerkingly noble decision not to disrupt the marriage of his former sweetheart to another man. Beside it the quiet masculine dignity of Crabbe's tale is both more realistic and more truly moving.

The parting itself is handled with fine realism, with the father facing it with the help of alcohol and the mother gazing intently at her son, but most importantly when the sweet sorrow of parting is marred by traces of a jealousy which at the end of the tale the lovers have grown beyond. Judith's is put in perspective by juxtaposition with the fear that she can already hear the boat coming. This is brushed aside as a lover's mistake, but there is some irony in that she can then go on to lecture Allen about the strength of the passions which invade his mind. Allen's own moment of jealousy, about 'fawning Philip', spoils the parting more: if the boat were not this time actually close, Judith would have expressed her displeasure in anger.

At Allen's return, the suspense is held at a very delicate pitch. The most obvious source of suspense has already been removed: we know from the third paragraph that the lovers will meet again. It is the mood of Allen that our attention is on, a mood which demands a 'strange and solemn sympathy'. The connection with the parting hour is emphasised by the insistence that the parting took place on the very spot where he now stands. The difference is indicated by the physical change from the youth who departed: Allen is now a worn-out man with withered limbs. In one sense this is not the youth who left forty years ago; in another it is. The awful strangeness of the moment, as he makes his lonely way up the familiar beach left half a lifetime before, is caught by the utter silence, broken only by the gentle flapping of a sail and the drowsy sound of distant bells. His confused but quiet meditations are suddenly shattered by the alien tumult of an unknown generation, in whose faces he searches for the features he knew in their youthful form, his pre-occupied attempts being interrupted by irrelevant joviality. The woman he asks about the past loses her concern after retailing the gossip she knows, and transfers her attention to her friends who are hastening to the beach. The friend who when he left had an ambition to own a hoy is even more unfeeling. The meeting with Judith is thus held back until Allen has come to feel an outcast in his own surroundings. But the meeting itself, offering an early nineteenth-century writer such possibilities of sentimental pathos, is quiet and dignified. Time has had an irreversible effect, yet fundamentally it is conquered. What they can share exists in the past, but they meet on a level of common humanity: 'his various fate . . . 'tis comfort to relate . . . she too loves to hear.'

The narrative of Allen's life abroad needs to be long in order to communicate fully the fact that it took up the greater part of his lifetime, that so much stands between the present and the time of the parting hour. But the writing has not the thick texture of Crabbe's best work. The major impression is of a restlessness alternating with a musing on the past. Finally we see him in a scene with Judith, which the summer heat and the shade of the trees links firmly with the other period of greatest peace, with his Spanish wife. This time it is not the parting hour he is dreaming about, but 'his best days', the time in Spain, which is more vividly present to him than anything before or since. So when he wakes and cries, 'My God! 'twas but a dream', he is only partly right. Beside the quiet reality of Judith laying down her knitting to attend to him, his memories are as insubstantial as the song of the night-birds or the fairy light of fireflies. But we also know that both he and Judith know it is his 'best days' that he has been dreaming of, and that they have a reality to him which permanently stands between them. Yet the final effect of having our involuntary sentimental wish that they be united in marriage prevented by the fact of his Spanish wife being still alive, is to emphasise the quality of a relationship which can endure without its most obvious fulfilment, a relationship which can survive not only shared misfortune but also unshared good fortune.

In 'The Widow's Tale' (Tale VII), the primary subject is Nancy's discovery, through friendship with the widow, of an adequate basis for a lasting relationship. But it is also concerned with the tendency of people to make premature judgements of each other and with the study of a mind which might, under other circumstances, have gone the way of Dinah. Nancy misjudges both her own family and the widow; the family misjudge both her and the widow. Her alienation from the family after her town-school education is very finely rendered in her reaction against their eating habits. The description captures both the sense of community, labourers and cook eating with the farmer and his sons, and her affected withdrawal from it: 'Rein'd the fair neck, and shut th'offended eye' (l. 28). The mixture of diction conveys both the physical reality and her perspective on it:

> The swelling fat in lumps conglomerate laid . . .
> Fill'd with huge balls of farinaceous food.   (ll. 15, 20)

We can share her revulsion, yet remain detached from it as we note also the masculine vigour of what it rejects:

> Where by the steaming beef he hungry sat,
> And laid at once a pound upon his plate.   (ll. 9–10)

She wants to withdraw totally from this communal life, to a small parlour, 'And there to dine, to read, to work alone' (l. 35). When her father throws out a coarse hint about future marriage, her reaction is again withdrawal, to sigh and pray in her own room. Harry Carr is immediately established as an eligible young man by his capacity to see both aspects of the situation, that Nancy would not do on his farm, and that it is a pity she would not. Beside his sense, Nancy is clearly sickly. The seemingly 'pensive' widow

> Pleased the sad nymph, who wish'd her soul's distress
> To one so seeming kind, confiding, to confess.　　(ll. 72–3)

The break in the couplet, '. . . wish'd her soul's distress', indicates the pleasure she is taking in her role as delicate maid among coarse hinds. Her judgement of the widow as one likely to sympathise with her is initially no more inaccurate than her brother's but she indulges her fantasy to the point where what she projects on to the widow is what she would like to become herself. She sees no incompatibility between romance and widowhood: 'Here you enjoy a sweet romantic scene' (l. 108). The garden is approximated to Catherine Lloyd's – 'These twining jess'mines, what delicious gloom . . .' (l. 110) – and is seen as a refuge from the world which recalls those of other spinsters in Crabbe:

> 'What lovely garden! there you oft retire,
> And tales of wo and tenderness admire.'　　(ll. 112–13)

It is Dinah who comes, in fact, most clearly to mind: 'In that neat case your books, in order placed' (l. 114) is on the route to 'In level rows, her polish'd volumes stood'. ('Procrastination', l. 169)

But the widow can balance this view of herself against that of the farmer and his sons, and reject both. She is not so much delicate as 'feeble'. The garden 'Tempts not a feeble dame who dreads the cold' (l. 124): the health Nancy affects to despise is necessary to the indulgence of a contempt for it. But she is not embittered: she is magnanimous enough to generalise from the irony that the farmers 'see what you admire, and laugh at all they see' not to counter-scorn, but to advice not to scorn the farmers. Nancy expects the widow's smile to be 'At those who live in our detested style' (l. 140). In fact it is at her own affectations and the self-pity which dares 'not show/Ills that would wound her tender soul to know' (ll. 143–4), but compulsively dwells on them, anticipating a shared maidenly 'shudder'. Yet despite her maturity, the widow has not quite come to terms with her own experience. The main function of the tale is, of course, to provide Nancy with a projection through time of her fantasies about romantic love. The widow loved a romantically 'thin and pale' youth, whose poverty prevented a successful marriage though it prolonged a romantic attachment. The experience leads the widow to make two criticisms of romantic love: 'no dream is more untrue' and

> 'Alas! my child, there are who, dreaming so,
> Waste their fresh youth, and waking feel the wo.'
>
> (ll. 194–5)

Her tale certainly shows the waste, but it also shows that the attachment was more than a dream. Nancy's projection of her resentment towards her own father – 'The tyrant's power who fill'd your soul with dread' (l. 249) – is shown to be a falsification by the charitable good sense of the widow's father's actual words and action. The widow thinks she has located a more real enemy in the falsifying dream of romantic love, and, given her experience, there is much to be said for her view. She has lived through the dismal reality of 'all for love' for many years,

> 'When, being wretched, we incline to hate
> And censure others in a happier state;
> Yet loving still, and still compell'd to move
> In the sad labyrinth of ling'ring love.'   (ll. 289–92)

For year after year, though the love endured, the 'pains and vexations' grew greater. The image of the labyrinth is an ironic projection of Nancy's wish to withdraw from the coarse outer world and a fine image of the introversion forced on the lovers by their refusal to accept the conditions of the larger world. The waste of life caused through the myth of romantic love by the poverty and exclusiveness which might ostensibly seem to enhance its stature is conveyed with the authentic note of a experienced process. As the widow's father pointed out in his essentially sympathetic speech, the survival of the love under conditions of inescapable poverty 'doubles every pain'. But that romantic love can be dismissed simply as a falsifying dream, is to some extent a myth itself, developed by the widow in self-defence. It is simply inadequate to say,

> 'Passion to reason will submit – or why
> Should wealthy maids the poorest swains deny?'   (ll. 198–9)

When Nancy suggests that perhaps the lovers were united at last, the widow's first reaction is a smile, 'But soon a starting tear usurp'd its place' (l. 258). Similarly, when she speaks of her lover's grave, the common-sense perspective is confined to a parenthesis: 'when I die,/ There – but 'tis folly – I request to lie' (ll. 309–10). Nancy urged her, 'let not memory lose the blissful view': the view was not very blissful, but the widow is so far from losing memory of it that she still wants to cling to it in death.

Nancy is quick to seize on the romanticism of this and thinks that to have become a widow she must therefore have been 'in a tyrant's power'. The widow replies drily, with the wisdom which was brought home to the ageing Arabella:

> 'Force, my young friend, when forty years are fled,
> Is what a woman seldom has to dread.'   (ll. 315–16)

But although it did not drive her into the 'sweet romantic' withdrawal Nancy had in mind, her first relationship had hopelessly crippled her emotional life. The man she married was clearly eligible in every respect: he 'spoke of love as men in earnest speak' and through a period of years 'with assiduous love my pleasure sought', so she was sensible to marry him. But on her side there was no more than sense: there was no emotional response –

> 'That heart I gave not; and 'twas long before
> I gave attention, and then nothing more . . .
> There was no fondness in my bosom left.'   (ll. 325–6, 334)

It is clear that if the widow had been less drained by her earlier experience the marriage would have been happy; as it is, all vitality is absent: 'Serene, though heavy, were the days we spent' (l. 345). But although she thus has good ground for feeling bitter towards life, she has seen, in retrospect, that there was a greater richness possible in the form of her second major experience than her emotional exhaustion allowed her to enjoy at the time. The 'blooming shrubs' and 'curious trifles' are not the collection of a Dinah, as Nancy thought, but tokens of an 'assiduous love' more actually fruitful than the romanticism of her first relationship, and instead of wanting Nancy to share the withdrawal which is now, at her advanced age, forced on her, she wants her to aim at the more rewarding form of relationship while she is still capable of fulfilling it. Nancy has to work hard at remoulding her personality to a form suitable for marriage to a farmer, but the widow is pleased when she becomes emotionally involved: it is not *merely* a matter of sense –

> This pettish humour pleased th'experienced friend –
> None need despair, whose silence can offend.   (ll. 369–70)

The result is a relationship which, like the new one between Nancy and her father, will be mutually enriching:

> The coarser manners she in part removed,
> In part endured, improving and improved.   (ll 379–80)

Through Nancy's flexibility, her father too can see that he was mistaken, in his judgement of the widow – 'She look'd as begging pardon of
the worm' (l. 418) was as inadequate a view as Nancy's own of both the
widow and the family – and the father, like Nancy, is capable of
acknowledging and correcting his mistake:

> 'people, when they know the fact,
> Where they have judged severely, can retract.'   (ll. 413–14)

All the obstructions to the emergence of 'real worth' – the half-truths
of romantic myth, the mincing 'arts' of town-school education, and
premature judgement – are removed by the widow's magnanimity. The
tale is optimistic not only in its hopes for the relationship of Nancy and
Harry, but in that from such potentially souring experience the widow
has emerged with such humanity.

In 'Jesse and Colin' (Tale XIII), the health of the relationship between
the two main characters is secured through Jesse's rejection of the con-
taminating influence of the wealthy lady who wishes to patronise her.
An experience, which might have distorted her nature even more radically than the widow's romantic disillusion might have warped her,
instead propels Jesse towards what has every promise of developing into
a fruitful married life. At the beginning, Jesse knows that Colin has been
educated to form a rich relationship, yet feels more drawn towards the
lady, once helped by her father, who now offers to help her. The basis of
the attraction is apparent in the resemblance between Jesse and the lady:
both are full of self-pity, both consider it may be better to be owed gratitude than to owe it, and the words 'kind' and 'generous' are used
ironically of both. Jesse is tainted by the values of the woman she is
preparing to admire. But when the lady makes it plain that she intends
Jesse to act as informer on her three other dependants, Jesse's thoughts
immediately and involuntarily turn towards the health of Colin. At the
lady's house, the arts of relationship are mutual suspicion and deception.
The three dependants, who try in turn to win the confidence of Jesse,
represent the limit, the terminus, of such a way of life, and in reaction
against the labyrinth of their manoeuvrings, Jesse's feelings are reorien-
tated towards Colin's cottage. Jesse quickly sees that the household are
long past the point of possible change, and that she cannot afford to pity
them since the danger of contamination is great so long as she remains
there. She is now prepared to acknowledge gratitude, but only in a
special sense, for the knowledge of the limit of a mode of conduct. When
she mentions leaving, the lady is reduced from hints to Jesse about her
unmade will to expostulating at one of the other dependants with impo-
tent rage carried to the point of fantasy. From this our attention is
switched suddenly to the wholesome Colin in his pleasant, unostenta-

tious garden. It is not until now that we learn that Colin's father came down in the world. The exposition is not very interesting in itself, but necessary to establish Colin as a man who has already seen through visionary hopes of gain and instead created for himself and his mother a real and stable relationship. He is kind in a sense far beyond the earlier Jesse's and her lady's condescension. When she returns to him, her earlier taint has been completely removed by her experience. Her 'No' to the suggestion of fetching the marriage licence is not feigning, but part of the traditional pattern of natural relationship, a pattern evoked by the hints of pastoral with which the tale concludes.

'Jesse and Colin' is not one of the best conceived or best written of the *Tales*, but it represents quite powerfully Jesse's original taint, the deep-rooted corruption of the lady and her three dependants, and the natural retraction of Jesse away from the corruption towards the health of Colin. The title suggests the world of pastoral, and despite the strong danger of contamination that is where the tale concludes. It stands among Crabbe's celebrations of the possibility of fruitful relationship.

'The Confidant' (Tale XVI) is one of Crabbe's most sophisticated fictional structures. The character of Anna is revealed in four stages, corresponding to the successive stages of Stafford's knowledge of her; Eliza's blackmail, which deeply threatens their relationship, occupies the central and most direct section of the tale; and the resolution is achieved through Stafford telling a tale within the tale, which parodies Eliza's blackmail in a way that both dismisses her and shows his mature, humane forgiveness of Anna's mistakes.

The first description of Anna is of her appearance and of the blush which shows an apparent innocence and a real lack of contamination:

> Though this fair lass had with the wealthy dwelt
> Yet like the damsel of the cot she felt.   (ll. 11–12)

Although her experience is very different, in this respect she resembles Jesse. In the second stage of the description we are taken into the nature of her experience immediately before the marriage to Stafford. As a lady's companion, she has dissimulation forced upon her:

> She play'd at whist, but with inferior skill . . .
> The lady's taste she must in all approve.   (ll. 23, 29)

She also has to deal with the men who try to take advantage of her dependence by making illicit offers. The future seems bleak, but she does not repine: 'She veil'd her troubles in a mask of ease' (l. 33). It is a situation which encourages hypocrisy, but as yet the veil is only what is necessary to perform her role with 'grace': when danger impends she is healthily 'shamed and frighten'd'. Stafford is introduced at the point

when we know as much of Anna as he would have seen at early
acquaintance. He is of mature years and not only 'gentle, generous . . .
kind' but also 'cultivated'. The money his benefactor 'lived to save',
Stafford uses to feed his mind 'with useful culture'. From the start, there
is a generosity in his love:

> Love raised his pity for her humble state,
> And prompted wishes for her happier fate.   (ll. 63–4)

The third stage in the description of Anna is the version of her past
known to the lady, a history of orphan childhood and attempts at
seduction. There is some irony when she admits that 'e'en with me
protection is not peace': she has in mind the continuance of 'men's
designs' rather than her own exploitation of Anna. But her final image,
foreshadowing Stafford's tale of the stolen fruit, emphasises the contrast
between Anna's single error and persistent soliciting:

> 'Like sordid boys by costly fruit they feel,
> They will not purchase, but they try to steal.'   (ll. 91–2)

The truth about her past is finally presented by the narrator, who has,
like Stafford in due course, sufficient objectivity to see it as an 'afflicting
tale'. A girl of fifteen was betrayed by a cowardly seducer of thirty.
That she was tainted at the time is clear not only from her acceptance of
her mother's advice – 'Let her to town (so prudence urged) repair' – but
from the very fact that, as we now learn, both parents were alive,
whereas in the version told to the lady she was orphaned as an infant.
But the emphasis is on her suffering: on top of the recent experience
and incipient fears of Eliza, she sees her father die 'gloomy and
distress'd' in debt, and her mother shortly follow. The scope for self-pity
greatly exceeds what she allows herself:

> Past time she view'd, the passing time to cheat,
> But nothing found to make the present sweet.   (ll. 43–4)

The narrative time-scale then settles on the early years of marriage.
Much is well: Anna feels grateful and is 'vigilant, and kind'; Stafford
feels extreme delight and a healthy degree of pride in both his wife and
his son. But as she nurses the child, Anna also has some feelings which
she cannot share with Stafford. Unfortunately instead of exploring these
feelings, Crabbe merely asserts that

> Between the married when a secret lies,
> It wakes suspicion from enforced disguise.   (ll. 166–7)

In this case it does not, until Eliza has done much.
   Eliza's first letter is ugly in its self-pitying blackmail –

'. . . poor Eliza had from place to place
Been lured by hope to labour for disgrace' –   (ll. 186–7)

but, even though it is 'received in dread/Not unobserved', it barely
threatens the relationship. Anna realises at once that she must disclose
it to Stafford, and Stafford responds with a mature 'sober smile', which
both places Eliza and reassures Anna. In dismissing what he takes to be
school-girl fantasies, he too foreshadows his concluding tale: 'Some
youthful gaspings for forbidden fruit' (l. 210). At the second letter, the
situation worsens considerably. Anna not only miscalculates more
seriously her approach to Eliza – 'With too much force she wrote of
jealous men' (l. 253) – but attempts to conceal her growing confusion
from Stafford: 'For looks composed and careless Anna tried' (l. 257).
Stafford, perceiving her in trouble and devoutly loving her, tries to
break through the secrecy which seems to be spoiling the relationship.
But she denies there is any secrecy with a 'look so kind' that by an
ominous irony Stafford chooses to ignore his perception that she is lying:
'the fond man determined to be blind'. They are already deeply
entangled in mutual deception. In the third letter, Eliza's self-pity takes
on a new note of hurtful self-righteousness:

'She with her child a life of terrors led,
Unhappy fruit! but of a lawful bed.'   (ll. 271–2)

Anna is driven to a futile appeal to the fellow-feeling of a mother, and
her outward manifestations of distress become so clear that Stafford feels
obliged to interfere. His language is manly, but although Anna respects
him for it, the stronger feeling remains fear. When she tries to cover
up, she becomes more deeply tainted, condoning the self-pity with a sentimental indulgence which would be weak even if it were not also hypocritical:

'This plaintive style I pity and excuse,
Help when I can, and grieve when I refuse.'   (ll. 315–16)

She has become able to weave a fabric of lies, maintaining that she will
renounce this indulgence of her sympathies for the sake of Stafford's
love. 'My useless sorrows I resign' is a double lie: she knows she cannot
stop, and her sorrows are not at all for Eliza. Stafford doubts. He continues to play the matter down, answering Anna as if she were speaking
the truth, telling her to resign such 'useless sorrows'. But he is clearly
affected: 'he was kind but cool'. Outwardly there is calm, but the relationship is radically contaminated by secrecy:

A secret sorrow lived in Anna's heart,
In Stafford's mind a secret fear of art.   (ll. 331–2)

Although she is so deeply tainted, Anna reacts strongly against the particular form of Eliza's inhumanity when she writes that she has been freed by the death of her child: Anna's exclamation, 'Heartless wretch!' is in response to this rather than to Eliza's arrival. But her relationship with Stafford is paralysed –

> She must petition, yet delay'd the task,
> Ashamed, afraid, and yet compell'd to ask –   (ll. 349–50)

and in this extremity Stafford himself is shaken: 'once suspicious, he became unkind'. The relationship is in grave internal peril even before Eliza comes laughing in: 'They sate one evening, each absorb'd in gloom' (l. 353).

On Eliza's arrival, Anna attempts to continue the secrecy: 'And meeting whisper'd, "Is Eliza kind?"' (l. 357) The situation forces Stafford too into secrecy and deception:

> To nought that pass'd between the stranger-friend
> `  ` And his meek partner seem'd he to attend.   (ll. 360–1)

Both are anxious, yet, their confidence gone, they have to suffer alone. With poetic justice Anna is now is a situation parodying her life with the lady. Eliza has the manner of the unfeeling would-be seducers:

> Her friend sate laughing and at ease the while,
> Telling her idle tales with all glee
> Of careless and unfeeling levity.   (ll. 371–3)

This time Stafford can at first only look on with 'wounded pride', since Anna does not veil 'her troubles in a mask of ease', but conveys by her whole manner, 'I am a slave, subservient and afraid' (l. 377). But as the weeks pass and he assimilates the situation, a more healthy attitude begins to develop in the form of a sense of humour. When Anna maintains that she loves Eliza,

> "'Tis well,' said Stafford 'then your loves renew;
> Trust me, your rivals, Anna, will be few.'   (ll. 392–3)

Anna naturally cannot find this very funny, though Eliza is shrewd enough to see the strength of love which lies behind it and prepares for a change of tactic. Anna is still paralysed between conflicting impulses, between the courage deriving from desperation and the urge to conceal deriving from 'a parent's pride'. But Stafford, although temporarily driven to 'measures indirect', is not radically tainted any more: 'He held all fraud and cunning in disdain' (l. 417).

In the description of his overhearing the coversation between Anna and Eliza there is none of the relish of the father in 'The Learned Boy'. The focus is on Anna's suffering and we only learn through the passive voice that Stafford saw it:

> In Anna's looks and falling tears were seen
> How interesting had their subjects been.   (ll. 428–9)

Eliza's new threats are ironical in the light of what follows: it becomes true

> 'That you and Stafford know each other's mind;
> I must depart, must on the earth be thrown,
> Like one discarded, worthless and unknown.'   (ll. 431–3)

But meanwhile Anna is driven to despair. From the climactic sense of danger as Stafford overhears both the threats and the expression of despair, the focus shifts suddenly to his mature perspective: 'Stafford, amused with books, and fond of home . . .' (l. 462). The tension during the telling of his tale is maintained by the reminder of Eliza's 'flattering smile' set against Anna holding the sleeping boy whose stable home would have been shattered if his father had been less wise. But it is clear that there is no actual danger, from the enjoyment Stafford gets from the telling: Caliph Harun, he says, with an ironic glance at himself, 'Ruled, for a tyrant, admirably well' (l. 473). Similarly, there is clearly a raised eyebrow at Eliza when he says, 'wo to all whom he found poaching there'. He shows a thorough understanding of Anna's failing and the consequent suffering:

> 'He sigh'd for pleasure while he shrank from wrong . . .'
>   (l. 481)

> 'He felt degraded, and the struggling mind
> Dared not be free and could not be resign'd.'   (ll. 520–1)

The forgiveness is equally thorough, based not only on pity, but on both self-knowledge – 'his own failings taught him to be kind' – and reason:

> '. . . if his morals had received a stain,
> His bitter sorrows made him pure again.'   (ll. 556–7)

Both women realise the application of the story, but Stafford continues with the clinching description of Eliza's closet in order to give them both time to sort out their 'hurried passions'. The second cycle of Anna's troubles is like, the first, buried in Stafford's frankness and generosity of mind, and Eliza does not have to be expelled by force: she has been so thoroughly placed by Stafford's larger humanity that her own reflections are enough to make her seek 'unseen her miserable home'. The structure of the tale is thus the reverse of 'Advice'. In 'Advice', a prevailingly comic tale takes a sudden turn at the end towards an unexpected seriousness; in 'The Confidant', a situation which seems grave for much of the tale is resolved by largely comic means. The gravely threatened relationship is restored to stability through the wise forgiveness of Stafford, and holds every promise of future richness.

In 'The Frank Courtship' (Tale VI), there is never any serious threat that the relationship between the main characters, Sybil and Josiah, might go wrong, but its health is defined partly by opposition to the marriage of Sybil's parents. Jonas Kindred is too much the head of his household to see the best of his wife. When he is not there, she has 'a firm presence and a steady eye'; when he is present, she drops her 'look and tone', and although he rules 'unquestion'd', he is also 'alone'. Peace reigns in his house: not the kind 'Where all with one consent in union move' (l. 28), but the kind based on an imperative which 'Commands, by making all inferiors still' (l. 30). An apparent digression on the family's form of puritanism takes to a limit the ironies of its 'independence'. In the little picture of Cromwell they keep are focused the ambivalent attitude towards pride –

> For there in lofty air was seen to stand
> The bold protector of the conquer'd land –   (ll. 57–8)

and the irony of all independencies – Cromwell, having rid 'the house of every knave and drone', is 'Forced, though it grieved his soul, to rule alone' (l. 62). But although the ironies are sharp – it was Cromwell who conquered the land he protected, and he created his own loneliness – the tone is not bitter. The irony of Cromwell forced to rule alone carries to a limit the irony of grave Jonas Kindred ruling his family of Independents, but the harmless little ritual with which they examine the portrait emphasises the reality of family life which manages nonetheless to survive:

> The stern still smile each friend approving gave,
> Then turn'd the view, and all again were grave.   (ll. 63–4)

It is, though, a way of life from which not only grace but also Grace is absent.[8] Gloom is the norm:

> No lively print or picture graced the room;
> A plain brown paper lent its decent gloom.   (ll. 49–50)

And Jonas is also aligned theologically with the old dispensation in the couplet,

Sarah called Abraham lord! and who could be,
So Jonas thought, a greater man than he?   (ll. 11–12)

The reference is to the several places, most notably to *St John* 8. 52 ff.
('Before Abraham was, I am'), in which Abraham is contrasted with
Christ as the representative of the old order of the Law which was
supplanted by Christian Grace. The first reaction against the family's
gloom – 'few yet lived, to languish and to mourn' (l. 77) – is that of the
aunt with whom Sybil is sent to live, who has shown a natural reflux
against a mourning way of life:

> Twelve months her sables she in sorrow wore,
> And mourn'd so long that she could mourn no more.
>   (ll. 81–2)

The criticism is again levelled more at Jonas:

> He knew her rich and frugal; for the rest,
> He felt no care, or, if he felt, suppress'd.   (ll. 89–90)

Sybil's reaction to the new situation is by no means passive, and she
begins to experience a way of living which is potentially more graceful:
'The light vocations of the scene she graced' (l. 108). It is also potentially dangerous: when Jonas wants to see his daughter again the aunt
encourages her to dissemble, to hide her now gay young mind beneath
a 'grave conformity' of dress and prim expression. But unlike weaker
characters in Crabbe, she is not radically contaminated by the temporary
hypocrisy:

> Vain as she was – and flattery made her vain –
> Her simulation gave her bosom pain.   (ll. 135–6)

With Josiah, too, potential faults are more in the eye of the observer
than actually in him. The 'treacherous' think his look is 'sly'; to the
friendly it is merely 'keen'. His 'brown locks' associate him with the
wall-paper of the Kindreds' house, but they 'curl'd graceful on his
head'. Those who think him material for jest, 'Upon his virtues must
their laughter found' (l. 165), and he is 'not of *this* ashamed'. The bargaining between Jonas and Josiah's widowed mother foreshadows the
major exchange between Josiah and Sybil. It is similar in that it is
partly a battle, but different in that it is conducted by deception –
'Pleased to comply, yet seeming to reject' (l. 179) – and in that money
is a major consideration:

> . . . she, like him, was politic and shrewd,
> With strong desire of lawful gain embued.   (ll. 176–7)

Love is of minor significance: if the bargain is sealed, 'The pair must love whenever they should meet' (l. 173). To Jonas the discussion is a purely formal matter: there is no room for the operation of Grace or grace.

Before she returns, Sybil has already begun to find playing cards with her aunt, which once seemed so daring and exciting, an arid pursuit. New feelings, 'not so well defined', draw her towards a different sort of gloom from her father's:

> Rather the nut-tree shade the nymph preferr'd,
> Pleased with the pensive gloom and evening bird.
>
> (ll. 204–5)

Poor Jonas is very shocked:

> 'She – O Susannah! – to the world belongs . . .
> And reads soft tales of love, and sings love's soft'ning songs.'
>
> (ll. 240, 242)

His dignity is a little undermined by his exasperation at Sybil's being 'vainly grave when not a man is near'. It is one thing to be angry at the conceit of her romantic–pensive role-playing, but another to wish she would put her gravity to more use as a means of attracting the right sort of man. When he thinks he is in control and apportions roles to his wife and himself – she will advise Sybil while he uses threats – Sybil's greater histrionic agility rapidly reduces him from 'Girl! I reject thee from my sober roof' (l. 260), to silence and theatrical gesture: 'Jonas then lifted up his hands on high' (l. 265). Her mother makes an even worse job of her part of the two-pronged attack: attempting to clarify the nature of Josiah, she incidentally gives away the true nature of her own kind of marriage:

> 'Union like ours is but a bargain made
> By slave and tyrant – he will be obey'd.'   (ll. 272–3)

Puritan commercial values extend to seeing marriage as a 'bargain', but hers seems not to have been a very fair one. In such a context, the climax of her argument seems less like a piece of prudent advice than a *cri de coeur*: 'Yield but esteem, and only try for peace' (l. 293). More revealingly still, she exposes what such a marriage means in terms of human feeling when she gives as a reason for not marrying for love:

> '. . . should your husband die before your love,
> What needless anguish must a widow prove!'   (ll. 290–1)

Even if Jonas had not, as we later see, made such a misjudgement based on Sybil's appearance, his wife would have been on very shaky ground saying,

> 'Can eyes and feelings inward worth descry?
> No! my fair daughter, on our choice rely.'   (ll. 282–3)

What they have chosen is a form of marriage which on her own showing leaves much to be desired. Sybil's preliminary conception of love is equally inadequate:

> 'At my forbidding frown, his heart must ache,
> His tongue must falter, and his frame must shake.'
>
>   (ll. 296–7)

As the frown suggests, it is merely the reverse of her father's. With characteristic naughtiness she goes on to shock her mother's sense of religious decorum:

> 'He kneel and tremble at a thing of dust!
> He cannot, child:' – The child replied, 'He must.'   (ll. 304–5)

But when he does, she finds her role is not so clearly charted as she now imagines it to be.

As a further touch to his officious preparation for the meeting of the young people, Jonas passes on to Josiah a secret, of which the chief effect is to discredit himself: 'Deign to wear a mask/A few dull days .../I wore it once ...' (ll. 315–16, 318). Against his fussing attempts to conceal what he takes to be Sybil's true nature and his concern to reassure Josiah that he will eventually 'rule unquestion'd and alone', as he does himself, Josiah's reply has a healthy note of honesty and directness: 'Can I cause fear, who am myself afraid?' (l. 326) Sybil, meanwhile, is beginning to move beyond her initial crude romantic views:

> 'Nothing shall tempt, shall force me to bestow
> My hand upon him – yet I wish to know.'   (ll. 329–30)

Since Crabbe treats so often of experiences and situations as they are affected by time, one regrets on occasion that the couplet form he chose to use is not particularly well adapted to rendering consciousness through time. The inadequacy is obvious on thinking, for example, of the dramatic flux of feeling in the 'If it were done, when 'tis done' speech in *Macbeth*. Sybil's words are a minor attempt to capture consciousness-in-time. 'Tempt' is corrected to 'force': she is, she discovers while she is speaking, open to tempting, and she does wish to know what this 'creature' is really like. The final comic preparation for the main dramatic scene is Jonas leading in the youth and hastening to retire, like an over-eager Pandarus, conferring one last 'meaning look' on his daughter.

The scene itself is one of Crabbe's major successes. In form it owes something to the tradition of courtship bargaining, of which the scene between Mirabell and Millamant in Congreve's *Way of the World* is one of the most famous examples; but it is no mere battle of wits. The fullness of human warmth engaged is emphasised by contrast with the bargains referred to earlier in the tale. The full fluctuation of feeling is caught as they each explore the other and try to throw him off balance, establishing in the process a relationship between equals which is more truly free than that of their elders. Dramatic tension accumulates rapidly as the silence is prolonged:

> The couple gazed – were silent, and the maid
> Look'd in his face, to make the man afraid.   (ll. 337–8)

Josiah is not so easily disconcerted, and they form their first impressions of each other under conditions of equality. Sybil notes the obvious integrity but also 'something of the pride/That indicates the wealth it seems to hide' (ll. 349–50) and the slyness which others had noted before her. Josiah notes, as well as the beauty and vivacity, a degree of 'scorn or pride' and – 'if his mind the virgin's meaning caught' – even some coquetry. As the silence is prolonged further, Sybil tries to restore her self-confidence by making one of her playful remarks to herself – 'I wonder if he speaks'. Suddenly he says, 'Slow in her ear – "Fair maiden, art thou well?"' (l. 367) She tries to recover from the shock produced by his quiet tones by wittily pretending to take it as a doctor's question:

> 'Art thou physician?' she replied; 'my hand,
> My pulse, at least, shall be at thy command.'   (ll. 368–9)

But she has shown her confusion by the blunder of 'hand', quickly corrected to the more modest 'pulse'. Josiah immediately takes advantage of her confusion and kneels to kiss the ironically offered pulse. The action has a spontaneity the older generation has forgotten about and breaks through the poses they have both assumed with a warmth of feeling which shows the role-playing to be only the surface expression of something much deeper. Sybil responds with equal spontaneity, 'The rosy colour rising in her cheek' (l. 372), before she again tries to field him with wit:

> Then sternness she assumed, and – 'Doctor, tell,
> Thy words cannot alarm me – am I well?'   (ll. 374–5)

'Thy words cannot alarm me' is slotted well into her vivacious response, but again shows her susceptibility to feelings 'not so well defined'. 'Am

I well?' is an invitation for compliments, which Josiah declines to take up. Instead he plays up to the role of doctor and uses it to make some very sharp criticisms of Sybil –

> 'Within that face sit insult and disdain;
> Thou art enamour'd of thyself . . .' –   (ll. 390–1)

while still retaining the tone of civilised, even gracious, conversation. She in turn is equally sharp:

> '. . . for a sinner, thou'rt too much a saint . . .
> So void of grace . . .'   (ll. 419, 433)

She has allowed exterior things to distort her sense of values; he has let his sober values assume an exterior form which is irrelevant to their real spirit. In outward appearance, if not in inward life, he seems as 'formal' (she uses the word four times) as her father. Both make their criticisms 'with good will' and with honesty in a way which establishes their relationship as both freer and more gracious than the older generation's.

The contrast is emphasised by the following scene, in which Sybil's mother suggests introducing a deviousness so conspicuously absent from the major dialogue:

> 'Can you not seem to woo a little while
> The daughter's will, the father to beguile? . . .
> Will you preserve our peace, Josiah? say.'   (ll. 458–9, 461)

Josiah replies that peace will rest more securely on his 'care and truth'. In the final scene Jonas again plays his role of angry father teaching a lesson to a daughter, 'Born', as he says without conscious irony, 'of wilfulness and pride.' In playing up to him, Sybil enjoys the comedy, but she is only meeting him on his own level of indirection, and by the end she has worked back not only to an admission that is 'of grace' in both senses of the word, but to a directness which shows how fully she has cut through the layers of role-playing to a level of real and pure feeling:

> 'Dear child! in three plain words thy mind express–
> Wilt thou have this good youth?' – 'Dear father! yes.'
>   (ll. 495–6)

'The Frank Courtship' stands as perhaps the highest point of Crabbe's achievement. The qualities of relationship found to be most valuable in the tales discussed in this chapter – sincerity, humility, trust, directness, honesty – are celebrated most vivaciously in it. The integrity of the young people has been so evident that when Josiah says to Sybil's mother, 'Rely securely on my care and truth . . . perpetual is thy peace' (ll. 463, 465), it is quite clear that the relationship will survive time, even though this is one of the few tales in which its passage is not of central significance. Having seen it develop in its early stages, we are left certain that it will continue to be a creative relationship, unlike, for instance, Dinah's and Rupert's, which suffers atrophy through time.

The writing is as graceful as the relationship. Crabbe's narrative skills are deployed in all the strength of their prime. As in many of the tales, a key word, in this case 'grace', is repeated at important stages of the poem in order to focus one of the levels of meaning. The pace of the narrative varies, with a flexibility characteristic of the best tales, from the rapid summary of the years of Sybil's childhood and adolescence, through the lightly sketched details of the scenes between Sybil and her parents before the introduction to Josiah, to the almost minute-by-minute rendering of the crucial interview between the young couple. The dramatic tension of the interview, built up by the fine stroke of the very protracted silence, is sustained through the rapid flow of the dialogue, made more pointed by the rhyming of the couplets. The quality of the relationship between Sybil and Josiah is emphasised by the careful contrasts with the deviousness apparent in the scenes with the older generation, and the lonely imperiousness of Jonas is taken, in a characteristic manner, to a limit in the portrait of Cromwell. The *Tales* of 1812 as a whole show a fecundity of imagination and a rich awareness of the possibilities of human relationship, of which 'The Frank Courtship' can stand as the most accomplished example. 'Procrastination', which is equally deeply imagined, can stand as the finest example of a failure in relationship. The collection as a whole establishes Crabbe as a short-narrative poet of a quality surpassed in English only by Chaucer. As Johnson said of Shakespeare in the words quoted in Chapter 1, 'he who has mazed his imagination, in following the phantoms which other writers raise up before him, may here be cured of his delirious extasies, by reading human sentiments in human language; by scenes from which a hermit may estimate the transactions of the world, and a confessor predict the progress of the passions.' No eighteenth-century novelist equals him in the range of contemporary moral and social attitudes he has dramatised, and for an adequate comparison, aside from Chaucer and Shakespeare, one has to turn to some of the major novelists of the nineteenth century.

6 *Tales of the Hall*, 1819 (1)

After the *Tales* of 1812, Crabbe seems first to have thought of attempting a larger-scale work, but abondoned the attempts before bringing them near completion. The material printed by Ward as 'Tracy', which is dated 1 January 1813, was, it is clear from some accompanying prose notes, to have been part of a long work bringing together several groups of characters and several themes. In one of the Murray notebooks there are some drafts and notes for two dramas, 'The Sisters' and 'The Husband', which date from November of the same year. To judge from what is extant, Crabbe was wise to discontinue these works, particularly the plays, which are melodramatic in conception and show none of the feeling for drama achieved, for example, at the end of 'The Frank Courtship' or in 'The Squire and the Priest'. A number of short stanzaic poems were written in 1814, but it seems, perhaps because of the recent death of his wife and the move to Trowbridge, to have been an unproductive year. On 2 February, he wrote to the Dean of Lincoln: 'I am so suspended in Mind that I can do nothing, not even rhyme' (Folger Shakespeare Library collection).

The gestation of *Tales of the Hall* probably began in 1815. In a letter written late in November to Miss Charter, he mentions writing 'at some Hours a Book on Divinity and at others poetical Recollections and there are times when I feel not dissatisfied, for the one is a Duty long fixed in my Mind and the other an Amusement of some standing also' (Broadley and Jerrold p. 115). 'Villars', eventually printed as the fifth of the *Posthumous Tales*, is written shortly after the date December 1815 in Cambridge Add. MS. 4422, and it is followed by an early draft of 'Infancy', which, with some linking lines beginning 'One of the Party whom I since have known', leads into what Ward prints as '[Susan and her Lovers]'. Although 'Recollections' seems very like 'Rembrances', the title Crabbe was still toying with as late as 28 December 1818 (Huchon, p. 405), the precise form of the work was slow to emerge. In the spring of 1816, Crabbe asked Miss Charter to send him 'any short stories, especially of Ghosts and Apparitions, but they must be singular and brief or I cannot versify them' (Broadley and Jerrold, p. 131). By the end of the year he was thinking already more of correcting than of composing.[1] A Murray notebook of 1816 gives titles or other means of identification to about thirty tales, not many of which are extant in full. Drafts of what became Books VI, IX, XV, XVI and XIX show that Crabbe had already cast some 'Recollections' in the form of conversations between two brothers, George and Joel, but some drafts have no introductory material and one discarded tale, 'The Doctor's Ghost', is introduced by, among others unnamed, a Boswell and a Dr Dillon. Correction continued through 1817: on 20 August he wrote to Miss Charter, 'I have copied 300 lines this day' (Broadley and Jerrold, p. 187). On the third of the same month he had written to Colburn about 'Remembrances' in a way which implies that it was already conceived of as a unified work: 'The Poem I have been about for a long Time past is a continued Relation and I have not attempted any Verses which do not relate to this Poem' (Princeton University Library). The Huntington notebook, which has the date of 9 December 1817 roughly half-way through, has for each of the complete tales some introductory lines of discussion between George and the brother now named Joseph, who eventually became Richard, but the relationship is much less developed than in the printed *Tales of the Hall*. At the front of the book there is another list of accumulated material which is again surprisingly large. From extant lists alone, it seems that Crabbe wrote over thirty tales between 1812 and 1819 which he did not print. Of these about one third survive in part or whole. The quality of what he rejected was probably not high – of the three unpublished tales in the Huntington notebook, 'The Squire of Eldon' is very routine work and 'The Coroner's Inquest' and 'The Laurel' are very poor – but he clearly remained a much more fertile writer than one might assume from such entries in the journal quoted in the *Life* as 'Make up my thirty lines for yesterday and today' (*Life*, p. 248). 'The Lover of Virtue', printed in *New Poems* from a Murray notebook, is characteristic of the surviving rejected material. The intention was to contrast the sentimental verbalising of the lover with the actuality of his cruelty. But there is a basic fault in the structure, making the irony very clumsy. The opening sentimental monologue of the lover, which is developed at length in order to make the sudden deflation at the end more effective, cannot on reflection be credited. In the later Huntington draft, the awkwardness is made even greater, for the tale is presented by Joseph relating to George what was told him by the lover as he was dying during a naval battle. Despite the letter to Colburn, Crabbe also worked on some poems not intended for 'Remembrances': on 30 October 1817 he wrote to Mrs Leadbeater of 'some few things in the Manner of Sir Eustace Grey' (*Leadbeater Papers*, p. 350). 'The World of Dreams', first printed in 1834, almost certainly belongs to this period. It is of some interest in representing the phantasmagoria of an opium dream.

The letters to Miss Charter of the earlier half of 1818 show that little more was achieved, though by April some decisions about excluding some of the accumulated material had evidently already been taken. The new collection was not to include as many ghost stories as he had envisaged previously: 'I have already Two Ghost-Relations, one serious and one of the more comic kind and these will I daresay be thought sufficient.'[2] It seems probable that the frame of the published work was developed quite late. On 28 December 1818 Crabbe wrote to Murray, 'I have ... introduced my elder Brother to his hall', and on 22 January 1819, 'I send the three next books and they will be followed by one more which you will either include or not at your pleasure. It is the story of the Elder Brother ...' (Huchon, p. 406). Some of the material concerning George and Richard definitely dates from before this period. Although the manuscript is lost, the 1834 notes use the name Joel in the variants of Book II, which means that it probably dates from 1816. A surviving fragment containing passages resembling parts of Books VI and VII is in a Murray notebook which also belongs to 1816. Book V is referred to in the Huntington list ('Books etc. in Ruth's House. Her Story.'); and further fragments of Books IV and VI in another Murray notebook can probably be ascribed to early 1818, as they use 'Richard' but precede a discarded fragment dated 23 March 1818. But the chief surviving draft of Book VII is in a Cambridge notebook (Add. MS. 4426) in which the only date is 6 November 1818, and in none of the extant manuscript work of 1816–17 is the relationship between George and Richard centred on Richard's visit to the Hall and his anxiety to return to his wife: introductory discussions are brief and concerned with the tales, not the brothers. It seems probable, therefore, that the material relating to the brothers was expanded and focused more clearly at a late stage, perhaps very late.

The manuscript evidence is confirmed by the general impression given by the printed work that Crabbe's intention at the time of writing the introductory books was to work up a more fully integrated opus than he in fact produced. When in the first book we are given a brief introduction to the rector, the 'sister-pair' and the 'sage physician' (who never appears again) it seems that we are to encounter as the work progresses an integrated social group, which in fact we do not meet. The material on the brothers themselves, although it fits with the histories we hear in Books IV, VI, and VII, is given at such a leisurely pace that we are led to expect the brothers to figure more largely in the work as a whole than they do. Only a few of the tales are related at all closely to the characters of the brothers, and many of the introductory conversations clearly, and in a number of cases demonstrably, belong to the period when the characters were less sharply distinguished than they are, for example, in Book I. The books in which George and Richard are most clearly characterised will therefore be discussed separately from those which are really as independent as the tales of 1812. As an attempt to give unity to the whole of the *Tales of the Hall* the framing device of the two brothers must be judged a failure. The histories of George and Richard really form a separate subject, which, except in certain tales discussed in this chapter, is not constructively developed through the stories they narrate or the comments they make about them.

Our impression of George in Book I is of a man whose active life is past. He formerly led a busy life, but once loved rashly and was disillusioned. His emotional conservatism is rendered in his love of trees which take many years to mature. His political conservatism derives partly from a reaction against his own youthful experience: he now reproves those who love a political cause with boyish ardour, as he himself had once loved a woman. But it associates naturally with a basic reverence for the constitution. Unlike the previous owner of the Hall he is uninterested in 'improvements' to the property: he values it as the work of past ages. He loves the gloom of the interior with its broad brown stairs and, outside, the ancient lead on which boys, who have since died as old men, once carved their initials. But he is not fully reconciled to his present condition, for he recognises its loneliness in a way which prepares us for his final acceptance of Richard:

> Sighing, the works of former lords to see,
> 'I follow them,' he cried, 'but who will follow me?'
>
> (ll. 82–3)

That he is rather aloof is shown by his tenants' inability to give more than a physical description, but to those who are better acquainted with him, he is known as a man of integrity.

Richard's nature is more volatile: 'clashing notions and opinions strange/Lodged in his mind; all liable to change' (ll. 218–19). Unlike George's 'solemn and . . . serious view', his religion is in some disarray and largely in his wife's keeping, yet he instinctively shuns the sordid or base. His relationships are spontaneous, quickly formed and frank. With such a temperament he can afford a less conservative political position than his brother: he 'had more youthful ardour to be free'. The book concludes in a way which anticipates the end of the whole collection. Richard is conscious of his comparative poverty and apprehensive lest George meet him as a stranger. Before the meeting he tries to reassure himelf by rehearsing both the means by which the invitation reached him and a little speech in which he will declare all the ways he is not going to flatter his brother. But the fears and the prepared expression of dignity are made irrelevant by the emotional reality of the reunion. George's aloofness is almost broken by his feeling: he scorns the thought of tears, so has to turn away to hide his eyes. Richard is unable to deliver himself of his declaration of independence. It takes time before both half-brothers are in a fit condition to greet each other properly:

> At length affection, like a risen tide,
> Stood still . . .
> Each on the other's looks had power to dwell.   (ll. 342–4)

Natural human feeling asserts itself against the prepared faces of both brothers.

As an introduction to *Tales of the Hall*, the first book has not enough zest to be successful. The actual reunion is well-handled and the differences between the two brothers are gradually established, but the writing is too diffuse. It is already clear that the new collection has not the conciseness or the lively ironic structure of the *Tales* of 1812.

In Book II we learn a little more about the brothers and their meeting, but as a whole it is a badly organised book, with no sense of direction to it.

In Book III, 'Boys at School', the after-dinner conversation is interestingly focused on the question whether men are determined from an early age or whether education and experience can change them. George and the rector, Jacques, take opposite sides. To Jacques the world is a school; to George school already provides a model of what the world merely projects on a larger scale. Jacques wins the argument, and Crabbe is clearly on his side: character changes through time. George opens the conversation by sketching the history of a man he nicknames Hector, who was a bully at school and, having briefly modified his behaviour while gaining his fortune, continued later in life to bully his wife, children and servants. Jacques suggests in reply that vice is often reduced by experience. As an example he adduces another Hector, Sir Hector Blane, once the strong-armed blockhead of the school, who became a notable naval captain. At this stage, Jacques' argument is merely a version of Mandeville: the individual vice has happened to prove socially useful. Pugnacity is of benefit to society as someone has to defend the realm. George will not let this pass. He admits Sir Hector's public achievements, but insists that as an individual his shortcomings remain the same. In reply Jacques modifies his position, using Locke's image of the growing plant, and suggesting that it is the role of the educator to prune away the valueless shoots and encourage the fruitful ones.

The centre of the book is occupied by the example of Charles, whose history George asks Jacques to relate. Jacques hesitates before beginning, aware of the complexities of the case. Charles as a boy was capable of development in many directions: he was modest and civil, yet possessed of a certain basic pride. As his illusions about his talent were fostered by the lord who decided to become his patron, the pride steadily grew. When Jacques met him after the passage of some years, the pride cut him off from the comfort of human company which he needed. When Jacques next saw him, in the workhouse, he remained isolated, the pride which made him hide his wretchedness directly increasing it. Only at the point of death was he so exhausted and so relieved by the company of Jacques that the pride left him and he was able to call Jacques 'Friend!' George's summary comment is very inadequate:

> 'The man,' said George, 'you see, through life retain'd
> The boy's defects; his virtues too remain'd'.   (ll. 325–6)

At the level of cliché, it is true that the boy had seeds of both the pride and the civility which eventually overcame it. But if it had not been for Jacques' tactful but assiduous husbandry, continually seeking him out in the isolation of his pride and waiting for the moment when he was ready to renounce it, he might easily have died in the pride which was all the patron succeeded in cultivating in him.

Thinking his case here established, George then asks rhetorically whether a noble youth could help becoming a noble man. The punctuation in all editions gives the concluding tale of Harry Bland to George, but it seems much more probable that it was meant to be Jacques' final reply. If it is taken to be George's, he undermines his own argument without showing any awareness of what he has done; but the pause is parallel to Jacques' pause before relating the history of Charles, and the tale constitutes an answer to George from Jacques' established point of view. In boyhood Harry Bland was rather a prig, unable to tolerate the mistress his father took after the death of his mother, even though she evidently did all she could to conciliate the boy. But when tempted himself, his perspective altered and he kept a married woman. He retained traces of his former self, but they had been disastrously uncultivated: 'His mind approves the virtue he forsakes,/And yet forsakes her' (ll. 433–4). Jacques' view of man's potentiality for regeneration carries with it the equal possibility of degeneration.

The book is interesting in that it takes Crabbe's usual presupposition, that character is cultivated or deteriorates through the passage of time, and by challenging it against the contrary view of George explicitly vindicates it.

In a letter to Miss Charter of 25 August 1819, Crabbe said that of the *Tales of the Hall* he preferred 'the Relation of the Brothers, Richard's Education if I may so call it' (Broadley and Jerrold, p. 235). The reason was presumably that it contains much autobiographical material, for

Books IV–VI are not particularly well organised or tightly written. The description of the ageing George at the beginning of Book IV is clearly meant to contrast with the youth of Richard which is the main subject of the book. George feels that he has to buy female company with the 'costly trifles' which decorate his rooms, whereas Richard as a boy loved solitude. George cannot summon the interest to read more than half a page of a book and skips through the newspapers looking only for the conclusions, whereas Richard's interest was absorbed by the sailors' yarns and by Ruth's books. George shows some awareness of his own condition: he knows he is 'Urged by the strong demands of vanity' (l. 6). But there is a strong self-pity in the degree of his self-preoccupation: his is a 'mind diseased'. At the end of his description of his ennui, he snaps out of it, but then falters into hypochondria before acting up to his role as host:

> 'But how the day? No fairer will it be?
> Walk you? Alas? 'tis requisite for me –
> Nay, let me not prescribe – my friends and guests are free.'
>
> (ll. 43–5)

The mild autumn day on which the brothers go for a walk prompts George to think, 'Yes! doubtless we must die.' Richard's response, on the other hand, is to enjoy the present moment, transient though it is:

> '. . . we yet taste whatever we behold,
> The morn is lovely, though the air is cold.'   (ll. 67–8)

He sees harmony even in what is apparently destructive and disruptive, *because* it is transient:

> 'That gun itself, that murders all this peace,
> Adds to the charm, because it soon must cease.'   (ll. 76–7)

George translates the charm into economic terms:

> 'Look at that land – you find not there a weed . . .
> They have no – what? – no *habitat* with me.'   (ll. 80, 87)

His attitude is reductive, over-tidy: the weeds are held at a distance by the botanical term. As he continues, he briefly becomes so enthusiastic about his sheep that Richard is surprised to detect a note of delight, but George checks himself and resumes the pose he was striking at the beginning:

> 'So says my bailiff: sometimes I have tried
> To catch the joy, but nature has denied . . .
> Worn out in trials, and about to die,
> In vain to these we for amusement fly.'   (ll. 94–5, 98–9)

In the draft quoted in the 1834 edition, the conversation drifts irrele-
vantly towards a misanthropy in George, which Richard challenges; in
the final version, the emphasis returns to George's introspection and
self-pity:

> ''Tis not in trees or medals to impart
> The powerful medicine for an aching heart.'   (ll. 114–15)

But he is at least turning outwards to some extent when he speaks of
his friends enriching him and wants to hear Richard's own history.

Despite jokingly distinguishing Richard's from fictitious travellers'
tales, George is clearly expecting some sort of far-fetched yarn. He wants
to push Richard's experience to the comfortable distance of 'crocodiles
and apes'. But Richard has learnt more 'mild good sense' not only than
George expects but also than George has. In the experience Richard
relates, there is an element of mystery – 'some maddening power my
mind possess'd – but the setting is very mundane: merely the high spirits
of a young man responding to a break in a calm accidentally tipped over-
board. Instead of the clear-cut exotic creatures George imagined, 'All
was confused . . . no distinguish'd sound/Could reach me . . . An un-
defined sensation stopp'd my breath' (ll. 209, 210–11, 213). His thoughts
whirl as the waves wash over him, but there is no romantic vision of his
whole life compressed into an instant:

> '. . . such confusion on the spirit dwelt,
> That, feeling much, it knew not what it felt.'   (ll. 240–1)

There is only the 'indistinct' sense that 'hope, youth, life, love, and all
they promised' are drowned. It is in retrospect that the experience has
meaning. Clearly it is not something he *can* forget, but he knows also
that he *ought* not to forget its implications:

> 'For what to us are moments, what are hours,
> If lost our judgement, and confused our powers?'   (ll. 248–9)

The perspective provided by the threat of sudden death in a state of
confusion affects his view of day-to-day life even 'when reason slumbers'.
Richard's perspective on life has been deepened by his experience,
whereas George's was only narrowed by his.

The note of condescension in George disappears now that he sees that
Richard's mind is rich in experience, but the self-preoccupation has not
wholly gone:

> 'Thou couldst but die – the waves could but infold
> Thy warm gay heart, and make that bosom cold –
> While I – but no! Proceed, and give me truth . . .'   (ll. 275–7)

Richard relates how he was educated not so much in school as through the tales of the sailors and their wives. The young boy's sensitivities were aroused by the tales of whaling: catching cold-blooded fish seemed harmless enough,

> 'But so much blood! warm life, and frames so large
> To strike, to murder – seem'd an heavy charge.'   (ll. 333–4)

His sense of wonder was stimulated by the description of the arctic sun, which

> 'Red, but not flaming, roll'd, with motion slow,
> On the world's edge, but never dropt below.'   (ll. 337–8)

His sense of pity was cultivated by watching the bereaved women as they waited on the beach for the bodies of their men to be washed ashore: 'Strange that a boy could love these scenes, and cry/In very pity' (ll. 383–4). His mother was anxious lest such experience might be bad for him – 'My Richard, do not learn to grieve' – but his sensibility was clearly developed by such vicarious experience, much as Crabbe's own must have been. He even begins to learn to make moral discriminations –

> '... some, the fond of pity, would enjoy
> The earnest sorrows of the feeling boy' –   (ll. 321–2)

though he fed promiscuously on whatever he could find – 'The food I loved, I thought not of its kind' (l. 346). None of these details about Richard's education, except lines 383–4, is in the Murray draft of this passage, though the general drift is similar. Nature, too, helped to develop his sensibility. His favourite spots were memorised 'not by the marks they bare,/But by the thoughts that were created there' (ll. 461–462). The sea-gulls in the storm that 'calmly rode the restless waves among' fostered his 'dreams of princely power', while the lapwing and curlew 'with wild notes my fancied power defied,/And mock'd the dreams of solitary pride' (ll. 457–8). Unlike George as described at the beginning of the book, Richard clearly remains as capable of enjoying the present moment as he had been when a child, for at the end of the book he breaks off his narration: 'this soft autumnal gloom/Bids no delay – at night I will resume' (ll. 486–7).

In Book v ('Ruth'), Richard tells George in more detail about two particular sources of his rather irregular education, the books in Ruth's mother's house and the pathetic history of Ruth herself. Like George, Ruth's mother had had a traumatic experience in earlier life, but unlike George she had been able to digest it, and the young Richard wanted to find out how. Unfortunately, Crabbe does not pursue the question: he

only reproduces the story of Ruth. Ruth's is a case in which character
and history are not so closely related as they usually are in Crabbe: she
is essentially a passive victim. But the meaninglessness of her suffering
is not really faced in the tale, and it remains obscure how her mother
regained serenity and what the young Richard learnt from the story.

At the beginning of Book VI, George again recurs to his own experience, which he describes as a 'disease; a poison'. In contrast, Richard's
experience of love is fundamentally healthy, though a little eccentric.
The eccentricity is emphasised by Matilda's father, who wonders why
the lovers delayed so long in coming to an open understanding –

> 'More had he wonder'd had he known esteem
> Was all we mention'd, friendship was our theme.'
>
> (ll. 117–18)

The central episode of the Book is an incident entitled in several manuscripts 'The Happy Day'. The title was in some degree ironic, for
although the day is the memorable one on which love was first declared,
Richard's vacillation of mood makes him several times far from happy.
The major vacillation has already been discussed in Chapter I above
(pp. 7–8). From the sense of being totally in command of the situation
which he gains from the view on the upper of the two routes to Brandon
of the 'spacious bay' and the fleet in 'full sail', under man's 'full
control', he is thrust suddenly into confusion by seeing a 'rival soldier'
with his Matilda. His wavering impression of Matilda is suggested by a
'but' clause within a 'yet' clause:

> 'She was all coldness – yet I thought a look,
> But that corrected, tender welcome spoke.'   (ll. 215–16)

He is vaguely aware that he must not 'violate the social law', but from
pleasure at the way man's power 'guides the ship man's art has made'
he has moved to 'guideless rage'. As his fantasy grows, he casts himself
in the role of stooge used to feed her vanity, and he is seized by a com-
pulsive voyeurism: 'I must the pair attend,/And watch this horrid
business to its end' (ll. 245–6). Every slight action is twisted to fit in
with the illusion which now has him in its grip:

> 'O! you will make me room – 'tis very kind,
> And meant for him – it tells him he must mind;
> Must not be careless: – I can serve to draw
> The soldier on, and keep the man in awe.'   (ll. 253–6)

Even after he has realised that the soldier is no rival, but a friend's
husband, he is far from being in control. His peevishness becomes such
that

> 'Vex'd and unhappy I indeed had been,
> Had I not something in my charmer seen
> Like discontent.'   (ll. 300–2)

But again his mood fluctuates and the happiness becomes so intense that they feel the need to 'veil the gladness in a show of grief':

> 'There is between us and a watery grave
> But a thin plank, and yet our fate we brave.'   (ll.312–13)

The place where he eventually declares his love and asks for Matilda's reply is one in which it is easy to lose one's way, and after his success he again works himself into a state of illusion: 'There are no woes, and sorrows are but dreams' (ll. 361). So he feels in need of some sort of experience of pain in order to bring him to himself again. The sight of 'a shepherd old and lame'

> 'seem'd my blood to tame:
> And I was thankful for the moral sight,
> That soberised the vast and wild delight.'   (ll. 385–7)

Many critics have noted that the texture of the writing in *Tales of the Hall* is in general much looser than in the *Tales* of 1812. This book is not even among the best of the later collection, but in its leisurely manner it conveys much of the strangely vacillating mind of a timid, imaginative young man in love.

Book VII, more than the books concerning Richard, is in a form approaching the 'progress'. We do not see the final stage of George's development, for that is reserved until the concluding book, but his history as a young man is given in a more straightforward chronological form. When it is his turn to relate his experience of love, George can no longer sustain his quasi-avuncular attitude. He has to confess to a far greater folly than Richard's and he fears contempt. He gave his youth to a particularly fruitless form of the romantic dream, and his subsequent life was soured by disillusion. 'Then was I pleased in lonely ways to tread' (l. 66); now, as a consequence, he remains lonely. The episode in which George protected Rosabella from the cows survives in an earlier form in Cambridge Add. MS. 4422, printed by Ward as 'The Amours of G[eorge]'. The draft is not distinguished, but its octosyllabics have a pace which was lost in rewriting.

> And, plucking forth an oaken Bough,
> I ran like Guy to fight the Cow,

for example, becomes laboured into:

>'Was each a cow like that which challenged Guy,
>I had resolved t'attack it, and defy
>In mortal combat! to repel or die.'   (ll. 245–7)

On the whole, a scene which might have been very comic is actually rather dull.

The second significant influence on the young George was his thrifty uncle, a type characterised well by his banter of bad puns. For him 'golden numbers' were more important in ledgers than in verse. George absorbed something from him which showed more fully later. But meanwhile the romantic dream had seriously reduced his capacities for normal involvement in human life, and in fact its effects are still with him at the time of relating his history to Richard.

In the central episode of the book, this preoccupied, introspective young man is sent on a trivial commercial errand to a firm with the bathetic name of Clutterbuck and Co. He notes some lack of cleanliness in the house he is sent to, but his first reaction is chiefly resentment at the intrusion of the maid on his romantic self-preoccupation. Left to await the representative of Clutterbuck and Co., his response shifts steadily towards a moral condemnation of the condition of the room. The slow build-up of the scene makes the reader anticipate the reappearance of Rosabella, and her first words fit the expectations the description of the room has aroused, but suddenly she switches to George's own idiom: 'Art thou come at last?' She falters only slightly – 'A thousand welcomes' is not the right tone – and easily picks it up again. George meanwhile is simultaneously aware of the present tawdriness and the former beauty it overlays, 'the same and not the same'. The outrageous question, 'has your heart been faithful?' momentarily stings him into self-defensive anger; but most of Rosabella's arguments are so strong that he is sufficiently perplexed for her to attempt a seductive song. This cools his anger, but his reason will not be blinded by decadent romantic pastoralism. What really moves him is the truth. Although there is much self-pity in her attitude, her repentance is genuine.

Rosabella's repentance creates a crux for Crabbe's ethic: the pattern of habit culminating in a trap is brought into collision with the basic Christian concept of a permanently accessible forgiveness. The allusion in the Cambridge draft (quoted by Ward) to the forgiveness of the woman taken in adultery was probably made less specific in the final version to avoid associating George too closely with Christ, but his forgiveness is a truly Christian response, made convincingly unsaintly by the prudent reservation that she must change her way of life. It is a reservation which releases him from the obligation to marry, for habit proves too strong; but it does not release him from the obligation to pity. As a result of his assiduity, she is saved from despair, even though she is incapable of changing her way of life before death confronts her. The death of Rosabella challenges George too to a revaluation of 'the end of man'; but he is equally bound by habit and reverts to the values of his uncle. A physical illness of his own is necessary to bring him to fuller knowledge of his spiritual poverty. He is, finally, the man we met in Book I, 'The future fearing, while he feels the past' (l. 826), unable as yet to live adequately in the present, but ready to absorb the enriching influence of relationship with Richard.

Books IV, VI and VII are not among Crabbe's best work, and Book VII especially is too long, but the difference between the two brothers, caused largely by their very different histories of experience, is developed interestingly. The interest would have been greater if Crabbe had gone on to show the difference as it manifested itself in varying responses to subsequent tales. The progress of the influence of Richard on George also remains untraced, though something of it can be inferred from Books XVIII and XXII. At the beginning of Book XVIII, we are given a foretaste of the change in George. When Richard is worried that Matilda's letters do not seem to show their usual degree of affection, George brushes his illusions aside with an ease which shows he has fully come to terms with his own past behaviour – ' "Fancy!" said George, "the self-tormentor's pain" ' (l. 12) – and he introduces the tale of Ellen with a remark more relevant to himself than to her:

> 'Nor dare I take upon me to maintain
> That hearts once broken never heal again.'   (ll. 110–11)

The change in his attitude towards the future is indicated in his description of the house he sends Richard to inspect. The previous owner died before he had time to complete his planned alterations: 'Something he wish'd, but had not time to do;/A cold ere yet the falling leaf...' (ll. 44–5) George warns Richard to 'guard well against the falling leaf': his fear is no longer of the future, but that the future may be all too short.

Book XXII, 'The Visit Concluded', is the best of the frame books. One of its strengths is the representation in Richard of the disproportionate effects of temporary depression. At the beginning, George again asks Richard to look at the house with the intention of finding out its best aspects: 'Find out the something to admire in all' (l. 13). But when he receives a cold farewell from Jacques, Richard broods on it, magnifying his adverse impression out of all proportion until he can call Jacques heartless. At this stage, he can console himself for the apparent fickleness of friends with reflections on the permanent friendship of marriage.

But when he meets the sisters (described in Book VIII), he goes beyond the proper limits of sympathetic friendship and projects his own mood on to them:

> He judged they must have many a heavy hour
> When the mind suffers from a want of power.   (ll. 52–3)

In fact, 'few and short such times of suffering were/In Lucy's mind' (ll. 60–1), and Jane's 'flights' 'were always pure, and oft sublime'. Even in his present mood, Richard cannot misinterpret their manner towards him – 'Their tone was kind, and was responsive too' (l. 73) – but he is too preoccupied with his own thoughts to pay much attention to what they say. They know George's love for him and represent Richard's staying longer almost as an obligation: 'your Brother knows you now,/ But to exist without you knows not how . . . you can give/Pleasure to one by whom a number live' (ll. 76–7, 80–1). But Richard neither says nor listens very much, for he is preoccupied with brooding about his own illusory view of the situation. His mood imposes on George a way of feeling which the sisters have rightly said is not really his at all:

> 'He kindly says, "Defer the parting day,"
> But yet may wish me in his heart away.'   (ll. 90–1)

The episode of the child serves to indicate the injustice of Richard's feelings more fully. Lucy has really been rejected, yet even so she does the favour to her former lover of futilely trying to educate his child. There is no external obligation, the child is 'unproductive', and Jane's view is dismissive – 'Train not an idiot to oblige a slave' (l. 131) – yet even so Lucy undertakes it. Richard has sufficient tact not to put questions about the present situation of Jane's former lover, but he is quite incapable of generalising from Lucy's behaviour to his own, of seeing that in his case too the heart should be ruling the head.

On Richard's return to the Hall, the brothers, 'sad themselves', naturally find themselves dwelling on 'saddening subjects', such as the sisters; but George has changed. With his plan for Richard's future now nearly complete, he has learnt not to live in the past or to let its suffering infect the present:

> George was willing all this woe to spare,
> And let to-morrow be to-morrow's care.   (ll. 144–5)

Richard had been unable to be blind to all the beauty of the new house, but he finds something to complain of: 'The price indeed. . .' George replies that money is not the main consideration: what matters far more is the kind of neighbours one has, the kind of people one puts oneself into relationship with. The awkwardness of the final morning is very finely

rendered. Richard's hand, eye, tongue and mind are all doing different
things, showing his disorientation and confusion:

> Richard his hand upon a paper laid, –
> His vacant eye upon the carpet stray'd;
> His tongue was talking something of the day,
> And his vex'd mind was wandering on his way. (ll. 176–9)

The situation is very tense, as each observes, conscious that he is being
observed:

> Each of his Brother took a steady view, –
> As actor he, and as observer too. (ll. 184–5)

Richard is torn between his petulance – George 'Appear'd not as his
Brother should appear' (l. 189) – and the recognition that he himself is
not feeling in the way he should – 'would I see/My Brother wretched
but to part with me?' (ll. 192–3). Instead of doing something to alter the
situation, he turns in on himself in 'sore division' and expects all the
effort to come from George. Yet when George does do something, suggesting they should 'fight like men with grief', Richard, stepping back
to judge, finds him 'rather wise than kind', although he cannot, even
when trying, locate anything specific:

> He thought some change appear'd – yet fail'd to prove,
> Even as he tried, abatement in the love. (ll. 221–2)

Unable to find anything real, he seizes on an absurd reason for dissatisfaction:

> George had been peevish when the subject rose,
> And never fail'd the parting to oppose. (ll. 227–8)

When George tries to break through the mutual reserve by talking of
his needs for someone to care for and to be looked after by, Richard is
thrown into further confusion:

> Something like war within his bosom strove –
> His mild, kind nature, and his proud self-love. (ll. 251–2)

His depression is too self-centred for him to be able to respond in terms
of George's needs, and his reply is concerned instead with his own
illusion that George's attitude towards him has changed. Briefly, he
entertains the possibility that 'something in my spirit lives' accounting
for the change, but he is quick to seek an external cause again: 'not in
thee I trace/Alone this change, it is in all the place' (ll. 293–4). As he
goes on, it emerges that this means only Jacques, for he has to admit
that the sisters were generous. Richard is not convinced about Jacques

by George's answer, but cannot think of an adequate reply, so he changes the subject:

> Even from his Brother's cheerfulness he drew
> Something to vex him – what, he scarcely knew:
> So he evading said . . .   (ll. 338–40)

But finding yet another apparent source for his depression –

> 'Matilda writes not; and, when last she wrote,
> I read no letter – 'twas a trader's note' –   (ll. 342–3)

he at last realises the absurdity of saying that all are out of step except himself:

> 'Madmen may say that they alone are sane,
> And all beside have a distemper'd brain;
> Something like this I feel . . .'   (ll. 348–50)

The depression is essentially causeless, and to search for a cause is merely to feed the illusion.

But, even now, Richard is too proud to withdraw his aspersions on George's hospitality: 'home has health, and that is comfort still'. It is George who fully commits himself, though he knows the vulnerability which is inseparable from fully engaged relationship. He speaks

> As one who to his friend his heart reveals,
> And all the hazard with the comfort feels.   (ll. 356–7)

He has learnt that life is impoverished unless the self is at risk. At first it seems as if he might want Richard as a kind of possession: 'a friend to gain,/And then to lose, is but to purchase pain' (ll. 362–3). But in fact he wants him 'To grow beside me as my trees have grown' (l. 381), to be beside him, yet to be free-growing, living his own life. He now explains that it was his recognition of Richard's independent life as husband and father which made him finally desist from his repeated requests to prolong the stay. If Richard had shown himself dependent George would indeed have been indifferent towards him; if he had thought in terms of money, George would have paid his 'debt' and sent him home, 'Nor glad nor sorry that he came or went' (l. 395). Richard has not seen George as an object to be exploited –

> 'Till every girl and boy had learn'd to prate
> Of uncle George, his gout, and his estate' –   (ll. 398–9)

so they are both to keep what they have learnt to value in each other. They will fulfil mutual need but will have mutual independence as well: freedom is not to be lost but encompassed in their way of life. As he gives him the house, George asks Richard's pardon: "'twas not my design/To give surprise; a better view was mine' (ll. 453–4). It is not clear what his design was: perhaps it is left deliberately obscure in an attempt to conceal the awkwardness in naturalistic terms of George allowing Richard to go through the unnecessary motions of an apparent parting. But although it is a little clumsy, the device is fully justified by the way it enables Crabbe to face and reject one of the possible false inferences from 'The Lover's Journey': misunderstanding through projection of mood is very easy, but through frankness and generosity it can be overcome and the truth known, the comedy having gone full circle. Secondly, it can act as a diagram of the complete relationship of the brothers, which we are not given in full: the coldness of former years has been replaced by a warm, mellow relationship as conclusively as Richard's illusion is destroyed by George's generosity. Thirdly, although it takes a temporarily sour form, Richard's independence is established beyond doubt: unless he is wanted for himself he does not want to stay, so George's judgement of him is demonstrated to be accurate. Fourthly, George having shown through his action that he now knows where true value lies, Richard can show in a temporarily distorted way that he also knows: he is wrong about Jacques, but at least his mistake manifests a true sense of what friendship should be.

In conclusion, George emphasises his own need and repeats that it will only be fulfilled through a free relationship: if he became the 'patron' instead of the 'friend' he would quickly degenerate into the capriciousness we saw at the beginning of Book IV. So he freely shows where he is vulnerable: if he ever does behave like a superior, they must be cold towards him to demonstrate *his* dependence on *them*:

'Then shall I woo forgiveness, and repent,
   Nor bear to lose the blessings Heaven has lent.'   (ll. 509–10)

'But this was needless', and so is reply from Richard: 'All felt the good that all desired t'impart' (l. 512). They have all found and know that they have found what enriches life. Crabbe concludes by wishing his reader equal health: 'Health, reader, and repose!' Like some of the tales of 1812, this concluding book is a celebration of the fruits of good human relationship. Although there is very little outward drama or event, Richard's temporary depression and George's new-found maturity are very finely rendered.

'The Natural Death of Love' (XIV) is a book which Crabbe tried to relate to the frame material, but not very successfully. The opening paragraphs on Jacques are perhaps more relevant than they may seem: his emphasis on moral action at the expense of 'higher points' of doctrine is parallel to the discovery of Henry and Emma that the future of their marriage lies in collaborative effort rather than the romantic dream which time has proved to be insubstantial. The reliance which, to the confusion of his parishioners, he nonetheless places on inspiration is similarly parallel to the couple's realisation that the more stable basis for relationship which they work out for themselves does not preclude love. But the relation between the tale and the state of mind of George, who is supposed to relate it, is uncertain. When he sees that the letters from Matilda to Richard are obviously letters of love, he offers Henry and Emma as a contrast; yet the dialogue in which the tale is cast shows them working towards a successful relationship. Possibly it was intended to show a stage in George's own development from disillusion to hope, of which he is not fully conscious as the tale unfolds itself; but if so, the intention is obscure and inadequately fulfilled.

At an early stage in their alteration, Henry realises that it is folly to spend their time in recrimination; but it is not easy in practice to hold the distinction between recrimination and a sensible search for the truth. Emma points out that Henry's romantic illusion was self-imposed; but Henry can easily produce the counter-argument that the illusion was fostered by deception on Emma's part. He accuses her of having exaggerated her sensibility in several ways in the manner of Augusta in the witty but rather shallow tale, 'The Preceptor Husband'. Now she no longer shows any interest in books or any extraordinary sensitivity to the beauties of romantic scenery or the suffering of paupers: clearly, he infers, she exaggerated in order to impress him. Emma's reply is penetrating: the language of flattery forces the girl to live up to it. Given that deception is built into the very language of romantic love and that therefore disillusion of some kind is inevitable, Henry urges again that it is futile to continue recrimination. Taking the wider perspective, the pattern of romantic disillusion can be reversed: England, now cultivated and beautiful countryside, was once a barren waste, and in the same way marriage may be improved by cultivation. In response to this, Emma offers true obedience: she will live up to his present language just as she previously lived up to the false language of romantic flattery. To cement the relationship between Jacques and the present tale, Henry uses the image of cultivation which Jacques had used in Book III. Like Richard and George at the end of the collection, Henry and Emma will live in a relationship of mutual dependence without subservience. Whatever the relationship between George and the tale, Henry and Emma have argued their way to a relationship of substance and value.

Although this is another tale which cannot stand with Crabbe's best work, the exchanges between the couple are kept lively and the sense of dramatic tension is maintained by the asides implying imminent interruption: 'Nay, do not frown ... Nay, hear me further ... Once more permit me . . .' Through a dialogue which initially releases much mutual animosity, Henry and Emma shape for themselves a relationship which will have permanent stability and has the potential for further fruitful development. Crabbe's views on the fragility and the inherent self-delusion of romantic love are absorbed into his vision of the possibilities of love within marriage.

Apart from Jacques and, briefly, the bachelor of Book X, the only characters from other books who are brought into the social world of the frame are the sisters of Book VIII, but here too Crabbe made little attempt to involve the brothers. The first thirty-two lines were added at a stage later than the two extant drafts, one of which, now in the John Rylands Library (owned in Ward's time by Mrs Mackay), is dated April 1817, and the other, in the Huntington notebook, is a little later. In the opening lines, George, having faced his trauma in Book VII, is represented as rising from bed in a happy frame of mind, feeling something to be admired, in a way remote from his apathy at the beginning of Book IV, and indeed wanting to share it, no longer wallowing in his loneliness. In Book IV the walk was 'requisite'; here he is anxious to start. This addition also alters the emphasis of the part of the introduction which does occur in the drafts. In the drafts, the direction of thought is 'Nor the Proud only . . . The very Vertuous suffer . . .' (Huntington); in the printed version, George speaks of a strength in facing distress which needs 'not the resources of our pride'. He is now able to see in Lucy what he was unable to achieve in his own experience.

The tale of the sisters itself is very routine material and not worth dwelling on. The intrusion of George at the end in both the Huntington draft and the manuscript quoted in the 1834 edition provided a welcome relief from the overcharged atmosphere of the ending, but was presumably omitted because it made George more assiduous in his personal relationships than he was supposed in the final version to be before the influence of Richard had taken effect. The opportunity of relating the sisters' disappointments in love to George's was missed.

The only book in which the relation between the tale and the frame of *Tales of the Hall* is fully satisfactory is XX, 'The Cathedral-Walk'. Unlike the long and dull 'Lady Barbara; or, The Ghost' (XVI), it is not a serious ghost story; but the irony is extended in the first part of the book to include George, haunted by his romantic dream in a more general sense than Emma, the heroine of the tale, is haunted by the hope of seeing the ghost of her dead lover. The ironic relationship is fully present in the Huntington draft of 1817, but it gains added point from the history of George's amatory affliction in Book VII. He opens the book by describing his 'hypochondriac State'. There is a degree less reality about his case than Emma's: her lover really dies, whereas

George's case is only 'call'd consumptive'. But they both resemble the old mansion in which he is staying, of which only part is occupied by the concerns of the living:

> 'The rest – who doubts? – was by the spirits seized,
> Ghosts of all kinds, who used it as they pleased.'   (ll. 17–18)

His loss of health is metaphorical as well as actual: a 'fresh assemblage' is seen daily when the weather is fine and the walks are 'clean', but George is content to lurk among the shadows, the furtiveness of his action rendered by a verb used significantly at the end of the tale – 'I stole the yew-tree shades among'. The others treat him patronisingly as part of the landscape – 'The man is harmless . . . we no notice take, we let him go and come'. But George thinks his withdrawal from life is to a superior level:

> 'Much it amused me in the place to be
> This harmless cipher, seeming not to see,
> Yet seeing all, – unnoticed to appear,
> Yet noting all . . .'   (ll. 50–3)

The repeated 'all', absent from the draft, gives him a sense of omniscience which feeds his preoccupation with himself: what he likes to hear is 'them speak of the forsaken man'. He is enjoying the role of the 'forsaken', though actually he is assiduous 'unnoticed to appear'. The introduction concludes by relating George's self-absorption – 'for many an hour/I walk'd alone' – to the ghost stories which perplex the timid minds of the other visitors at the mansion: both have 'witching power'.

The scene for the ghost stories is set by two contrasting descriptions, the first of which puts the emphasis on ordinariness – 'The sun just dropp'd beneath a distant hill' (l. 76) – and on the pleasantness of the moonlight:

> 'And pleasant was the chequer'd light and shade
> Her golden beams and maple shadows made.'   (ll. 79–80)

The second translates into the Gothic equivalent:

> 'Then all was silent, save the sounds that make
> Silence more awful, while they faintly break;
> The frighten'd bat's low shriek, the beetle's hum,
> With nameless sounds we know not whence they come.'
>   (ll. 83–6)

In the Huntington draft this gently mocking contrast is not focused: in the first description instead of an 'ancient tree' throwing a 'fair picture' on the gravel, there is a 'trembling Tree' which throws a 'dark Shadow', and in the second we hear the less mysterious 'injured Bat's soft Shriek ... And faint low Sounds'. When the effort of human activity is absent, the force that takes over is a natural, not a supernatural one –

> '... vegetation, that with progress slow
> Where man forbears to fix his foot, will grow' –   (ll. 91–2)

or, more mundanely, to emphasise the point: 'dust repell'd the ray/Of the moon's light and of the setting day' (ll. 93–4). But in the absence of exterior light, the imagination is as ready as the brushwood to display the objects in the room 'with its own wild light in fearful forms array'd'.

Each of the ghost stories is deflated in the telling. The tale of the warrior and his spirit is told flatly and made ridiculous by the last line: ' "I fall!" he cried, and in the instant fell' (l. 117). The tale of the witch is mocked by the ambiguity of the last couplet:

> 'The hag confess'd it when she came to die,
> And no one living can the truth deny.'   (ll. 122–3)

One cannot doubt that she truly confessed to making fetishes, but one can doubt whether she told the truth, and there is no one living who can decide the question. The heroine of the third tale, the beauty, is a 'thoughtless girl' indeed to keep three lovers without letting anyone know which she prefers, because one of the two who fall in the desperate duel *à trois* is her favourite, so she has to haunt the survivor 'every Thursday night'. In the debate which follows, about the possibility of ghosts returning after death, the argument that they do is made deliberately bathetic:

> 'It may not be intelligence to bring,
> But to keep up a notion of the thing.'   (ll. 167–8)

But to preclude a wholly mocking attitude Crabbe registers a qualification through two speakers, one of whom is Emma, who is about to tell the most extended mock ghost-story: 'Our prudence had been better shown/By leaving uncontested things unknown' (ll. 189–90).

Emma, having lost her lover through death, is a more extreme case of romantic melancholia than George. Like Johnson's Nekayah, she 'resolved to grieve', but romantic death does not come so rapidly as death by disease:

> 'I wish'd to die, – and grief, they say, will kill,
> But you perceive 'tis slowly if it will.'   (ll. 237–8)

When her uncle, a widowed dean, invites her with 'congenial gloom' to live with him, she has all the machinery for romantic indulgence she could wish for in the dimly-lit seclusion of the cathedral. As a matter of choice, she isolates herself from outside reality:

> 'I took the key, and oft-times chose to stay . . .
> Till I perceived no light, nor heard a sound,
> That gave me notice of a world around.'   (ll. 255, 257–8)

Like George she enjoys, exults in her isolation, and her pride becomes such that she begins to align herself with 'a nobler place':

> 'Then had I grief's proud thoughts, and said, in tone
> Of exultation, "World, I am alone! . . .
> And I shall leave thee for a nobler place." '   (ll. 259–60, 262)

The situation is generalised to include George – 'Nor should romantic grievers thus complain' (l. 265). In the Huntington draft, the reference to George is less pointed: 'And I do think if People will complain . . .' The serious side of it is that she becomes metaphorically haunted in a way which directly reduces her capacity for life:

> 'In company with him alone I seem'd,
> And if not dreaming, was as one who dream'd.'   (ll. 292–3)

But the ecstasy of her visions is comically deflated by the 'congenial gloom' of the dean's response:

> 'He ask'd no question, but would sit and weep,
> And cry, in doleful tone, "I cannot sleep!" '   (ll. 286–7)

On the night of her meeting with the 'ghost' she characteristically sets herself , like George, in a sphere above mortality, 'Where lofty minds celestial views explore' (l. 314). The language partly deflates her arrogance – 'I was borne on visionary wings . . . But rising, walk'd'. But the main irony operates in retrospect: she will shortly have an experience which will ironically answer her prayer,

> 'Thou canst make clear my sight, or thou canst make
> More gross the form that his loved mind shall take.'
>
>   (ll. 328–9)

The form will be more gross than she anticipates. She assumes blandly that she is a 'favour'd mortal', 'bless'd beyond mortals', using the ortho- dox image of paying a debt to mortality, yet taking it for granted that she will shortly be enjoying 'heavenly converse'. She is like George, who at the beginning 'every impulse of the mind obey'd': she half-concedes that she is out of her depth – 'I cannot judge what laws may spirits bind' (l. 355) – yet has already begun to arrange the details of the meeting – 'ere my love can speak, he should be first address'd'. When she makes her grand speech to what she takes to be the ghost, the rhetoric – 'Dear, happy shade! companion of the good . . .' – sweeps her easily past such inconvenient questions as 'do I on thee intrude?' As self-preoccupied as her uncle the dean, she will not go to take leave of him before rejoining her lover for ever. The anticlimax is managed extremely well, with the routine Gothic horror of the 'hideous form',

> 'Pale, and yet bloated, with distorted eyes
> Distant and deep, a mouth of monstrous size',   (ll. 375–6)

developed in routine fashion until the very last line of the paragraph, which suddenly destroys romantic expectations of all kinds: 'Bah! – bother! – blarney! – What is this about?' (l. 379)

But the irony goes deeper than simple deflation. Emma expects, when her visions have fled, to meet 'vice and impudence', still thinking in terms of sexual relations, though of a different kind; but the intruder is on a completely different wavelength: 'Would'st hang a man for peeping in a grave?' (l. 385) Behind the comedy lies the bald irony that he is only desecrating the graveyard in a more literal way than Emma. In retrospect her behaviour is worse than arrogant. Both of them have been 'peeping in a grave'; both have attempted to steal from the dead, thinking they would gain 'enough/To pay the hazard'; both have found nothing. When John, the intruder, exposes his intentions of aggression, the light increases and Emma for the first time sees clearly. She is at last sufficiently awake to reality to see that she must hide her fear in order to gain command of the situation, showing a degree of self-control she did not possess before:

> ' "Come, John," I said, suppressing fear and doubt,
> "Walk on before, and let a lady out!" '   (ll. 397–8)

She easily outwits him, but in doing so is forced to admit that she too is transgressing and to associate herself with stealing:

> '. . . I transgress, and am in trouble too . . .
> Each other's counsel therefore let us keep,
> And each steal homeward to our beds and sleep.'
>   (ll. 407, 410–11)

The young lady who thought herself about to enjoy 'heavenly converse' is forced ignominiously to keep counsel with a graveyard thief. The word 'steal' lodges in John's conscience, but he again relates it to Emma as well:

> ' "Steal!" said the ruffian's conscience. – "Well, agreed;
> Steal on, and let us to the door proceed." '   (ll. 412–13)

The scene plays itself out on the bathetic level of the actual: briefly he thinks again of violence, but she is able to outwit him, since 'Escape alone engaged the dreadful man' (l. 417). Emma, too escapes, but in a wider sense:

> 'So I escaped, – and when my dreams came on,
> I check'd the madness by the thoughts of John.'   (ll. 420–1)

Emma does not offer her tale simply as a form of anti-ghost-story ('say I not what can or cannot be') but as an ironic comment on the moral effects of fantasy; and in this form it reflects back also on George, who is not haunted by even an imaginary ghost, but, in the more general form, haunted by romantic self-indulgence. Living with ghosts, or being haunted by the past, is not compatible with living adequately in the present.

'The Cathedral-Walk' is, however, an isolated success. In the other tales, apart from those devoted to the brothers, there is little or no attempt to relate the characters or experiences of George and Richard to what happens in the tales. This confirms the manuscript evidence which suggests that most of the tales were written before the idea of the framing device of the brothers in its present form occurred to Crabbe. The result is not wholly to be regretted: the books about the brothers, especially 'The Visit Concluded', contain some interesting material of kinds not handled elsewhere by Crabbe (for example, Richard's mundane depression and the semi-autobiographical parts of Books IV and VI, which are much better than 'Infancy'). But looked at as a complete opus, the *Tales of the Hall* is not sufficiently integrated by the device to form more of a unity than the *Tales* of 1812. Such unity as it has is more a question of a mellowness of tone which permeates most of the tales, but which has a concomitant disadvantage in its comparative lack of variety.

7 *Tales of the Hall*, 1819 (2)

Although it is possible to see connections between some of the tales which are not explicitly related by means of the frame, Crabbe leaves the perception of them almost as much to the reader as in the *Tales* of 1812. There is, for example, no attempt to indicate, by juxtaposition or some other simple structural means, that 'The Preceptor Husband' can be seen as a comic version of 'The Natural Death of Love'. All the tales in *Tales of the Hall* deal in some way with love, and in almost all of them the passage of time is of considerable, often crucial, importance. The mood of the brothers looking back across a lifetime of experience, with feelings in which acceptance plays a large part, is one which suffuses the whole collection. The far slower pace at which the narratives move, although making them much less powerful than the *Tales*, also helps to sustain a consistent tone of quiet reflectiveness. But the total effect remains that of a collection of tales, not, as has sometimes been claimed, of a novel in a verse.

The only two books which are clearly linked are x and xi, 'The Old Bachelor' and 'The Maid's Story'. George says explicitly in his introduction to the former, 'Then by her side my bachelor I place' (l. 15). From the fragment of Book x in Cambridge Add. MS. 4422, it is clear that at an earlier stage the relation between the two was to have been even closer, for the two characters are introduced together: 'They came and both with Talents formed to please . . .'

The bachelor shows very little capacity for coming to terms with the crises in his life. To his first disappointment in love, for example, he responds with a romantic pose, and after his third he takes to travelling not to develop his mind but to waste time. When, at the age of sixty, he begins to form another romantic attachment, to a much younger woman, he is inclined to blame fate, but it is clear to the reader that his motives are self-pity and the lack of anything to do. The relationship is broken not by any growth of responsibility on his part, but simply because the girl finds a man of her own age. The only real interest in the bachelor's story lies in the contrast it forms with that of the maid.

At the beginning of Book xi we are again invited, by Richard, to relate the two tales. The chief conclusion to be drawn from such a comparison is that the maid is throughout her life more stable and resilient than the bachelor and at the end of it much more mature. Her story is the longest of Crabbe's tales and like all his later work it could to advantage have been shorter. It attempts to cover the whole of her adult life at far too even a pace for any of it to remain in the mind with the clarity and vividness of the best work of Crabbe's prime. He certainly took much trouble over it. The Huntington draft differs very greatly indeed from the final version throughout the long passage from the lovers introduced by Martha's mother to Frederick's last appearance. Frederick dies young, her mother does not remarry, there is a long, dull passage about a dissenting couple, and, most importantly, there is no real maturing of the maid. But although much weak material was excluded, the revised version is some two hundred lines longer.

The first trial the maid is subjected to is the influence of her mother, who wants her to take a purely financial interest in marriage. Yet despite herself, the mother teaches Martha the beginnings of a valuable self-discipline. To her mother this is part of her equipment as beguiler of some wealthy man, but when she teaches her to keep her temper under control, she is achieving more than she realises. The mother's ethic is agreeably, though definitively, defeated when she proves as vulnerable to time's reversals as she warned Martha not to be and becomes emotionally attached to a young physician. Having warned Martha against 'soft emotions', she succumbs to a 'soft address'. The focusing of the irony by the repetition of the word 'soft' was achieved after the Cambridge draft (which is subsequent to the Huntington).

When, after her mother's marriage, she is sent to live with her grandmother, Martha's feelings are mixed: she feels some resentment at being called 'child' by such a mother, but on the other hand she suppresses an incipient pride. In the Huntington draft she is in a very different state of mind at the equivalent stage. Staying with her aunt, after her mother's death, she refuses to join the aunt in running a shop, being too contaminated by her mother's influence:

> But I had often heard of Fortunes made
> In very honest way – and not in Trade
> Then turned me to the Glass . . .

When the grandmother dies, the sudden shock of poverty brings out the worst in Martha: she feels superior to Biddy's naïve prayers and indulges in some self-pity. But she is helped towards a more mature attitude by her stepfather, a humane man who has had to come to terms with grief himself and can therefore teach her the kind of knowledge her mother lacks.

As a result of the grandmother's death, the mother's views undergo a radical change and she becomes a dissenter. In the Huntington draft, Martha herself is half-attracted by a dissenting preacher, but in the final version she resists her mother's new attempt to impose an alien set of values on her as successfully as she resisted the money-values at the beginning. In the Huntington draft, she indulged at this stage in romantic melancholy:

> Oft as the Moonbeam on the Ocean shone
> I walked at Morn and Eve and thought alone ...
> Dreaming of Hope indulged, of heavens pure bliss
> And Joys that are not in a World like this.

In the printed version, she is more mature and deliberately avoids the settings which might draw her thoughts in that direction: 'seldom walk'd alone,/Nor when the moon upon the waters shone' (ll. 610–11). When the moon does shine, 'my window closed,/My needle took, and with my neighbours prosed' (ll. 612–13). Unlike the bachelor she is not seduced by romance.

In the episode with Priscilla, Martha's new degree of maturity is shown further by means of contrast. Unlike Martha, Priscilla is carried away by the landscape to a vision which is a very suspect mixture of the religious and the romantic. Her emotion includes a good deal of the pride Martha has learnt to reject. She is so carried away by fantasy that she thinks she would reject her long-lost lover even if he returned as a young man. More gently than in the Cambridge draft, Martha tries to deflate the vision. When the lover does return, no longer young and very worldly, Priscilla professes dismay. Martha perceives Priscilla's self-deception but does not bluntly expose it. She reserves for later, private reflection her more penetrating insights into what Priscilla will do.

The last episode is in the Huntington draft, but without the gradual maturing of Martha it has little of its eventual point. Unlike the bachelor, Martha is not merely inactive, but actually does what she can to prevent a last romantic attachment, unsuited to her years. She admits that she was pleased and flattered by young Rupert's attentions, but she has already inured herself to romantic moonlight settings and is aware of the comic side of the situation. When he kneels abruptly and launches into a romantic strain, she briefly exploits the comedy, but not long enough to be cruel. He asks for pity on his romantic woes; she offers him real pity, imagining for him the consequences through time of a marriage such as he proposes. The relationship would inevitably turn sour and disable him for another after her death. Through her maturity, a life which might easily have been seriously disabled is left able to develop normally. No such reflections occurred to the bachelor in the last adventure of his story.

'The Maid's Story' gained most of its point, the maturing of Martha, after the Huntington draft was written. In this case, as with most of the *Tales of the Hall* Crabbe evidently started with plot material and only gave it moral shape in the process of rewriting. Even in its final form the tale is diffusely written and contains much material which does not sufficiently contribute to the basic structure. However, some of the details, for example the descriptions of the grandmother's card-playing and of her butcher, are lively in themselves, and although they would have found no place in the economy of one of Crabbes major tales, it would be a pity if they were absent. There are occasional compensations for the dilution of the later work.

'The Widow' (Book XVII) is better than 'The Maid's Story'. Crabbe is more famous for his studies of deranged minds, but he is equally interested in weak ones. The widow is so weak that she might almost be said to have no character at all. Hers is an extreme case of a person's nature being formed through the influence of others. George is amused when Richard is flattered by her 'come hither' look: she has been married three times and is clearly on the market again. The reason for her success, he thinks, is that

> '. . . there is that in her
> That easy men to strength of mind prefer;
> She may be made, with little care and skill,
> Yielding her own, t'adopt a husband's will.'   (ll. 52–5)

In the draft quoted in the 1834 edition, which is very close to the one in the Huntington notebook, George says it is he who prefers such minds to those of 'stronger cast'. The alteration makes it clearer that this is an inadequate view. The tale by implication provides a better one.

Harriet's first husband is an 'easy man', who is so weak that he fears 'of mind such strength' as she possesses, and who therefore brings out the worst in her. She comes to enjoy the process of victory in domestic conflict even more than its results:

> It was such pleasure to prevail o'er one
> Who would oppose the thing that still was done.
>
> > (ll. 99–100)

But as time passes and she becomes habituated to the pleasure, it loses its effect:

> Was she a child to be indulged? He knew
> She would have right, but would have reason too.   (ll. 145–6)

These lines are not in the Huntington draft, but there is a marginal note, 'It was less Pleasure'. When he begins to suffer from depression as a

result of her behaviour, she can only see his gloom through the filter
of her own ego: 'His nerves were shook like hers'. She expends all her
sympathy on fiction:

> Better for Lady Julia's woes to cry,
> Than have her own for ever in her eye.   (ll. 155–6)

Her husband's woes evidently do not count at all. This quiet irony is
another detail subsequent to the Huntington draft. When he turns to
her for 'comfort', she sends him away with a cliché – 'Time would dis-
orders of such nature heal!' (l. 173) – or meets him only with talk of her
own sleepless nights, mimicking his depression in an attempt to manipulate him, but clearly finding comfort more easily herself:

> 'With pangs like hers no other was oppress'd!'
> Weeping she said, and sigh'd herself to rest.   (ll. 177–8)

After his death, the word 'comfort' takes on a more obviously material
sense for her:

> Fortune not now the means of comfort gave,
> Yet all her comforts Harriet wept to have.   (ll. 185–6)

'As weak as wailing infancy', she is capable only of moaning, 'My
helpless babes ... Can I do without? ... What will people say?' The
poles of her apprehension of her situation are self-pity and self-satisfac-
tion:

> It was so hard on her, who not a thing
> Had done such mischief on their heads to bring;
> This was her comfort, this she would declare,
> And then slept soundly on her pillow'd chair.   (ll. 197–200)

Yet she continues to consider herself as depressed as her dead husband
was: 'death she sometimes woo'd, and always fear'd'. In the draft it is
less clear that she is mistaken, for the irony is less pointed: 'death she
sometimes wished and sometimes feared'.

The second husband is a very shrewd man who sees that she needs
to act out easy roles and allows her scope for them:

> Now thought our clerk – 'I must not mention love,
> That she at least must seem to disapprove.'   (ll. 221–2)

In the Huntington draft, 'must' in the second line of this couplet is
'will', making it a less penetrating psychological observation. Instead he
puts his emphasis on setting her muddled affairs in order and even, in a
couplet added after the draft, provides her with a self-justification: 'It is
my wish to guard your husband's fame' (l. 234). She flounders at once,

and, unable to speak of her 'nerves' with as much conviction as before, falls back on 'what will people think?' – which he dismisses brusquely: 'people's thinking is not worth a straw'. With similar ease, once they are married, he can reject all the luxuries she achieved with the first husband, persuading her it is for her own good:

> She wanted air; and walking, she was told,
> Was safe, was pleasant! – he the carriage sold.   (ll. 267–8)

It is good for her: he prevents both the aimless acquisitiveness and the repining she indulged in during her first marriage:

> For when she saw that her desires were vain,
> She wisely thought it foolish to complain.   (ll. 285–6)

In this marriage she really finds comfort: 'Her heart had comfort, and her temper rest' (l. 278). In the Huntington manuscript she does recover her capacities and think the clerk right, but her recognition is not focused by the ironic recurrence of the word 'comfort'. But although the clerk is good for Harriet, she is very bad for him. 'All in order and sub-jection moved': it may be desirable that all is in order, but it is not good that she should be in such total subjection, for the consequence is that 'ambition now began/To swell the soul of the aspiring man' (ll. 291–2). The habit of getting his own way leads him to indulge in fantasies of continuing to get it. He becomes as unfeeling towards Harriet as she was towards her first husband: 'Harriet, of course, not many years would live' (l. 296). He sees himself as farmer, magistrate, protector of the 'weak and the oppress'd' and even, specifically, of the (as yet unor-phaned) orphan children of Harriet. The dreams are shattered very abruptly by his own death. Despite the greater success of this second marriage, the view of the 'easy men' of George's introductory speech is already seen to be inadequate. Domination of a weak woman is not a good basis for marriage. This time she does not consider it necessary to demonstrate her depression, but the irony is even more cutting:

> Nothing, indeed, so much will discompose
> Our public mourning as our private woes.   (ll. 333–4)

The sense of the couplet remains concealed until the last phrase, which reduces 'public mourning' to the most superficial of façades.

The third husband uses more obvious techniques of manipulation than the second. He flatters her vanity about her appearance, and offers to restore the old comforts: 'he desired his wife/To have the comforts of an easy life' (l. 380–1). Again, the focusing of the irony by means of repeating the word 'comforts' is a touch subsequent to the Huntington draft, in which the line reads: 'To have the just Indulgences of Life'. He

panders to the 'nerves' which the clerk had played down, and instead of
bluntly offering to put her affairs in order, he prefaces his hints that he
has wealth to spare with the flattering cliché that 'his was pure, disinterested love'. Harriet naturally relishes the role of reluctant bride:

> She kiss'd her children, – and she said, with tears,
> 'I wonder what is best for you, my dears?'   (ll. 402–3)

It is as much a façade as her grief:

> The widow then ask'd counsel of her heart –
> In vain, for that had nothing to impart.   (ll. 407–8)

She catches the habit of flattery, couching it in transparent disclaimers:

> She could not praise him for his taste a bit;
> And yet men's tastes were various, she confess'd.   (ll. 414–15)

She has absorbed her second husband's attitude to the question of what
people will think: 'she judged them fools/Who let the world's suggestions be their rules' (ll. 439–40). Her concluding cliché, deriving from
him, –

> 'The changeless purpose of a steady mind,
> In one now left alone, but to her fate resign'd' –   (ll. 444–5)

is quietly undermined by the beginning of the following paragraph,
'The marriage follow'd . . .'
   All she has learned from her first two marriages is the half-truth that
she was more comfortable when she obeyed: 'when indulged she was
but more distress'd' and 'by her second husband when controll'd,/Her
life was pleasant'. According to the formulation at the beginning, the
decision to obey this time should lead to a happiness she found neither
with the indulgent nor with the self-centred husband: the third one is
'kind, but would have no dispute;/His love and kindness both were
absolute' (ll. 458–9). But she finds the fact that 'she must be pleased'
more of a curse than a blessing. There is no hypocrisy in his offer that
'She should share all his pleasures as her own' (l. 469), but enforced
pleasure becomes onerous and obedience eventually 'sad'. Yet characteristically she learns nothing of permanent value from this marriage
either. 'Her courage rising with her fear', she is at one point bold
enough to protest against the excess of pleasure, but after the death of
the third husband she is 'Disposed to think "whatever is, is right"'
(l. 524), just as the husband himself thought,

> 'I ever trusted in the trying hour
> To my good stars, and felt the ruling power.'   (ll. 503–4)

One major irony is that in each of the three marriages, whatever is, is wrong in some important respect. Another is that whatever her husband has been like has directly but only temporarily determined her own nature. For her, the pose in which we leave her is the elegant expression of a delicate sensibility:

> she in the autumn finds
> The sea an object for reflecting minds,
> And change for tender spirits; there she reads,
> And weeps in comfort in her graceful weeds.   (ll. 526–9)

But hers is indeed a 'reflecting mind', as changeful as any autumn sea, which has taken its colour from the men she married, and shown no marked tenacity in the pursuit of anything except 'comfort'. The manuscript ending quoted in the 1834 edition emphasises the idea of the husband creating the wife, which George touches on at the beginning –

> As men of skill the ductile clay command . . .
> So may the future husband here survey
> The mind he models –

but does not make the main point, implicit in the tale and briefly indicated in the moral at the end, that a wise husband will not merely create an obedient member of his state, but 'his power divide'. In the manuscript ending women are to have only the 'ensign' of power; in the final version they are to share the reality. But although the final version of the moral takes the second and third marriages more adequately into account, it is improbable that *Harriet* would have been a more successful wife even if she had attempted to practise its ideal. The main implication of the tale is that character in marriage should be a mutual creation, and Harriet is too weak a person to have developed a more adequate role in any relationship.

'The Widow' is one of the later collection which approaches most closely to what one might expect from the tired author of the 1812 *Tales*. Some of the major ironies are pointed by the repetition of a key-word, 'comforts', and the three husbands are set against each other in a way which both defines Harriet's nature more clearly and points towards the basis for a more adequate marriage. The writing, too, is less diffuse than in 'The Maid's Story', and has more of the wit of the earlier *Tales*. But there is none of the concentration on particular, dramatised incidents which focuses the work of 1812 so sharply. The character of Harriet was difficult to portray, being so negative, but although she lives in the reader's mind as a clear type, there is no episode in which she is involved vivid enough to provide a definitive representation of her.

'Smugglers and Poachers' (Book XXI) is a very different sort of tale from the widow's. The plot was suggested to Crabbe by Sir Samuel Romilly, presumably as a tale about the severity of the game laws. In some prosaic lines at the end, Crabbe says that one effect of the tragedy is that the landowner no longer 'takes such dreadful vengeance for a hare'. But the difference between the two brothers, James and Robert, is deeper and more interesting than their merely finding themselves on opposite sides of the game laws. To put the difference in the most abstract and developed terms, Robert values life for its own sake above all moral considerations, whereas James lives by the law, prepared when pressed to use it for selfish ends. The two sides of the game laws are particular cases of these general positions: the operation of the laws shows a striking degree of selfishness in those who have the law on their side, and the poacher implicitly questions the status of a law which denies the natural right of a hunter to his kill: 'Were not the gifts of heaven for all design'd' (l. 193). Crabbe clearly thought that the game laws were too severe: his sympathies are with Rachel when she feels

> That he would shoot the man who shot a hare,
> Was what her timid conscience could not bear.   (ll. 527–8)

But he is equally careful to spell out his judgement that poachers are 'guilty, rash, and desperate' wretches who can only justify their activity 'with perverted mind'. We are not invited to side with either brother: it is only Rachel who has full moral approval, for her respect for obligation regardless of private interests, whether sanctioned by law or not.

The opening contrast between the brothers swings our sympathy back and forth between them. The first point tells in Robert's favour:

> Robert would aid on any man bestow,
> James would his man and the occasion know.   (ll. 42–3)

But the second sounds a note of warning about Robert:

> Robert would all things he desired pursue,
> James would consider what was best to do.   (ll. 45–6)

The preference swings towards James – 'He could himself command, and therefore could obey' (l. 59) – while Robert's love of freedom includes freedom from law: 'he sometimes made/An active partner in a lawless trade' (ll. 68–9). But the balance levels up when James begins to look rather a prig with his talk 'of virtuous labour, of a sober life', beside Robert's vivacity. At first the love of both brothers for Rachel is wholly innocent. The love between Robert and Rachel is almost as between children:

> She loved his stories, pleased she heard him play,
> Pensive herself, she loved to see him gay.   (ll. 109–10)

James, more distant but equally innocent, has her constantly in mind. But as the relationship develops, both brothers begin to become tainted. James waits awhile, ostensibly to consider the right course of action but actually because if he committed himself to Rachel he would have to renounce the pleasures of more general female admiration, 'and he from all had praise/Enough a young man's vanity to raise' (ll. 142–3). In the relationship with Robert, the caution comes from Rachel, put on her guard by the art of rival girls, but the effect on Robert is to destroy his innocence: 'The simple common pleasure that he took/Grew dull' (ll. 150–1). From the start he 'loved to run/ And meet his danger', but now he becomes dependent on it – 'danger only could repose produce' – and consequently he joins 'th'associates in their lawless trade'. With no moral anchor, his conscience is set completely at ease by the hypocrisy of respectable society, the ladies he sees at church who 'whispering, deal for spicery and lace'.

Rachel is confused in her attitude towards the new Robert, partly by her father's sharing in the general hypocrisy and partly by the bias of love: 'There was some ill, – but he, she knew, was good' (l. 179). James purports to educate her in the way vice can take over the mind of an apparently good man, but the way he puts it shows a kind of moral fastidiousness which is itself far from creditable:

> He sigh'd to think how near he was akin
> To one reduced by godless men to sin.   (ll. 186–7)

Rachel wavers, finding it difficult to believe that a man 'So kind to all men, so disposed to pray' (l. 207) could be wicked, yet then seeing that the alternative is equally difficult, 'for she could not believe/That James could lie, or purpose to deceive' (ll. 209–10). Under the pressure of the situation James becomes more devious:

> Robert, more generous of the two, avow'd
> His scorn, defiance, and contempt aloud.
> James talk'd of pity in a softer tone,
> To Rachel speaking, and with her alone.   (ll. 221–4)

The image, 'he her bosom fenced with dread about', recalls by contrast the image of the relationship with Robert, 'they were in Love's high-way', and briefly highlights the metaphorical significance of James's occupation. But the repressive tactics of the gamekeeper cannot suppress love: 'love he could not with his skill drive out'. At several points this tale resembles *Measure for Measure*. Like Angelo, James says before the event that he will stand rigorously by the law, resisting any appeal to

'Love, favour, interest, tie of blood'. But Rachel knows instinctively that
there is something wrong in his attitude towards his brother:

> There was a generous feeling in her mind,
> That told her this was neither good nor kind.   (ll. 253–4)

The flaw is exposed fully when Robert is caught poaching. Rachel's
response is expressed in very mannered language –

> A thousand acts in every age will prove
> Women are valiant in a cause they love –   (ll. 308–9)

in order to contrast with James's crude abuse of his legal power:

> James knew his power – his feelings were not nice –
> Mercy he sold, and she must pay the price.   (ll. 317–18)

James is not given the stature of an Angelo. There is no conflict in him
between his integrity and his desires, and from an earlier stage he has
been accustomed to a degree of hypocrisy. But Rachel's dilemma is
explored more fully than Isabella's. She knows what she would choose if
she were in Robert's position: 'she could not their contract break'. But
she also knows that she is not, like him, actually facing death, and that
his guilt will be making him more likely to fear it:

> . . . he was man, and guilty, – death so near
> Might not to his as to her mind appear.   (ll. 331–2)

So although she would not break her obligation herself, she must grant
him the opportunity to break his: *he* might prefer life to moral obligation.

Having made her decision she maintains it firmly and openly: 'She
spake with firmness . . . she her full intent/Proclaim'd'. With Robert's
openness and James's strength of purpose, she carries out a duty which
neither of them would have felt bound by. James's reason for not
wishing her to see Robert to put the alternatives to him must be that he
fears Robert might recognise her stature and rise to it: the sight of him
would be more likely than not to make her want to save his life by
agreeing to James's demand. But Crabbe's attention is on Rachel and
Robert rather than James. Rachel puts the question to Robert in very
factual terms –

> 'Wilt thou die, Robert, or preserve thy life?
> Shall I be thine own maid, or James's wife?' –   (ll. 355–6)

leaving it to him to see either in his own perspective, life against loss of
Rachel, or in hers, honour against prostituted marriage. As usual, Robert
reacts spontaneously, and one takes it to be the noble reaction until one
reflects that he is seeing the conflict only in his own terms, not hers:
'His wife! – No! – never will I thee resign.' (l. 357) In her reply, Rachel

completely encompasses him: she knows he is 'rash and guilty' but with only a hint at her own position in the matter, which he has ignored ('to thee/I pledged my vow'), she develops the other side of the case, remaining within his perspective: 'the life that God has lent/Is thine, but not to cast away'. Robert's response is ignoble in the extreme: instead of perceiving her magnanimity, he makes the ugly accusation, 'Perhaps my brother may have gain'd thy heart?' (l. 365) Rachel is momentarily angered, to the point of indicating the risk to her own reputation in coming to see him. Capable of seeing so fully through his perspective she quickly forgives him, but reminds him that the decision remains to be made: 'thy spirit has been tried,/And thou art weak, but still thou must decide' (ll. 371–2). Again Robert can only see in his own perspective, unable to imagine what is involved for Rachel: in lines clearly drawing on Claudio's decision that he prefers life to his sister's shame, Robert says finally:

> 'O! sure 'tis better to endure the care
> And pain of life, than go we know not where!'   (ll. 383–4)

He can speak of enduring 'the care/And pain of life' himself without thinking of what Rachel will have to endure in order to buy his life. He even has the insensitivity to add, and repeat, 'love him not'. It is the decision of a man who values life above all other consideration: 'death torments me, – I to nature cling'.

As soon as the decision is made, Rachel's obligation is transferred to James: she 'was no longer free – she was his brother's bride'. James knows that he 'on her worth and virtue could depend'. But there is no security for Robert: he fears that James might deceive him and he cannot be content with his decision: 'all the promise hope could give,/Gilded not life, – it was not joy to live' (ll. 417–18). When he escapes from the prison, he cannot accept the consequences of his choice for life at the cost of all right to Rachel's hand:

> He look'd around in freedom – in delight?
> O! no – his Rachel was another's right!   (ll. 443–4)

Even he recognises that Rachel's virtue is distinct from mere external law –

> 'Alas! her virtue and the law prevent,
> Force cannot be, and she will not consent' –   (ll. 449–50)

but the reflection leads him to think in terms of actually murdering James. The reference to Claudio's speech is continued: 'I am all a tempest, whirl'd around/By dreadful thoughts' recalls the winds Claudio imagines will blow his spirit 'with restless violence about/The pendent world' (III, i ll. 124–5). The difference is that Robert's hell is present. The storm during which his 'lawless clan' hold their meeting echoes that in his own mind. But although James is by nature steadier and has the security of possessing Rachel, all is not well with him either. If his informer got close enough to the poachers to hear their plans, he must have known that Robert was among them, so James's taking arms 'Not all defensive' is the counterpart to Robert's thoughts of murder. During the short sleep before the attack he evidently dreams about him: he asks 'in fancy's terror, "Is he dead?" ' The ethics of both men fittingly end in violence.

When James has left home, we follow the movement of Rachel's thoughts as she first uses the word 'loved' of her feelings for Robert, then corrects herself to 'pitied', and then wonders whether even that is compatible with her marriage vows to James. She forces herself to think well of James – 'James too was civil' – but drifts into reflecting on the moral distance between them, his readiness to carry the use of law for protection of his interests to the point of shooting a man for shooting a hare. The final couplet of her meditation refers ambiguously to both brothers:

> But still she loved him – wonder'd where he stray'd
> In this loud night! and if he were afraid. (ll. 529–30)

When she sleeps, her dream is of Robert, but when she is awake and in control of her mind, she focuses it on James, anxious to learn 'Aught of her husband's safety or return' (l. 548). It is perhaps a weakness in the tale that we learn little about Rachel's state of mind when she finds both dying. But an excess of pathos would clearly have spoilt the ending and Crabbe was probably wiser to rely on understatement. She attends to the dying Robert 'ere her feelings were awake', and as they wake to anguish our attention is suddenly and jarringly transferred to the 'loud-speaking, eager men', explaining to the landowner where the attack took place, and then commenting rather insensitively on her actions.

> Now, more attentive, on the dead they gazed,
> And they were brothers: sorrowing and amazed,
> On all a momentary silence came,
> A common softness, and a moral shame. (ll. 596–9)

'And they were brothers' refers not only to James and Robert but also to the onlookers, shaken to a new degree of moral awareness. It is a pity Crabbe did not end the tale with these lines.

'Smugglers and Poachers' does not resemble Crabbe's earlier work in its basic form. It is really an adventure story with a quite different conception of plot from Crabbe's own. But on the whole he succeeded in bringing his own moral concerns to it, representing Robert and James not merely as figures in a rather melodramatic tale, but as opposing moral types whose inadequacies are pointed by the more truly humane Rachel. The effort of transmuting the material evidently also stirred Crabbe to write in a tauter style than in most of the *Tales of the Hall*. It is one of the best of the collection.

Three minor tales, 'Sir Owen Dale', 'Gretna Green' and 'William Bailey', are worth dwelling on briefly for very different reasons. 'Sir Owen Dale' (Book XII) is interesting in conception, but tedious in execution. Sir Owen is a man whose passions lie dormant for forty years, but who is then taken in by a coquette, Camilla, and channels all his feelings into a revenge which he nurses for four years. He asks his nephew, Charles, to make her in turn 'Desperate from love, and sickening with desire' (l. 304) and then to jilt her; but Charles falls in love with her himself and cannot fulfil the second stage of his undertaking. Sir Owen refuses to forgo his revenge until he meets one of his tenants, Ellis, who has seen the objects of his own revengeful feelings reduced to such a state that all wish for vengeance has left him. Sir Owen is sufficiently affected by the vicarious experience to forgive Camilla and Charles. There were thus strong possibilities in the tale for developing an interesting parallel between the situations of Sir Owen and Ellis, but the pace is much too slow in general, and in particular the tale of Ellis is developed in more detail than is strictly relevant to the main story of Sir Owen. Ellis might have been seen more precisely as the limit of Sir Owen's feelings, but the relationship is insufficiently focused for the tale to be more than an interesting failure.

'Gretna Green' (Book XV) is, conversely, a tale more interesting in execution than in apparent intention. From the introductory conversation between the brothers it seems that the book is to centre on Belwood, a rich young man of a weak nature, who elopes with his tutor's daughter and finds that the marriage becomes a prison. This part of the tale is, as might be expected, handled in a very routine fashion by Crabbe; the interest lies in the development of the character of the tutor, Dr Sidmere. It is his wife who first suggests that they encourage the couple to elope in order to gain some control over Belwood's money. The Doctor a weak character, vacillates in response: he

> Wish'd it to be – then wish'd he had not heard;
> But he was angry – that at least was right.   (ll. 164–5)

In the Murray draft (of late 1816 or early 1817) he vacillates between fear and hope, but does not take refuge in this way in the easy reaction of anger. Once the basic decision is taken, the Doctor begins to elaborate for himself the role he will adopt, the stern father who will only slowly be appeased. Yet striking the right balance will be a matter requiring great tact. If he is too stern they may decide not to elope after all, but if he is not stern enough, he will have compromised himself. Weak man as he is, the final decision he takes is to appear non-committal, leaving the dirty work to his wife. Instead of facing his problem responsibly, he spends his time in dramatising a denunciation and reconciliation scene, placing himself at the centre.

The transformation of the romance between Belwood and the Doctor's daughter into a disillusioned marriage is too rapid to be effective. The greater interest is again focused on the parallel scene of the Doctor exchanging recriminations with his wife. Left to reflect by himself, the Doctor quickly becomes calmer, since he can pursue his self-dramatisations in peace. In the Murray draft he merely imagines his daughter falling at his feet to beg for mercy: 'Of course my Daughter at my feet would fall/And call for Mercy'. In the printed version he has developed a whole scene:

> 'Suppose me there – suppose the carriage stops,
> Down on her knees my trembling daughter drops;
> Slowly I raise her, in my arms to fall,
> And call for mercy as she used to call.'   (ll. 339–42)

The couple work out for themselves a relationship of mutual self-defeat; but the final emphasis lies with the Doctor who is also responsible for the situation. The feeling one is left with is regret that the tale was not more radically altered in revision, putting the Doctor at the centre. As it is, the passages about him have to be culled out by the reader from an otherwise undistinguished performance.

'William Bailey' (Book XIX) underwent considerable alteration in revision. The main interest of a rather mediocre tale lies in the fact that we can trace the process of change from the beginning. Among Crabbe's extant notebooks there are a number of prose plot-notes, some of them very short, but a few extending to several hundred words. From one of the plots in a Murray notebook it seems probable that what was printed in *New Poems* as 'In a neat Cottage' was closely related to what Ward printed as 'The Deserted Family', despite the fact that the former is in blank verse and the latter in couplets. But the only case in which a plot-note for a completed tale survives is 'William Bailey'. There are in fact two prose versions in the same Cambridge notebook (Add. MS. 4422), separated by notes for six other tales, including 'Tracy'. The first is entitled, in cipher, 'William', the second, 'Story of W^m reviewed'. The second is dated 'Dec. 31' [1812]; the first is not dated but the nearest date, given to another of the plot-notes, is 18 November 1812. There is also a verse draft of the tale, called 'William and Frances', in one of the Murray notebooks, which dates from late 1816 or early 1817. The most interesting difference between the notes and the final version is in the ending. In 'William', Frances, then called Phoebe, went further astray after her initial seduction by Sir Henry Neville: 'She listened to a handsome Lieutenant and left Sir Henry: not heard of for many years'. Subsequently, 'one Phoebe Gleek was found exhausted and emaciated in Staffield Canal Side. was nursed and fed recovers feebly and imperfectly ... finds exquisite Pain in viewing the House of her lover. And that of Sir Henry still living with a favourite.' At the end, William feels 'Pity and Recollection as it arose from all the Incentives to Love Romantic Fancy and Imagination...' The second version is considerably closer to the eventual tale. Fanny (as she now becomes)

> is to be here represented with recurring Sentiments of Love and Virtue and her old Conduct must be softened. W^m frequents ... his old Haunts – In his old Dress. Sees Fanny in a favourite one of hers. They meet and repeat their Meetings Innocently no question. his Piety Her Songs and recovered Manners They retire to an unvisited Hamlet and small Cottage, live in Habits of Harmony and Charity. She dies first and he survives a short Time.

The final version carries this reversal of the normal 'progress' pattern even further: William and Frances do not merely meet again 'in Habits of ... Charity', they actually marry and settle happily to the management of an inn. The verse draft is fairly close to the final version, but the introductory passage stressing the eventual happy ending is shorter. Richard, in asking George about the couple, says, 'They seem to dwell in Plenty Love and Peace', but in his reply George does not say that Frances has been 'virtue's self since she had made her vows', nor that William calls 'her self-correction too severe'. Crabbe even altered the introductory description of Frances's fall: 'her Adventures! and her Weakness shown' became 'some awkward trials of her own'. The main change in the conception of the tale was towards gradually more forgiveness towards Frances for her infidelity to William.

Unlike the three tales just discussed, 'Delay has Danger' (Book XIII) is an assured success. It is the best of the *Tales of the Hall*, an achievement comparable with, though distinctively different from, the *Tales* of 1812. The characteristically slower pace enables Crabbe to capture the gradual drifting of a weak man into a relationship which is not positive enough to be represented by a small number of significant scenes. The only developed scene comes towards the end, as an equal shock to the reader and to Henry, as he suddenly discovers the consequence of his irresponsibility. But even in this tale some of the leisurely writing is not really contributing to the overall effect. The reference in the opening paragraph, which was not in the Murray draft, to the 'nameless worms',

> Whose generations lived and died ere man,
> A worm of other class, to crawl began,   (ll. 15–16)

arguably provides a perspective on the small pathos of Henry's fate, but the long prosaic discussion of the 'Danger in Delay' merely weakens the beginning of the tale. Again, there seems to have been a basic failure of self-criticism in Crabbe: the totally irrelevant 'short excursion' on the meaning of a lady's 'Nay' (which extends to thirty-five lines) was added after the Murray draft (which probably dates from late 1816). It is not the work of a man who was feeling his way as he wrote: it was added after the tale had taken something close to its final shape.

The first insight into Henry's weakness comes when his father proposes to send him to their patron while he arranges the financial side of the marriage. This proposal is made in the draft, but there is not the ironic mention of Henry's ineffectuality: 'as you must be dumb,/You may be absent'. Cecilia (Harriet in the draft) does not approve of the parting, but she does not make the strong objection she expresses in the final version, so there is not the tug-of-war situation in which Henry is left looking rather foolishly silent in the middle:

> Thither must Henry, and in vain the maid
> Express'd dissent – the father was obey'd.   (ll. 154–5)

This comic perspective on him affects the tone of the lines on his romantic posturing:

> In all his walks, in hilly heath or wood,
> Cecilia's form the pensive youth pursued.   (ll. 181–2)

There is a note of relief in his voice as he remarks on his freedom to indulge in romantic reflections which is also a freedom from interference:

> 'Here none approach,' said he, 'to interfere,
> But I can think of my Cecilia here!'   (ll. 188–9)

'But there did come' not the formidable Cecilia, but Fanny, 'a mild and blue-eyed lass', who happens to be wandering about the house 'speaking softly to herself alone,/Or singing low in melancholy tone' (ll. 241–2) in a way very much in tune with the mood of the 'pensive youth'. In the draft, the narrator openly accuses Fanny of engineering the situation – 'here I am ashamed/Of Truth itself and Fanny must be blam'd'. In the printed version, he increases the comedy with a Chaucerian avowal of ignorance – 'what has chance to do/With this? – I know not:

doubtless Fanny knew' (ll. 251–2). This tone, once established, is sustained by further rhetorical questions:

> And when a girl's amusements are so few
> As Fanny's were, what would you have her do?   (ll. 255–6)

But the development of the relationship is handled with a delicacy which the comedy does not dispel: they 'look together at the setting sun,/ Then at each other – What the evil done?' (ll. 259–60) There is a subtle ambivalence in Fanny's actions:

> Then Fanny took my little lord to play,
> And bad him not intrude on Henry's way.   (ll. 261–2)

It would seem gauche to suggest she need not have taken him at all: the only possible response is 'O, he intrudes not . . .' Yet the manoeuvre has provided the relationship with a focus on which outward attention can be centred while the real development takes place unnoticed:

> . . . man with woman has foundation laid,
> And built up friendship ere a word is said.   (ll. 271–2)

When a 'chance' meeting in the dark seems particularly surprising,

> The youth in meeting read the damsel's face,
> As if he meant her inmost thoughts to trace;   (ll. 283–4)

but Fanny deflects his attention with an apposite blush, enabling them to part with a silent smile which still carries the question. 'Do tell me what you seek?' yet with a transformed tone. The draft is comparatively crude, representing them both as more full committed than Henry as yet is: 'Afraid of Words unfit and Accents weak'. When they meet again in the same place, speech is inevitable, and such is the situation they 'chance' to be in that it takes only the briefest hint to propel Henry towards a commentary on the scenery which verges on the romantic:

> 'All so delightful, soothing, and serene!
> Do you not feel it? not enjoy the scene?
> Something it has that words will not express . . .'   (ll. 297–9)

'Poor Fanny's heart' responds not in kind but with a well-timed flattery – 'How well he painted, and how rightly guess'd' (l. 303) – which encourages Henry to look for a place to sit down. But Fanny is astutely 'afraid' to sit:

> 'Not, sir, of you; your goodness I can trust,
> But folks are so censorious and unjust . . .'

> At this she wept; at least a glittering gem
> Shone in each eye, and there was fire in them.
>
> (ll. 308–9, 316–17)

Poor Henry is entangled three times over: he does not only feel 'emotions very warm and sweet' at the sight of the tears, but is both lulled by her general concern for her reputation and flattered by her particular trust of him –

> 'What evil in discourse
> With one so guarded, who is pleased to trust
> Herself with me, reliance strong and just?'   (ll. 323–5)

The answer to his question is implict in the opening words of the following paragraph – 'Our lover' – but Cecilia is comfortably distant enough for him to feel confident in defining a proper response for her:

> It would be wrong in her to take amiss
> A virtuous friendship for a girl like this.   (ll. 330–1)

At this point, having represented the early stages of Henry's seduction with an ironic sympathy for his predicament, Crabbe begins to sharpen his criticisms. When Henry vaguely wonders why Fanny's guardians uncharacteristically seem to share her confidence in his honour, Crabbe added, after the Murray draft, the explicit comment, 'He said in folly and he smiled in pride' (l. 369). The wandering in which the couple indulge begins to take on a stronger metaphorical significance: in the line, 'Familiar now became the wandering pair' (l. 372), the word 'wandering' was originally merely 'youthful'. After the draft was completed, Crabbe decided to take us into the psychology of Fanny's tolerance of Henry's slowness to respond:

> The gentle dames are ever pleased to find
> Their lovers dreading they should prove unkind.   (ll. 376–7)

But Henry's vanity is flattered by fear in much the same way: weak as he is, he is gratified by being able to cause her pain:

> Her fondness sooth'd him, for the man was vain,
> And he perceived that he could give her pain.   (ll. 383–4)

In the draft, 'His Harriet scrupled not to own her Love', but in print, 'Cecilia liked not to profess her love' (l. 385): Cecilia has perceived that frequent professions of love feed his vanity, so she avoids them. On the contrary, 'Fanny ever was the yielding dove', and the degree of her success is registered quietly by the use of the possessive pronoun: Henry wishes Cecilia were 'like *his* Fanny, kind'. In the draft there follows a digression on Fanny's guardians, her aunt and uncle, steward and house-keeper of the hall, partly concerning Henry's not being worried by their social station and partly concerning some slander about the uncle. For the final version Crabbe discarded this irrelevance and instead dwells with effective repetitiousness on Henry's vacillation, in the long passage from line 389 to line 452. Henry is now deep in self-deception: despite the pleasure he gets from perceiving he can cause Fanny pain, he can conceive that he wrongs 'no creature by a kindness lent/To one so gentle, mild and innocent' (ll. 415–16). He can even persuade himself that his behaviour is justified in that it brings Cecilia to the forefront of his mind: 'By feeling thus I think of her the more' (l. 418). He is so far from the imaginative capacity of guessing what he might feel if Cecilia become involved in a similar relationship that he can actually write to her about Fanny as 'one in whom Cecilia would delight'.

> But what he fear'd to lose or hoped to gain
> By writing thus, he had been ask'd in vain.   (ll. 430–1)

The tone of the narrative voice has changed from a comic mock-innocence to direct mockery of an outright fool. Again his thoughts wander to the strange silence of Fanny's guardians, and the oddity of it is emphasised in the narrative voice, but the thought drifts as easily out of his head as it drifted in:

> 'They can have no design, or plot, or plan . . .
> Why do I vex me? I will think no more.'   (ll. 441, 452)

The manuscript begins to correspond to the printed text again at the reference to the letters passing between the lord and Henry's father, but in the draft the passage is not interrupted by Henry's reflections on why Fanny seems less afraid: the final effect is of the bemusement of Henry's mind as it fails to grasp the significance of any of the facts which drift through it in succession, the silence of the guardians, the letters between lord and father, Fanny no longer seeming afraid, and 'remonstrance strong' from Cecilia. The only positive response he is capable of is the anger of a coward at Cecilia's remonstrance:

> 'Unjust, injurious, jealous, cruel maid! . . .
> O! how unlike this dear assenting soul.'   (ll. 478, 481)

A quiet irony was added to Cecilia's letter after the draft: 'You know your Interest, now your Hazard learn' became 'You know your heart . . .' But the tone shifts again briefly to indicate that although Henry is a self-ignorant fool he is also a suffering fool: 'Uneasy, anxious, fill'd with self-reproof . . . He buys distress . . . and every time/ They met, increased his anguish' (ll. 483, 496, 499–500). The irony of 'conscious'

when in fact they mean very different things by 'speak' no longer has
the effect of mocking Henry:

> Again, yet once again, the conscious pair
> Met, and 'O speak!' was Fanny's silent prayer;
> And, 'I must speak,' said the embarrass'd youth.   (ll. 489–91)

The effect is to emphasise his isolation. The weakness is his own, but
he is nonetheless a victim of it, pathetic as well as shameful: 'daily he
became/The prey of weakness, vanity, and shame' (ll. 505–6).

One purpose of this shift of emphasis, which is largely absent from
the manuscript, is to form a contrast with the major scene of the tale,
the encounter with the guardians, in which the consequences of Henry's
folly are shown in the light of broad comedy. The new tone is struck
immediately in the description, added after the draft, of the uncle's
appearance:

> He was a man of riches, bluff and big,
> With clean brown broad-cloth, and with white cut wig.
>   (ll. 513–14)

The ineffectual Henry seems unlikely to cut much of a figure beside this,
and any remaining

> Doubt was dispers'd by – 'My esteem'd young man!'
> As he with condescending grace began.   (ll. 527–8)

The speech is not only so grand but so nicely calculated – 'Though you
have not, with craving soul applied/To us . . .' (ll. 531–2) – that Henry
can only splutter inarticulately,

> 'Sir, were the secrets of my soul confess'd,
> Would you admit the truths that I protest
> Are such – your pardon',   (ll. 549–51)

in a way which can easily be swept up into the rhetoric – 'Pardon!
good my friend,/I not alone will pardon, I commend'. Henry's feeble
attempts to stem the flow of words can only deflect a condescending
geniality into an ingratiating self-importance:

>   'In mercy hear me now!'
> 'I cannot hear you, time will not allow:
> You know my station, what on me depends,
> For ever needed – but we part as friends . . .'   (ll. 557–60)

Left briefly to himself, Henry can barely articulate, 'I something must
effect', before the even more loquacious aunt hurries to assail him. She
speaks to him, appropriately, as if comforting a woman:

'What! has he grieved you! Yet he, too, approves
The thing! but man will tease you, if he loves.'   (ll. 572–3)

But the flood of words can also include the sinister – 'There are who
bring/To me all secrets'; the fussily admonitory – 'now do remember
this,/Never to chide her when she does amiss' (ll. 584–5); and a brief
hint at the expression on Henry's face – '. . . such looks – Yes, yours are
just the same.' The comedy increases as the prattle takes in, in rapid
succession, irrelevant details about their interview with the lord –

'We saw my lord, and Lady Jane was there,
And said to Johnson, "Johnson, take a chair" ',   (ll. 598–9)

Johnson's ponderous witticism –

' "Let them go on," our gracious earl began;
"They will go off," said, joking, my good man',   (ll. 607–8)

a gossipy aside about the countess – 'she's a lover's friend', the glee of
operating the plot – 'O! we have watch'd you on from day to day' (l.
613), reported gossip between Fanny and her aunt about Cecilia's letters,
and some deliberately ill-concealed threats about 'th'effect of Johnson's
rage'. Punctuating the flow are a series of hints at Henry's reactions as
he fails again to get anything significant said: 'be you more composed
. . . But why that look? . . . do clear that clouded face'. The scene was
already close to the final version in the Murray draft: only a few details
were added, such as the ingratiating qualification to the threats about
Johnson's rage, 'But I assured him there was no deceit' (l. 636), that is
also absent from the Huntington draft of 1817, which begins in the
middle of Mrs Johnson's speech.

After the high-spirited comedy of the scene with the two guardians,
the tone shifts abruptly back again as the implications of what has
happened begin to register more fully with Henry:

Henry was lost, – his brain confused, his soul
Dismay'd and sunk, his thoughts beyond control . . .
All was a gloomy, dark, and dreadful view.   (ll. 645–6, 649)

His reaction is quicker in the printed version than in either of the drafts.
In the drafts, the substance of Cecilia's letter is given before Henry
relieves his feelings in an outburst of anger against her: 'Unjust and
cruel, insolent and proud . . .' (l. 677). In the final version he is already
reacting along these lines in the first paragraph after Mrs Johnson has
gone: 'He felt him guilty, but indignant too . . . he felt the high disdain/
Of injured men' (ll. 650–2). Unable as he was to achieve any effectual
reply to the Johnsons, he characteristically takes refuge in the easiest
response to hand, anger against the safely absent Cecilia. The change in

timing has the effect of limiting the degree of sympathy we feel for Henry: in the Murray draft he is too simply a pathetic figure as he stands 'afflicted, terrified, dismaid . . . And Hope in Harriet or her favour fled'. In print, there is certainly considerable pathos, but it is qualified by some contempt for the manner in which his weakness vents itself. This double response is sustained in the description of Fanny's character-istically well-timed entry. In the Murray draft, the narration of the interview is rather flat:

> In that soft Moment he embraced the Maid
> And said be Mine and joyful she obey'd
> And tenderly the Speech and the Embrace repaid.

In both the Huntington manuscript and in print, Henry's weakness is again emphasised –

> In that weak moment, when disdain and pride,
> And fear and fondness, drew the man aside' –   (ll. 688–9)

and so, equally, is the pathos of the situation as he responds with horror to what he is doing –

> 'I will!' she softly whisper'd; but the roar
> Of cannon would not strike his spirit more.   (ll. 692–3)

But everything has happened too quickly for the reality of the situation to have impressed itself fully on Henry's consciousness: the bizarre interviews with the Johnsons, the hasty response to Cecilia's letter propelling him into proposing to Fanny and the 'evening all in fond discourse was spent'. The full impact is registered only the following morning, in the masterly description of Henry's response to the scene from his window, which Crabbe was inspired to write after the Murray draft. The hour traditionally associated with hope and promise is one of utter desolation:

> Early he rose, and look'd with many a sigh
> On the red light that fill'd the eastern sky . . .
> But now dejected, languid, listless, low,
> He saw the wind upon the water blow.   (ll. 701–2, 705–6)

In the Huntington draft, Crabbe first wrote 'heard the wind' and then corrected it to the more literally accurate 'saw'. But the impression is aural and tactile as much as visual. The wind dominates the paragraph, communicating a sense of desolation – the gale which 'blew harshly' and the 'rough wind' which 'alone was heard to move'. It is autumn, the time when established relationships are broken up and individuals stand alone –

> When now the young are rear'd, and when the old,
> Lost to the tie, grow negligent and cold –   (ll. 713–14)

and when all seems finished or decaying –

> And near the bean-sheaf stood, the harvest done,
> And slowly blacken'd in the sickly sun.

But little is said explicitly about Henry's state of mind and to labour parallels between the scene and his feelings is to violate the tact with which Crabbe communicates the utter bleakness of both. It is the one point in the tale when there is nothing qualifying the sense of pathos at what this young man has brought on himself.

The postscript, five years after the marriage, is substantially similar in the Murray draft to the final version, but is less powerful without the contrast of tone with the landscape paragraph. Fanny's vapidity has naturally come to pall: Henry 'her weakness (once her kindness) sees,/ And his affections in her languor freeze' (ll. 745–6). Henry himself, 'The most repining of repenting men' (l. 734), has learnt very little. In the Murray draft he calls himself 'Fool!' three times in self-blame:

> Fool! to be taken by a Crimson Cheek . . .
> Fool! to be taken by the Tears of one
> Whom Love as well as Duty bade me shun . . .
> Fool! that to such Contempt thy Honour gave.

In the printed version the emphasis has shifted: he partly blames himself for being 'taken by a rosy cheek', but he also blames Fate and tries to make out that his assent was forced:

> 'What fiend possess'd me when I tamely gave
> My forced assent to be an idiot's slave.'   (ll. 755–6)

His attitude is not so much self-blame as self-pity:

> 'Fool! for this child my freedom to resign . . .
> While from this burthen to my soul I hide,
> To think what Fate has dealt, and what denied.'   (ll. 751, 753–4)

But the tone of the conclusion is dominated by the final episode which is already present, though less polished, in the Murray draft. Called to another town on business,

> There at a house he gave his luckless name,
> The master absent, and Cecilia came;
> Unhappy man! he could not, dared not speak.   (ll. 769–71)

It is an ironic parody of his former failure. He is not simply 'luckless': 'he could not, dared not speak'. Absurdly, he looks in Cecilia's face

As if he sought for sympathy and grace;
As if some kind returning thought to trace   (ll. 776-7)

of the kind he found and has come to despise in Fanny. Cecilia neatly
brings out the comedy of his situation by leaving him in shameful silence
awhile before saying to her servants, 'Attend this person out,/And, if
he speaks, hear what he comes about' (ll. 782-3). He can no longer
dramatise himself as 'Fool!' but palpably is one.

Apart from the beginning, 'Delay has Danger' is a beautifully calculated whole. In mode it varies flexibly from the rapid drama of the
scenes with the Johnsons to the slow brooding melancholy of the famous
psychological landscape of Henry on the following morning. Our response to Henry is carefully shifted several times between mockery and
pathos and various intermediary stages, in order to achieve a complex
of attitudes towards him which cannot be simplified into the single tone
of the conclusion, accurate though that tone is as a concluding comment.
Crabbe has managed with extraordinary subtlety to communicate the
character of a particularly spineless and mentally vacuous young man
and his gradual entanglement in a relationship for which he had little
real inclination, but which will blight the remainder of his life. Henry
is a fool, but so weak a man that our mockery is tempered with much
sympathy.

In general, the greater length Crabbe allowed himself in the *Tales of
the Hall* discouraged the concentration of language and the correspon-
dingly witty contrasts and comparisons in narrative structure that he
achieved in the *Tales* of 1812. It is unfortunate that in a number of
books he chose to repeat the life-history form of the basic 'progress'
tradition, rather than to develop the organisation around one or two key
episodes or situations which drew out his characteristic strengths to the
full. In some of the weaker books much of the narrative material achieves
no real significance and remains merely on the level of factual information. Even in 'William Bailey', a book to which we know he gave
thought over a number of years, not only is there much aimless narrative, but in revision Crabbe added to it: William's encounter with the
petty revolutionaries, which has no function in the economy of the tale,
was added after the verse draft in the Murray notebook. Again and
again in these tales, Crabbe seems to have lost his capacity to integrate
narrative interest with moral or psychological insight. 'The Widow'
achieves considerable competence of a predictable kind and 'Smugglers
and Poachers' shows Crabbe bringing his own concerns in an interesting
way to unfamiliar material, but the only tale discussed in this chapter
which shows real creative development is 'Delay has Danger'.

8 Posthumous Tales

After the completion of *Tales of the Hall*, Crabbe does not seem to have felt the enthusiasm for attempting new kinds of work which he experienced after the *Tales* of 1812. In a letter to Murray of 20 November 1819, he says, 'I wrote a few Pages, in Consequence of the Hints, for such they were, between us, but I did not so well approve what I had done as to feel any Alacrity in the Labour. Tales of fashionable Life would certainly suit better, had I those Materials which you suppose me possessed of. Characters might indeed by [sic] found, but Anecdote that fits them is wanted' (Fitzwilliam Museum, Cambridge). From a letter to Mrs Leadbeater of December 1820, it seems that he was doing some writing, but not with much sense of purpose: 'I scarcely know whether at this time I can be said to be about anything of the kind; just of the kind, certainly not, but the mind, accustomed to its mode of employing itself, will not suddenly be quiet, unless taken off or agitated by some important avocations' (*Leadbeater Papers*, p. 370). The extant evidence suggests that it was not until 1822 that he began to think more definitely of further publication. 'In a neat Cottage' (*New Poems*, p. 59) is dated February 1822, the Murray draft of 'The Deserted Family' (printed from a later draft by Ward, Vol. III, p. 477) is dated 16 June 1822, and the plan for the 'Farewell and Return' (printed in *New Poems*, p. 175) is dated 24 July 1822. Writing to his son John on 9 August 1822, during his visit to Scotland, he says, 'I should like to earn a little money during this excursion and will if possible make a little volume, like a thin one of the Tales of the Hall' (Bodleian Library). From a letter to Mrs Leadbeater of 26 March 1824, it is clear that he was then still actively working on 'A Farewell and Return', the 'Deserted Wife/or Family' and 'The Flowers' (*Leadbeater Papers*, p. 386), and in mid-1825 he was still thinking of publishing a final collection himself: 'I . . . look forward – late as the Time is – for a final publication. If I do not effect this I shall at least leave my Verses with my Sons . . . one Month's Severe Attention, exclusively given to the work would terminate my Labour' (Broadley and Jerrold, pp. 276–7). The work seems to have been delayed, though, for on 28 June 1826, he wrote to George of setting 'about the Duty I have long prescribed to myself of

correcting what is worth it and destroying the rest of my Miscellanies'
(Yale University Library), and according to the *Life* (p. 311) it was not
until 24 October 1831 that George learnt that another 'series of stories'
was 'quite prepared for the press'.

The best of the pieces written after *Tales of the Hall* and not printed
in 1834 as part of *Posthumous Tales* is 'The Deserted Family'. From the
Murray draft it seems that it was once intended to be a more ambitious
work, for much of the exposition is given in the form of gossip between
servants of the family, but in the draft printed by Ward it has the
characteristic shape of a late Crabbe tale. Another interesting omission
from the *Posthumous Tales* is what Ward prints as 'The Funeral of the
Squire' (Vol. III, p. 489). In the Murray Collection there are some loose
leaves consisting of a fragment called 'The Squire', beginning, 'I leave
our Manor's Lord...' In the Ward fragment, the later history of the
squire is narrated not by the poet's Friend, but by the sexton; but despite
this slight departure from the procedure of the 'Farewell and Return'
series, it is clear that the two fragments together form a complete tale
which must at one time have been intended for the series. Why it was
rejected remains obscure: it is not outstanding, but it is superior to
several of the accepted tales.

The original idea in the 'Farewell and Return' series, of showing the
change after a period of years both in the observer and in the people he
observed, was an interesting one, but as Crabbe failed in the event to
show the change in the observer, the form became a rigid 'before and
after' view of the people observed. The rich variety of Crabbe's vision
of the ways in which the moral effect of time is manifested was narrowed
down to a simple repetitive pattern of twin portraits. In some cases the
writing is extremely poor. 'The Dean's Lady', for example, is merely
dull satire against a blue-stocking. The only successful irony lies in the
contrast between the end of Part I, where she is living on future fame,
and the end of Part II, where she 'lives on past applause'. There is no
attempt to explore the significance of the passage of time in relation to
her experience, or to show any feelings she might have as she contem-
plates her failure: there are merely juxtaposed portraits of her in her
prime and in her decline. The general sense of monotony in the series is
increased by the fact that the change is for the worse in all except two
cases, Tales XII and XIV, neither of which is very memorable. In some
instances the failure is due to the imposition of the form of a tale on
material which is really too slight to carry it. Tale X, 'The Ancient
Mansion', for example, contains an accomplished description of the
changing seasons (lines 67–99), but the surrounding framework is too
insubstantial to form anything which could reasonably be called a tale,
and the concluding attempt to bring in some human content is ex-

tremely clumsy. Tale VIII, 'Barnaby, the Shopman', is memorable for
the single image of Barnaby's sweeping, described at the beginning –
'Cleaning his way, for cleanliness he loves' (l. 8) – and repeated at the
end to signify his failure to rise in the world in the way both he and the
poet had expected:

> Warn'd by the past, he rises with the day,
> And tries to sweep off sorrow. – *Sweep away!*   (ll. 164–5)

It might have made an effective short poem, but the narrative material,
which the form of the series requires, gives too obvious a sense of
having been worked up for the purpose of filling out a tale.

The best tale in the 'Farewell and Return' series is XVI, 'The Dealer
and Clerk'. It is a carefully structured whole in which the pattern of the
dealer's experience represents a simple form of poetic justice and the
clerk's a more subtle form, and although the language is not so taut as
in the best work of Crabbe's prime, it is much stronger than in most of
the other posthumous tales. At the Farewell stage, the dealer is in a
situation of gross injustice: he is evil but wholly successful. All his
relationships are in terms of money. He lends 'his darling money' to
'his unhappy friends'. In his marriage, his wife made 'A losing bargain;
she with scorn was paid/For no small fortune' (ll. 12–13). Neglecting
her, he 'bribed' another woman to leave her husband. The dealer responds
to him too in terms of money: 'The cruel spoiler to his need would lend/
Unsought relief' (ll. 25–6). Neighbours are outraged by the injustice of
the dealer's success and the husband's suffering and long for the adminis-
tration of a providential justice. Crabbe answers them with a direct
statement of ignorance about the problem of evil:

> Alas! my grieving friends, we cannot know
> Why Heaven inflicts, and why suspends, the blow.   (ll. 33–4)

The dealer will be dealt justice before the end of the tale, but the
husband he wronged will not. The one thing certain is that the dealer's
state is not truly enviable, though at this stage of the tale this can only
be registered by strength of language, by the scorn concentrated in the
phrase 'rich, wretched man' and the sudden twist in the use of money
imagery:

> Adieu! can one so miserable be,
> Rich, wretched man; to barter fates with thee?   (ll. 44–5)

To complain at the injustice of the dealer's situation is in effect to adopt
his values, to 'barter fates'.

Whereas the dealer is completely corrupted by money, his clerk is
suspended in a state of half-corruption by a balance of fears. The dealer

is prepared to back his evil actions with 'daring'. But the clerk is on the one hand 'full sore afraid/Of his own frailty', afraid that his conscience might fail him, and on the other hand he has 'instinctive dread of being poor'. The balance of fears keeps him in a state of equilibrium until a new fear occurs to him: 'a fear began/To break his rest – He served a wicked man' (ll. 58–9). The reaction against evil rapidly becomes a calculation about the degree of danger involved, and once he has started on the calculation he has lost hold of the terms in which he should be thinking. The opposite fear naturally asserts itself:

> 'If I should quit – another takes the pen,
> And what a chance for my preferment then?'   (ll. 86–7)

As he continues in his calculations, he becomes less honest and more contaminated by hypocrisy.

> 'Religion nothing by my going gains;
> If I depart, my master still remains.'   (ll. 88–9)

That his master would not change as a result of his going clearly has nothing to do with his own decision about whether he is justified in collaborating. Eventually he works his way round to thinking it is right to stay – 'It checks him, doubtless, in his fearful way' (l. 95) – though we know, and so must he, that such a man as the dealer is not going to be checked by so weak a man as the clerk.

At the beginning of the 'Return' section, the extent of the dealer's evil is increased by the 'murder' of his wife. At this stage the tone is kept at a mundane level: the murder is of the kind 'that human eye/Cannot detect, – which human laws defy' (ll. 102–3). Characteristically, the dealer's final action in the relationship is to pay the cost of the funeral. He tries to remain unaffected by time: 'He paused a while, and then the way resumed,/Ev'n as before' (ll. 131–2). But time has changed his situation nonetheless: 'yet was he not the same;/The tempter once, he now the dupe became' (ll. 132–3). Conscience begins to assert itself against the dealer even though he has hitherto ignored it:

> His dreams – 'Twas strange, for none reflected less
> On his past life – were frightful to excess;
> His favourite dinners were no more enjoy'd.   (ll. 148–50)

The final stage of the dealer's progress is clearly marked off by a change of style to that of the Gothic novel. His 'cur' is predictably 'gaunt' and 'savage', and its eye like a 'live coal' becomes a little comically Gothic when we are solemnly told that it 'possess'd but one':

> Gaunt, savage, shaggy, with an eye that shone
> Like a live coal, and he possess'd but one.   (ll. 173–4)

It is given a mock-genealogy – 'The son of Fury, famed in days of old,/
From Snatch and Rabid sprung' (ll. 189–90) – which is deflated by the
mundane proverb that concludes the paragraph: 'and noted they/In
earlier times – each dog will have his day' (ll. 190–1). The death of the
dealer is surrounded with Gothic mystery and machinery.

> Of outward force, they say, was not a sign –
> The hand that struck him was the Hand Divine . . .
> While grinning imps the body danced about,
> And then they vanish'd with triumphant shout.
>   (ll. 224–5, 228–9)

Suddenly Crabbe changes the tone again to indicate that the divine
retribution represented in the popular style of the Gothic is an over-
popularised version of reality:

> So think the crowd, and well it seems in them,
> That ev'n their dreams and fancies vice condemn.   (ll. 230–1)

But although the form is for the 'crowd' only, the attitude is fundamentally right: the reaction against evil must be a recoil of Nature, not
merely a calculation of Reason – 'not alone for virtue Reason pleads,/
But Nature shudders at unholy deeds' (ll. 232–3).

In the second half of the 'Return', the clerk is shown to be in a state
very similar to the dealer's, though less dramatic:

> His meals were troubled by his scruples all,
> And in his dreams he was about to fall.   (ll. 244–5)

In the representation of his quarrel with the dealer, it is his first reaction
which is best: 'John resisted with a stout good-will . . . the offer'd gain'.
Under pressure, his emphasis shifts a little towards a form of self-interest
deriving from one of his many fears: 'I dare not do it . . . I'm sure there
is a hell'. When the dealer puts it in the form, 'the fool that dared/Not
join a venture which he might have shared' (ll. 262–3), there is not
much that he has failed to take account of. The clerk half of the tale
represents not only a more refined version of poetic justice, but also a
commentary on the ethic embodied in the dealer half: an ethic based on
the fear of 'the Hand Divine' is useful in the absence of anything else,
but it is dangerous to balance fears. In leaving the dealer, the clerk is
doing the right thing for a barely adequate reason; later he will be put
in a situation where the balancing of fears will not so fortunately lead
to the right result. The real test for him comes when he wants to marry

the widow of a subsequent employer, whose will anticipated the possibility by making her inheritance of his wealth dependent on her not remarrying. Once they have started to 'reason what it was that gave/ A husband power, when quiet in his grave' (ll. 300–1), the couple are lost: they have started a utilitarian calculation which removes them from respect for absolute law. Feeling the need for moral justification, they reduce law to legalism by picking on the wording of the marriage contract:

> 'Till death!' – you see, no longer – 'do us part.'
> 'Well! death has loosed us from the tie, but still
> The loosen'd husband makes a binding will:
> Unjust and cruel are the acts of men.'   (ll. 303–6)

So they drift into a utilitarian view of promises to the dead: 'Thus they – and then they sigh'd – and then – and then . . .' (l. 307) But conscience will not let the sophistry past:

> ''Tis not a marriage: either dare be poor,
> Or dare be virtuous – part, and sin no more.'   (ll. 316–17)

The issue is one in which the balancing of fears is not enough: it takes courage to make either of the virtuous decisions possible, and the clerk has none. So conscience punishes their 'fond evasion':

> If times were good, – 'We merit not such times;'
> If ill, – 'Is this the produce of our crimes?'   (ll. 322–3)

In retrospect the clerk romanticises his response to the earlier trial:

> Ah, John! bethink thee of thy generous joy,
> When Conscience drove thee from thy late employ.   (ll. 328–9)

'Generous joy' is not something within the actual range of his experience, but in retrospect his feelings then seem now a lost paradise. He knows the contradictions and subterfuges he is forced into: he knows he has no 'call', yet goes to non-conformist meetings 'just to hear, that we are sinners all'. He tries to convince himself of Calvinist doctrines which might relieve his sense of personal guilt, but even as he rehearses the teachings, he is confronted with his inability to carry them out: 'we must the work begin/By first attacking the prevailing sin!' (ll. 350–351) So his religion remains future: 'Faith, feelings . . . this will he embrace'. He perceives himself that 'he was scarcely tried/By the first conquest, that increased his pride' (ll. 357–8), and that whatever reward was owing for it already 'by his self-applause was amply paid'. Instead of the melodramatic poetic justice meted out to the dealer, he is left in

in possession of his 'plenty' and his 'credit', his widow and her money.
He is simply poised in his equilibrum of weakness:

> He mourns his weakness, hopes he shall prevail
> Against his frailty, and yet still is frail.   (ll. 363–4)

He needs no punishment beyond being what he is:

> Such is his life! – and so I would not live
> For all that wealthy widows have to give.   (ll. 371–2)

'The Dealer and Clerk' has not the narrative subtlety of Crabbe's
best work, though the change of style into and out of the Gothic is an
effective means of registering the comparative crudity of the dealer's
progress. The form of the tale, with its division into twin histories of
the two men enables Crabbe to criticise the ethical assumptions underlying the simpler of them, and he was sufficiently engaged by the form
for his imagination to work much more strongly on the representation
of their feelings than elsewhere in the 'Farewell and Return' series.
It is not a form he had attempted before, though it is related to the sort
of internal contrast between, for instance, Arabella and her spinster
friend. But the degree of imagination engaged is insufficient for the tale
to be regarded as a distinctively new kind of achievement. Like 'The
Widow' of *Tales of the Hall*, it is accomplished work, but not a new
creative departure.

Of the five posthumous tales not in the 'Farewell and Return' series,
at least two were written many years earlier. There is a late draft of
'Rachel' in one of the Murray notebooks in which the two speakers are
the George and Richard of *Tales of the Hall*, and 'Villars' was written
in the Cambridge notebook Add. MS. 4422 a little after the date December 1815. The chief interest of 'Villars' (Tale v) is in the revision of the
ending. The version printed by Ward as a variant is written considerably
later in the manuscript than the version printed in 1834. Whether the
first attempt was deliberately preferred or the existence of the second
was forgotten when the tale was transcribed cannot be known, but the
second is certainly much better. Tale ii, 'The Family of Love', is probably Crabbe's last tale: a working draft in one of the Murray notebooks
is dated January 1827. It is an extremely long and shapeless tale, of no
intrinsic interest.

The best of the *Posthumous Tales* is 'Silford Hall'. Its main strength
lies in the representation of the consciousness of a young adolescent as
he lives through a day so affecting to his youthful imagination that he
remembers it for the rest of his life. A fine sense of the ambivalence of
adolescence runs through it. At the beginning, the atmosphere evoked

in his father's house is one of oppressive mundanity. Not only is there
the dull routine of a village school but

> If, now and then,
> His boys for play laid by the book and pen,
> For Lawyer Slow there was some deed to write ...   (ll. 24–6)

The boy, Peter, has a premature responsibility thrust on him: 'though
yet a Boy, he shares/Their many Tasks and multifarious Cares'. The
last quotation is from the very late draft in the Forster Collection of the
Victoria and Albert Museum. In revision 'Their many Tasks and' was
changed to 'In staid Nathaniel's', further emphasising the pedestrian
atmosphere of the house. When the boys are playing, Peter 'Has sums
to set, and copy-books to rule' (l. 50), and he resents the ambivalence of
his position, having

> To miss the master's dignity, and yet,
> No portion of the school-boy's play to get.   (ll. 61–2)

His methods of coming to terms with his position are also ambivalent:
one reason why he does not try to run away is that he 'felt the Mother
clinging at his heart'; the other is that he is helped to bear 'it as a man
should bear' by the miscellaneous collection of books which provides
release into a world with broader horizons. The reading is indiscriminate
– along with fragments of Shakespeare, Spenser and Milton, he takes in
Robin Hood and Hickerthrift – but an escape is needed from his father's
staid and arid pursuit of his duties: 'His hungry mind disdain'd not
humble food'. Under his mother's tutelage, his moral responses are not
at all ambivalent:

> He shrank from vice, and at the startling view,
> As from an adder in his path, withdrew.   (ll. 154–5)

But he feels the strange vacillation of mood and the objectless melancholy of the young adolescent: he often feels the joy of the lark,

> Yet oft with this a softening sadness dwelt,
> While, feeling thus, he marvell'd why he felt.
> 'I am not sorry,' said the Boy, 'but still,
> The tear will drop – I wonder why it will!'   (ll. 160–3)

The trip to Silford Hall, which forms the body of the tale, is from the
start represented as an ambivalent experience. The Hall is linked with
the exoticism of Peter's reading –

> Fruits of all tastes in spacious gardens grew;
> And flowers of every scent and every hue –   (ll. 183–4)

but his business there is very mundane – 'he must take the amount,/ And sign a stamp'd receipt!' He approaches it in a very mixed frame of mind:

> To this fair place, with mingled pride and shame
> This lad of learning without knowledge came.   (ll. 187–8)

The edge of the last line is missing in the Cambridge draft – 'This un-experienced lad delighted came' – and so too is the gentle irony against Peter's 'better knowledge' in the following lines, in which his mother thinks it too far for her 'darling Peter' to walk and he conceals his 'better knowledge', exploiting for once the ambivalence of his age, as he wants to ride his father's nag. While he is being dressed for the occasion, he is, through his mother's perspective, 'Her darling child':

> All in his coat of green she clothed her boy,
> And stood admiring with a mother's joy.   (ll. 203-4)

Through his own, he is an adult figure out of his adolescent reading, a romance hero being armed for the quest:[1] 'he was full proudly drest;/ Full proudly look'd, and light he was of heart' (ll. 217–18). There is a mock-heroic note to the description which fuses both perspectives:

> Forth went the pony, and the rider's knees
> Cleaved to her sides – he did not ride with ease.   (ll. 238–9)

As he sets off, he has the self-consciousness of the adolescent:

> The village boys beheld him as he pass'd,
> And looks of envy on the hero cast.   (ll. 242–3)

In the bailiff's office, he is disappointed by what he sees – 'a small room, with bare and oaken floor' – but is lost for words:

> 'Good day!' he said, but linger'd as he spoke
> 'Good day,' and gazed about with serious look.   (ll. 269–70)

It is the housekeeper, Madam Johnson, who rescues him with a phrase in his own ballad idiom, 'And what dost thou, my pretty lad?'

In his tour of the house his response is initially very child-like – 'There was such magic in the things he saw' (l. 305) – and he clings to Madam Johnson as a protectress: 'I'm safe', he thought, 'so long as you abide' (l. 316). The paragraph in which he catches sight of himself in a mirror was added after the Cambridge draft. It is not, as has been claimed,[2] a major step in a journey from innocence to experience. It is not his own form which captivates his attention but his clean new clothes. The reaction of 'our happier boy' is explicitly distinguished

from the corruption of Narcissus: it is simply the self-consciousness and
the temporary conceit of a child seeing himself in unaccustomed clothes
and in a mirror much larger than the ones at home. When he thinks
Madam Johnson might be going to leave him alone, he says in the
authentic voice of childhood, that he is not afraid, even as he expresses
his fear: 'Oh! do not leave me – I am not afraid,/But 'tis so lonesome.'
In the chapel his experience is coloured by his reading of fairy-tales:
'he felt/The cedar's power, that so unearthly smelt . . . candles tall . . .
such as the halls of giant-kings would light', and his faltering questions
are childishly inadequate to his feelings:

> 'Is this a church? and does the parson read' –
> Said Peter – 'here? – I mean a church indeed?'   (ll. 361–2)

Even when they leave the chapel he continues to feel the unattached
fear of a child: although his mind is free

> From every fear substantial and defined,
> Yet there remain'd some touch of native fear.   (ll. 368–9)

In the picture-gallery his mood changes substantially – 'He gazed
and thought, and was no more the boy' (l. 373). But even though his
knowledge about the figures portrayed in the paintings enables him to
impress Madam Johnson, it is emphasised in a line added after the
Cambridge draft that he remains essentially adolescent – 'So like a man,
and yet so like a child' (l. 382). She tries to exploit the ambivalence for
her own purposes by drawing attention to a painting of Joseph and
Potiphar's wife and asking, 'Had you been Joseph, boy!/Would you
have been so peevish and so coy?' (ll. 396–7). Peter is embarrassed, but
morally unshaken:

> Our hero answer'd, with a glowing face,
> 'His mother told him he should pray for grace.'   (ll. 398–9)

It is Madam Johnson herself who is more disconcerted – 'She seem'd
disposed to laugh – but knew not how' (l. 401). She tries to recover her
self-composure by dismissing him as a mere child – '"'Tis but a child,"
she thought, and all was cleared' (l. 403) – but she had been deeply
shaken by his moral innocence:

> No – laugh she could not; still, the more she sought
> To hide her thoughts, the more of his she caught.   (ll. 404–5)

She passes 'the offensive pictures silent by' and leads him quickly on to
others. She tries to reassert her dominance by drawing attention to some
scenes of other forms of vice:

> 'Observe the faces, forms, the eyes, the air:
> See rage, revenge, remorse, disdain, despair!'   (ll. 423–4)

But when Peter asks naïvely, 'is that Nature, too?' she can only reply lamely, 'Corrupted Nature', and take refuge in some guidebook information:

> She then display'd her knowledge. – 'That, my dear,
> Is call'd a Titian, this a Guido here,
> And yon a Claude – you see that lovely light,
> So soft and solemn, neither day nor night.'   (ll. 427–30)

The boy's sensibility is much more directly responsive: instead of the cliché about Claude's colouring, he notices,

> '. . . there is just the breeze,
> That curls the water, and that fans the trees;
> The ships that anchor in that pleasant bay
> All look so safe and quiet.'   (ll. 431–4)

In a passage added to the Forster draft after the transcription of most of the text, Madam Johnson's reaction is again to try to place him back in the position of mere child by impressing him with the money value of one of the paintings. She so manages the conversation that she can conclude it with the patronising, 'Why, thou'rt a reasoner, Boy!' Swept on by the impetus of her success, she points out 'A Babe so charming' in a Reynolds; again the 'Boy' responds more subtly:

> 'I wonder how he could that look invent,
> That seems so sly, and yet so innocent.'   (ll. 455–6)

Yet immediately afterwards we are reminded that he is barely more than a child: he responds to the statues not as art, but as the embodiment of one of his magical stories about a pilgrim who finds a city whose people have all been turned to stone. The sensitivity is acute, but it is in this case very child-like:

> 'Are you awake?' – 'I am amazed,' said he;
> 'I know they're figures formed by human skill,
> But 'tis so awful, and this place so still!'   (ll. 474–6)

His response to the billiard-room is also that of a child, but when he shows some concern at the use of bishops as the names of pieces in chess, Madam Johnson is careful to dissociate herself from the adult view, unwilling to be caught this time, as she was with the paintings, in a position of dubious superiority:

'Bishops, like Kings,' she said, 'are here but names;
Not that I answer for their Honours' games.'   (ll. 495–6)

Curiously, the episode in the library, which now seems central to the
tale, was not conceived of until some time after the Cambridge draft.
Throughout the episode there is a sense of threat: the books are not just
'food for every mind' –

> Above, beneath, around, on every side,
> Of every form and size were Books descried;
> Like Bishop Hatto, when the rats drew near . . .   (ll. 556–8)

Peter is explicitly dissociated from Bishop Hatto – 'guiltless he and fear-
less' – but the three tomes he selects from the shelves are filled with
menace, with serpents, 'battles dire, and dreadful' and 'Hydra and dire
chimera'. He still wants to see them, but 'happier had he been' if he
had not,

> For there were tales of men of wicked mind,
> And how the Foe of Man deludes mankind.   (ll. 592–3)

Just as he begins to admit 'the fear that shames the valiant man' and his
child-like need for protection, he realises that he is alone. At first he sees
the adventure in terms of his reading – 'a bold prince, with fifty doors
in sight,/Tried forty-nine before he found the right' (ll. 612–13) – but
as it is protracted his feelings turn towards a resentment expressing a
real fear:

> 'Was this her love,' he cried, 'to bring me here,
> Among the dead, to die myself with fear!'   (ll. 622–3)

His mind vacillates between recriminating recollection of Madam Johnson and observation of his situation:

> ' "We'll see the rooms," she said, "before we dine;"
> And spake so kind. That window gives no light.'   (ll. 627–8)

Finally, his child-like mind is completely dominated by the present
emotion:

> Anger and sorrow in his bosom strove,
> And banish'd all that yet remain'd of love;
> When soon despair had seized the trembling Boy.   (ll. 633–5)

Yet once he is found again by Madam Johnson, he feels with child-like
resilience a 'tumult of o'erpowering joy' almost immediately afterwards.
The episode is a convincing portrayal of a young boy's panic – resentment and anger complicating the basic response of sheer fear – but there

is no attempt to show in a Wordsworthian manner the lasting effect of
it on his sensibility.

The prevailing mood arising from the day's experience is:

> 'I am so happy, and have such delight,
> I cannot bear to see another sight.'   (ll. 661–2)

'Fleshless forms' occur among the various figures of his dreams, but the
boy is essentially happy – 'oh! the joy/That in his dreams possess'd the
happy boy' (ll. 665–6) – and essentially unchanged: he sits 'with equal
shame and pride' beside Madam Johnson at dinner, just as he originally
approached the Hall with 'mingled pride and shame'. The ending
clearly gave Crabbe much trouble: the Cambridge manuscript shows a
great deal of labour at it along the lines of the version quoted in the
1834 edition, and two separate fragments of it are also preserved in the
Bodleian Library. Peter was to have returned to the Hall later in life as
a resident guest in order that two morals might be deduced from the
tale. Firstly, 'Little didst thou know/How near approach the lofty and
the low'; and secondly that custom blunts the appetite:

> Where now the joyful expectation? – fled!
> The strong anticipating spirit? – dead!   (1834 edition)

In the final version, Crabbe draws no moral, but simply leaves the day
as a permanently memorable one to Peter:

> So deep the impression of that happy Day,
> Not time nor cares could wear it all away;
> Ev'n to the last, in his declining years,
> He told of all his glories, all his fears.   (ll. 714–17)

The obvious morals would clearly have spoilt the impact of the tale. In
essence it is not a tale with a moral, but an acute exploration of early
adolescent experience. As a representation of the consciousness of a
sensitive young adolescent, it cannot stand beside Wordsworth, but
among Crabbe's works it has in its present form a unique flavour. Only
in a few other works – 'The Lover's Journey' and some of the frame
books of *Tales of the Hall* – does Crabbe have a comparable interest in a
mode of consciousness for its own sake, and this is his only sustained
rendering of pre-adult life.

It is commonplace in criticism of Crabbe to remark that he has been
unfairly neglected. The body of criticism on him is extremely small, and
since the age of his contemporaries when he was very popular he has
not, to judge from the infrequency of reprints of his work, been a

favourite with the reading-public. There have always been small bands of admirers, protesting against the neglect, but they have not yet been generally heeded. Many reasons for this have been offered, of which the most obvious is the most probable: that he seems, on the face of it, anachronistic beside his contemporaries, Wordsworth and Coleridge. An attempt was made in the first chapter to place him in a tradition which by-passed the Romantic movement. But it remains true that he has not Wordsworth's kind of significance. The body of English literature would have much the same aspect if Crabbe were removed from it; without Wordsworth it would be a different corpus. But to measure Crabbe against the greatest poet of the nineteenth century is only one move in establishing his stature.

Although an attempt has been made in this book to place Crabbe's work on the line from Johnson's Shakespeare to the major nineteenth-century novel, it also remains in important respects *sui generis*. He was not drawing on any tradition of narrative verse, nor did one develop from him. The sort of integration of dramatic representation with moral or psychological insight which he achieved in verse passed into the prose, not the verse, tradition of the century. Although novelists as diverse as Jane Austen and Hardy admired him deeply, theirs were essentially different modes. Nor has he ever represented for anyone a kindred spirit in an alien world, in the way that Gray and Collins achieved disproportionate significance to certain nineteenth-century critics of the eighteenth century. The case is not just that, as is often said, he hovers between Augustan and Romantic, belonging fully to neither movement, but that in certain obvious respects nothing leads to him or from him. This isolation is probably another factor contributing to his neglect. But from another perspective, it establishes his claim to a unique place in English literature.

Whether the place is that of a major or of a minor poet is a nice question. Certainly he did not, in Eliot's terms, alter expression.[3] But neither did he inertly adopt the language of another. The point is made immediately by contrasting *The Library* with 'The Frank Courtship': the former is the work of a member of the school of Pope; the latter is that of an independent sensibility. Yet such independence has been achieved by poets who by general agreement are regarded as minor: for example, Gray. The comparison with Gray might be extended, too, if one adduced Crabbe's capacity for creative renewal: the capacity to perceive, after the success of *The Village*, the potentialities of narrative which culminated in the 1812 *Tales*, is matched in a different form by the extraordinary variety within Gray's small oeuvre. And one has to concede that, apart from some predictable successes, Crabbe's work after 1812 is a disappointment. 'Delay has Danger', 'The Visit Concluded' and 'Silford Hall' are the only distinctively different achievements which could be laid beside the *Tales*.

Yet setting Crabbe against Gray one is struck very clearly by a difference of scale – not only of bulk of really excellent work, but of human importance. One would not turn to a poet such as Gray if one wanted to sense the shape of human nature. Part of Crabbe's achievement is that he has vividly dramatised for us a particular phase of English moral and social culture; but he has done so with an insight which in his best work has carried him to the level of the permanent. In 'Peter Grimes' we are taken to the boundaries of what we would consent to call 'human'. 'Procrastination' presents us with a living image of a vice which is carried as near as possible to the point at which the word 'evil' would become appropriate. 'The Frank Courtship' celebrates the natural reflux of vital and gracious relationship against a mode of life which had become too formal and unfeeling. In 'Arabella' Crabbe explores the area of moral behaviour in which mature broad-mindedness is barely distinguishable from rationalisation. 'Delay has Danger' explores the area in which weakness of mind and spirit shade into actual folly and moral irresponsibility. Again and again in his poetry he examines the consequences on the life of the individual of the distinctive moral choices the individual makes. Occasionally he feels the need to interfere in the course of the action: for example in 'The Patron' the boy's aspirations to free-thinking are punished in a too obvious way by the whipping administered by his father. But usually Crabbe is content to see the consequences simply working themselves out through the passage of time. His characteristic criticism of life is to envisage what happens if a given moral choice or cast of mind is projected through time. Although some of his values (for example in 'The Patron') have dated, most of those present in his best work have remained centrally human. He is, in Wordsworth's magnificent phrase, a 'rock of defence for human nature'.

Notes

Chapter 1

1 Ch. 3, section 1. The 'Opinions' are in the Murray notebook which contains 'The Poet's Journal' quoted in the *Life*. They are a second draft of the 'principal work' referred to on p. 57 of the *Life*.

2 On 4 January 1814, Crabbe wrote to Miss Lewis: 'I also earn a little by Versifying, but this I shall leave off; I have a Prose Work but of too serious a kind to expect from it Money-profit, indeed I try to shut out the Thought' (Huntington Collection). It is clear what this work was from one of the notebooks in Cambridge University Library, in which there are some prose notes attacking Gibbon, dated 19 January 1814; and in one of the Murray notebooks there are many aggressive pages on Gibbon, of about the same date, and a reference of 27 March 1814 to Hume on miracles. On 25 November 1815 he mentioned to Miss Charter that he was writing a 'Book on Divinity' (Broadley and Jerrold, p. 115), and it is possible that he was referring to the same work as late as 20 November 1819, in a letter to Murray now at the Fitzwilliam Museum, Cambridge, when he wrote of a 'work of religious kind' he had in hand as 'a Matter of Conscience and feeling, an Engagement with myself.'

3 Annotation to 1834 *Works*, Vol. I, p. 45 (Trinity College, Cambridge).

4 Printed by F. M. Link in *English Language Notes*, Vol. II (1965), pp. 205–6.

5 Broadley Collection, University of Leeds: *Life*, Vol. IV, p. 157.

6 *Table Talk and Omniana*, ed. T. Ashe (1884), p. 276.

7 *Memoir and Letters of Sarah Coleridge*, edited by her daughter (1873), Vol. I, p. 75.

8 *Quarterly Review*, IV (1810), 281–312, reprinted in *Critical Heritage*, in which the quotations appear on pp. 118 and 125.

9 *Familiar Letters of Sir Walter Scott*, ed. D. D[ouglas] (1894), Vol. II, p. 343.

10 See, for example, pp. 118–19 in the *Critical Heritage*: '... it is precisely in order to escape from the world as it is, that we fly to poetry

... For this end new worlds have been framed ... [a] visionary creation. ... [Pastoral poetry] diverts the mind from ordinary life by soothing and gentle means.' The review was, of course, drawing on contemporary commonplaces.

11 Crabbe's irony was not registered. The *Eclectic Review* (VIII, 1812, pp. 1240–53) responded in a way which remained commonplace: 'if the end of poetry be to relax and recreate the mind, it must be attained by drawing away the attention from the low pursuits and sordid cares, from the pains and sorrows of real life, at least whatever is vulgar and disgusting in them, to an imaginary state of greater beauty, purity, and blessedness.'

12 *Shelburne Essays*, 2nd ser. (1905), p. 129.

13 Introduction to World's Classics ed. of the *Life*, p. xvii.

14 Murray notebook, parts of which are printed in *New Poems*.

15 Varley Lang, 'Crabbe and the Eighteenth Century', ELH, V (1938), 305–33.

16 *Blackwood's Magazine*, XXII (1827), 537–40. Reprinted in *Critical Heritage*, p. 313.

17 *An Essay on the Genius and Writings of Shakespear* (1712), *The Critical Works of John Dennis*, ed. E. N. Hooker (1939–43), Vol. II, p. 6.

18 'On the Origin and Progress of Novel-Writing', prefixed to her *British Novelists* (1810). The quotation is from the 1820 edition, pp. 52–3.

19 This is quoted from the earlier of the two drafts referred to in note 1. The sub-section is headed *Of Free Agency* but is not numbered.

20 This was a commonplace in Christian thinking (see, for example, Blair's sermon 'On the Progress of Vice', *Sermons* (1791), Vol. III), but perhaps most wittily expressed by Johnson in *Rambler* 113, where the writer declines marriage to a fatalist: 'Misothea endeavoured to demonstrate the folly of attributing choice and self-direction to any human being. It was not difficult to discover the danger of committing myself for ever to the arms of one who might at any time mistake the dictates of passion or the calls of appetite, for the decree of fate; or consider cuckoldom as necessary to the general system, as a link in the everlasting chain of successive causes. I therefore told her, that destiny had ordained us to part.' (Yale ed., Vol. IV, p. 239.)

21 There is a list of books owned by Crabbe in a notebook now in Cambridge University Library (Add. MS. 4425).

22 'On the Origin and Progress of Novel-Writing', p. 56.

23 Murray Collection, sermon first preached 27 June 1784. Compare, for example, Hastings, p. 216: 'when we offend in any one respect

against the holy commandment, are we not convinced, and does not
our conscience inform us, that *we* are transgressors?'

24 'A Dissertation on the Nature of Virtue', published as an appendix
to *The Analogy of Religion.*

25 A *Serious Call to a Devout and Holy Life* (1728), Everyman ed., p.
23. Like Crabbe, Law made very frequent reference to the parable of
the talents.

26 See, for example, D. M. MacKinnon, A *Study in Ethical Theory*
(1957), p. 134: 'the individual creates various relations with his
fellows, and in creating them creates himself.' Germain Grisez,
Abortion: the Myths, the Realities, the Arguments (1970), p. 320:
'Each single act is an engagement of one's freedom, a determination
of one's self by one's self.' Stephen Clark, 'The Use of "Man's
Function" in Aristotle', *Ethics*, LXXXII (1972), 283 (quoting E. W.
Strauss): 'Man has to become what he is.'

27 They were imitated, for example, by Blair in his popular *Sermons*
(Vol. I, pp. 201–2 of the 1791 edition, which was the fourteenth)
and by Secker, whom Crabbe particularly admired (see the letters
referred to in notes 3 and 45), *Works* (1811), Vol. II, p. 277. In *The
Doctrine of Philosophical Necessity* (p. 61), Priestley was able to
score a point against Price by quoting his use of the commonplaces
of habit theory in a way which seemed to commit him to necessi-
tarianism.

28 Page 80. See Owen C. Watkins, *The Puritan Experience* (1972), for
some qualifications to the patterns G. A. Starr attributes to the
autobiographies.

29 See the pair of prints of Louis XIV in *The Parish Register*, I, 43–50,
and the *Life*, p. 16. His son John was almost certainly modelling
himself on Hogarth in the drawing referred to on p. 127 above, and
Crabbe seems to have had Hogarth in mind in the tenth paragraph
of the 1812 Preface.

30 Ronald Paulson, '*The Harlot's Progress* and the Tradition of History
Painting', *Eighteenth-Century Studies*, I (1967–8), 69–92.

31 Sheldon Sacks, *Fiction and the Shape of Belief* (1967), p. 214.

32 See Robert D. Mayo, *The English Novel in the Magazines 1740–1815*
(1962).

33 According to Mayo (*English Novel*, p. 117) the tales from the
Adventurer were more often reprinted and imitated than those of
any other periodical. In her unpublished doctoral dissertation,
*Crabbe's Tales and the Theory and Practice of Narrative in the
Eighteenth and Early Nineteenth Century* (University of California,
Berkeley, 1966) Mary E. Nelson suggests (pp. 102–4) that White-
head's 'Variety' is more like Crabbe's work than any other

eighteenth-century preceptive narrative poem. This is probably correct; but the resemblance is slight. In Chapter 5 of her dissertation Dr Nelson discusses *Caleb Williams* and *Nature and Art* as influences on Crabbe's portrayal of the progress of passion.

34 Letter of 5 March 1813, published by H. J. C. Grierson in *Times Literary Supplement* (1932), 643.

35 T. N. Talfourd, *The Pamphleteer*, V, 10 (1815), 437; reprinted in *Critical Heritage*. T. Bareham, 'Crabbe's Studies of Derangement and Hallucination', *Orbis Litterarum*, XXIV (1969), 161–86.

36 *Hours in a Library* (1876), Vol. II, p. 52. Stephen qualifies his remark considerably, but, as Fitzgerald notes, is curiously unimpressed by Crabbe's sense of humour.

37 Preface to *Tales* (1812). Compare Johnson's Lives of Dryden, Akenside and Congreve.

38 Lines 208–19. They are also alluded to in 'The Patron', ll. 259–72.

39 See, for example, Johnson's life of Boerhaave and *Rambler* 114 on the death penalty – 'Who knows whether this man is not less culpable than me?'

40 Reprinted by George L. Barnett, *Eighteenth-Century British Novelists on the Novel* (1968), p. 95.

41 *Ibid.*, p. 123.

42 Sermon XXII, *Works*, (1811), Vol. I, pp. 342–3. The sermons were published 1770–1. On 10 June 1830 Crabbe wrote to his son George that he would bring a volume of Secker with him to Pucklechurch (Yale University Library). Compare also Mrs Barbauld, 'An Enquiry into those Kinds of Distress which excite agreeable Sensations; with a Tale', in J. and A. L. Aiken, *Miscellaneous Pieces in Prose* (1773), pp. 190–219.

43 Johnson does not use the word lightly: in the 'Life of Thomson' he says that originality is 'praise of the highest kind'. Henry Giles, *Lectures and Essays* (1850), Vol. I, p. 60, quoted by Walter E. Broman, 'Factors in Crabbe's Eminence in the Early Nineteenth Century', *Modern Philology*, II (1953), 42–9.

Chapter 2

1 These changes are discussed further by R. L. Chamberlain, 'George Crabbe and Darwin's Amorous Plants', *Journal of English and Germanic Philology*, LXI (1962), 833–52. Ward reprints the variants from the first edition.

2 Noted by Julia Patton, *The English Village: a Literary Study, 1750–1850* (1919), p. 106. The comparison is developed by Arthur Sale in the introduction to his edition of *The Village* (1950), by R. L. Cham-

berlain in *George Crabbe* (1965), and by W. K. Thomas, 'George Crabbe: Not Quite the Sternest', *Studies in Romanticism*, VII (1968), 166–75.

3 See the letter to Burke printed in *The Correspondence of Edmund Burke*, ed. Holden Furber (1965), Vol. V ,p. 208.

4 Isabel St John Bliss, in '*Night Thoughts* and Christian Apologetics', *Publications of the Modern Languages Association*, Vol. XLIX (1934), 37–70, discusses the tradition behind Young. The argument is equally common subsequently. Crabbe uses it in a Chicago sermon (p. 138) and the Murray sermons of 2 June 1816 and 24 August 1823.

5 The Preface to *The Borough*, in which Crabbe says of Abel and Jachin, 'nor would either have committed the offence of the other', shows a similarly unsophisticated willingness to entertain the possibility of a character acting outside his given literary context.

6 *Edinburgh Review*, XII (1808), 131–51; reprinted in *Critical Heritage*, p. 56.

7 See W. K. Thomas, 'Crabbe's View of the Poor', *Revue de l'Université d'Ottawa* (1966), 453–85. Thomas proves exhaustively that such a picture is fantasy.

8 Compare Howard Mills, p. xxxii of the Introduction to his selection of Crabbe, *Tales, 1812, and Other Selected Poems* (1967). The contrast with Tennyson indicates the chief point of difference between the present discussion of the matter and Dr Mills's.

Chapter 3

1 A note to the 1834 edition states that part of Letter XII ending at line 122 was written in 1799, but it seems to refer only to lines 97–122. It was probably one of the earlier letters, but it is most unlikely that it was completed before *The Borough* as a whole was conceived.

2 *Unum Necessarium*, quoted from *The Whole Works*, ed. Reginald Heber (1839), Vol. VIII, p. 505.

3 Howard Mills, in the Introduction to his selection of Crabbe (1967), pp. xvii–xviii, rightly says that the most vivid 'social description' in *The Borough* is in Benbow's monologue.

4 John Upton and Richard Stack. The quotations are from Stuart M. Tave, *The Amiable Humourist* (1960), pp. 126, 132.

5 Vol. XXX, p. 225, quoted from Tave, *Amiable Humourist*, p. 133.

6 The resemblance to Malvolio was noted but not explored by Arthur Sale in 'Chaucer in Cancer', *English*, VI (1947), 240–4.

7 As emphasised in the 'Advertisement' to the second edition (reprinted as a concluding note in the 1834 edition), Crabbe of course believed that evil was *also* external, not *only* external.

Chapter 4

1 Crabbe is explicitly absolutist on this point in a sermon: 'do not
  make, as it were, an agreement with your conscience, and promise
  yourself to be religious in many respects, so that you may indulge in
  something: you cannot do more than your duty in anything, and
  therefore what you do rightly *cannot excuse* what you do wrong.'
  (Hastings, pp. 60–1)
2 Sermon 10. 9. There follows the passage quoted in Chapter 1, p. 16.
  Crabbe reflects similarly, in a sermon written for 4 September 1803,
  on the lawyer who (in *St Luke* 10. 29) 'willing to justify his Omissions by confining the Bounds of his Duty, asks with some Hope of
  finding himself excused – And who is my Neighbour?' (Chicago
  Collection, p. 327)
3 The same sermon continues (p. 328): 'the Reply of our Lord both to
  his own Disciples and to the Jews in general, was not so much
  directed to their Question as to their true and real Meaning which
  they disguised.'
4 It is successfully controlled at the level of anecdote in *Tatler* 108. But
  Crabbe is writing in a different convention.
5 *Emile* (1762), trans. Barbara Foxley (1911), p. 48. Gwyn's dislike of
  priests and doctors resembles Rousseau's. Paine's thought on the
  relation between human 'rights' and 'power' is similar to Rousseau's
  (see, for example, *The Rights of Man* (1791–2), Penguin ed., p. 90).
  Crabbe's plot may owe something to the anti-Godwin novel by Isaac
  Disraeli, *Vaurien: or Sketches of the Times* (1797), though Disraeli's
  Mr Wilson is unlike Gwyn: 'It was thus, that *law* ruined the estate,
  physic the constitution, and *divinity* the understandings of the
  gentlest and most unoffending of men!' (p. 172)
6 Crabbe's early parodies of Pope left some very obvious marks on his
  later verse. The paragraphs preceding and following Gwyn's long
  speech have a strong flavour of the 'Where Angels fear to tread'
  passage of *An Essay on Criticism* (ll. 625–30).
7 An example in which the reversal is regarded as comic can be found
  in *The Glasgow Magazine and Review*, I (1783), 20–5, 74–7.
8 Hobbes is not in keeping, but given the company he is in, she could
  be counted on to know the orthodox replies.
9 The tone is perhaps too light for *The Dunciad* to come relevantly to
  mind – 'And heavy harvests nod beneath the snow' (Bk I, l. 78).
10 In a letter of 21 December 1812, Crabbe referred to his sons: 'the
  younger designs with some taste: I am to him indebted for my Gipsy-
  Scene in my Lover's Journey: it is a Drawing 7 years old and one I
  have nearly copied.' (National Library of Scotland)

Chapter 5

1 Chicago Collection, p. 509. The sermon continues in a way which fully supports the inference of the tale: 'One who has injured may from thy Kindness take Occasion to injure thee again, but even then persist, resent not nor revenge, win him by mildness and forebearance ... This is Christianity.'
2 In a number of sermons, Crabbe emphasises that charity is more than giving money. For example, in his printed sermon, *The Variation of Public Opinion and Feelings* (1817), he praises those who 'give more than money – their time and ease – to this good work of Christian charity' (p. 31).
3 Yale ed., Vol. IV, p. 55. The insight does not diminish Johnson's condemnation of fraud any more than Crabbe's: 'Whoever commits a fraud is guilty not only of the particular injury to him whom he deceives, but of the diminution of that confidence which constitutes not only the ease but the existence of society.'
4 G. R. Hibbard, 'Crabbe and Shakespeare', in *Renaissance and Modern Essays*, presented to V. de Sola Pinto, ed. G. R. Hibbard with G. A. Panichas and Allan Rodway (1966).
5 John Lucas, A *Selection from George Crabbe* (1967), p. 30.
6 George Crabbe, *Tales, 1812, and Other Selected Poems* (1967), p. xxv.
7 Lilian Haddakin, *The Poetry of Crabbe* (1955), p. 110. Fitzgerald's note on his copy of the 1834 edition, Vol. V, p. 196.
8 For the observation of the fluctuation in the meaning of the word 'grace' in the tale I am indebted to Myrddin Jones.

Chapter 6

1 *Leadbeater Papers*, p. 339: in a letter of 1 December 1816 to Mary Leadbeater, Crabbe writes of 'leisure for the composition, or, more truly, for the correction of another book of rhymes.'
2 Broadley and Jerrold, p. 208. The two tales are presumably 'Lady Barbara' and 'The Cathedral-Walk'.

Chapter 8

1 See D. N. Gallon, 'Silford Hall; or, the Happy Day', *Modern Language Review*, LXI (1966), 384–94.
2 See Carole T. Diffey, 'Journey to Experience: Crabbe's "Silford Hall"', *Durham University Journal*, XXX (1969), 129–34.
3 See T. S. Eliot, Introductory Essay to Johnson's *London: A Poem* and *The Vanity of Human Wishes* (1930).

Index